THE DEADLY DON

THE DEADLY DON:

VITO GENOVESE
Mafia Boss

ANTHONY M. DESTEFANO

CITADEL PRESS
Kensington Publishing Corp.
www.kensingtonbooks.com

CITADEL PRESS BOOKS are published by

Kensington Publishing Corp.
119 West 40th Street
New York, NY 10018

All Kensington titles, imprints, and distributed lines are available at special quantity discounts for bulk purchases for sales promotions, premiums, fundraising, educational, or institutional use.

Special book excerpts or customized printings can also be created to fit specific needs. For details, write or phone the office of the Kensington sales manager: Kensington Publishing Corp., 119 West 40th Street, New York, NY 10018, attn: Sales Department; phone 1-800-221-2647.

CITADEL PRESS and the Citadel logo are Reg. U.S. Pat. & TM Off.

ISBN: 978-0-8065-4094-8

First Citadel hardcover printing: June 2021
First trade paperback printing: June 2022

10 9 8 7 6 5 4 3 2 1

Printed in the United States of America

Electronic edition:

ISBN: 978-0-8065-4095-5 (e-book)

In memory of Leonard Levitt, my steadfast *Newsday* colleague and friend, who was always a source of encouragement. Len was an intrepid reporter, who wouldn't stop in his pursuit of a story and of justice. He was part of a special breed of solid journalists.

Introduction

IN HIS MASTERFUL WORLD WAR TWO black comedy *Catch-22*, novelist Joseph Heller described a scene involving the naïve bomber pilot Lieutenant Nately—we never know his first name in the story—and a lecherous old man in a brothel in wartime Rome, Italy. Nately, ever the image of the profoundly confident American soldier, couldn't seem to understand the old man who spent his days leering at the scantily clad buxom whores, sipping wine, and living what seemed to be an unprincipled philosophy of life.

What really seemed to incense Nately was the way the Old Man—he was never given a name in the novel—was so unprincipled and supported whichever army or dictator was on top at the moment. Italy would actually win the way by losing it, the Old Man crowed.

"You talk like a madman," scoffed Nately.

"But I live like a sane one," the Old Man replied. "I was a fascist when Mussolini was on top, and I am an anti-fascist now that he was deposed. I was fanatically pro-German when the Germans were here to protect us against the Americans, and now that the Americans are here to protect us against the Germans I am fanatically pro-American."

"But, you're a turncoat," exclaimed Nately. "A time-server. A shameful, unscrupulous opportunist!"

Well, that may have been, but the Old Man reminded Nately that he was 107 years old. The fresh-faced young American, only 19, wouldn't in the novel live beyond his 20th birthday.

The Old Man's philosophy for survival in the war by gauging the way the prevailing political winds blew and backing whomever was on top at the moment serves as a metaphor for the way Vito Anthony Genovese, Mafia boss, even with an IQ measured below 100, used his street smarts to negotiate the treacherous path of life in La Cosa Nostra. With the equivalent of a third-grade education and from an Italian family background of very modest means, Genovese developed into what one federal official said was a "suave, shrewd, cruel, calculating, cunning ruthless individual." It was a mix of the right traits to rise in the world of organized crime. The steely-eyed Genovese combined these traits with brutality and bided his time in the deadly world of organized crime to become one of the most important figures in the history of the mob in America during what was its golden period.

From the time he emigrated to the United States in 1913 on a steamship and decided on a life of crime, the Neapolitan-bred Genovese developed a keen sense of which of the key figures in the early days of the New York City mob it was best to align with. With killing after killing, Genovese proved his worth to those who held the power. When the mob was raking in millions of dollars with the advent of Prohibition, Genovese proved his loyalty and earned a reputation for making his own fortune. Then, when things became too dangerous for him with the cops in New York, Genovese fled to Italy in the years before World War Two, ingratiating himself with Italian dictator Benito Mussolini's clique and the Germans. When the defeat of the Axis became inevitable, Genovese craftily shifted his allegiance to the U.S. military, all the while continuing to run a lucrative criminal empire in the wartime black market. His instincts for survival were right out of the script of the Old Man in *Catch-22*.

Once called the "King of The Rackets" by legendary prosecutor Thomas Dewey, Genovese survived the mob wars of Prohibition by aligning himself first with Joseph Masseria, considered one of the first significant Italian organized crime bosses in America, and then Charles "Lucky" Luciano, the man who led the coup that carried dispatched Masseria to a mausoleum in Calvary Cemetery. It was a murder that some claim involved Genovese as one of the trigger-men, or at least his presence at the crime scene. The homicide wouldn't be the last to figure in Genovese's life.

As his reward for helping take out Masseria, Genovese became a key member of Luciano's crime family, one of five Mafia clans that emerged in the realignment of the mob in New York City orches-trated by Luciano after Masseria was blown away. By all accounts, Genovese acquitted himself well. He seemed to have become wealthy in both his legitimate and illegitimate enterprises and was considered by Luciano to be a major part of the family. With his early loyalty to boss Luciano, Genovese showed a certain adeptness in mob politics and thrived in a world where death at the hands of your friends was an all too common occurrence. Genovese wormed his way out of numerous arrests—and one assassination attempt—and was never convicted in this period of anything significant. So long as Genovese didn't screw up, he would be fine.

When Luciano was sent away to prison for up to fifty years in 1936 in a prostitution case, Genovese was one of the top men in the crime family to help run things in the boss's absence. But the over-all acting leader tapped by Luciano was Frank Costello, the mobster-diplomat whose entrenchment with the Democratic Party, conciliatory manner, and legitimate business interests made him a first among equals in the family. Passed over by Luciano, Genovese would har-bor a deep, lifelong resentment towards Costello. Genovese was no match for Costello's combination of political power and money-making ability. Costello recognized the benefits of cutting people in for a share of the rackets, although he was not above screwing his partners. So long as Costello was around, Genovese had a sense of inferiority.

In the late 1930s, Genovese was really not in a position to move against Costello, who had numerous mobsters in his corner. In any case, even if Genovese wanted to make a power play, he suddenly found himself in trouble. An old murder rap in Brooklyn stemming from a debt in a card game compelled Genovese by early 1937 to flee to Italy. He had wisely scouted out Europe during an ostensible vacation to the Continent in 1933, so he knew the lay of the land and likely explored some offshore banking havens. Taking with him a reported $750,000 in cash, Genovese settled back in Italy, leaving his wife, Anna, to take care of three children and to fend for herself in a mansion in New Jersey.

Genovese knew that staying on Mussolini's good side would definitely assure his safety, and he did so by giving money that helped the Fascist Party and by befriending Il Duce's son-in-law, Count Galeazzo Ciano, with whom he partied and allegedly supplied narcotics. When anti-Fascist editor Carlo Tresca was gunned down on Fifth Avenue in Manhattan on January 11, 1943, some investigators believed it was Genovese who arranged for mob killers in New York to do the deed as a favor to his protectors in Rome, a theory that is open to some doubt, as will be discussed within.

There were reports that Genovese curried favor with the German military, which in July 1943 had occupied Italy, and that he served as an intelligence source for the Nazis, although that has never been substantiated. Anna would relate during court testimony that Genovese would party with the likes of Hermann Goering. In any case, Genovese had no worries with the Axis powers. When the Allied forces invaded Sicily in 1943 as part of Operation Husky, the German and Italian forces were defeated in about a month. Some say that in Sicily the U.S. Army came of age, and soon, as Patton had predicted, it pushed on to Messina and the toe of the Italian peninsula. The Allies then engineered an amphibious landing near Salerno in September 1943, and the battle was joined on the Italian mainland, although the inexperience of the American commander, General Mark Clark, almost caused the landing to be withdrawn in defeat.

With continuing reversals, Genovese's ally Mussolini was soon arrested and would later be murdered by partisans. As the Germans were pushed further northward, the Allies formed the AMGOT, short for the Allied Military Government of Occupied Territories, and sensing a new opportunity for survival, Genovese offered his services to the new masters in Italy as a translator. The offer was accepted, and the crafty Genovese lived to thrive among the Allies, along with his lucrative black market operations, which he ran right under the noses of the American, British, and Canadian forces.

Eventually, thanks to an inquisitive American military policeman with the strange name of Orange Dickey, Genovese's life as a criminal and his open murder warrant were discovered. It took a year of legal and military wrangling, but Genovese was brought back under military escort on the SS *James Lykes* to stand trial for the Brooklyn homicide.

But even under the thumb of prosecutors in Brooklyn, Genovese's luck or his insidious ability to corrupt the criminal justice system worked to save him. Peter LaTempa, who prosecutors thought would seal the case against Genovese for the murder of Ferdinand Boccia, died in a jail cell after taking an overdose of gastric medicine. Other potential witnesses either wound up murdered, disappeared, or in the case of codefendants, legally couldn't testify under the legal rules because they were coconspirators in the crime. The case went all the way to jury selection, but at the prosecutor's request, Judge Samuel Leibowitz reluctantly ruled that the case had to be dismissed over lack of evidence, but not before he blasted Genovese for escaping the clutches of the law again.

"You are always one step ahead of Sing Sing and the electric chair," said Leibowitz after he was forced to order an acquittal in the case. "I believe that even if there was a shred of corroborating evidence you would have been condemned to the chair."

If Genovese could be smug with the acquittal in the murder case, his personal life was entering a phase that would lead to bigger problems. Anna Genovese, an attractive woman born in New York of Italian immigrant parents and distantly related to her husband, had accompanied him on his earlier trip back to Italy. There is also some evidence that she accompanied him for a time when he fled to Italy during the Mussolini years. For a while anyway, Anna, who was Genovese's second wife, was the jewel in his existence, raising three children and working the nightclub scene in Greenwich Village, where he had secret interests. But their marriage would in the years ahead become a disaster for Genovese. At one point, he claimed she sold some of his business interests right out from under him after she traveled to Italy in 1939 and he gave her power of attorney over his American businesses. Then, in a highly publicized marital action which commenced in 1950, Anna gave damning court testimony in which she proclaimed he was raking in tens of thousands of dollars in illegal activities, from the Italian lottery to labor shakedowns, and parking the cash in banks as far away as Switzerland and Monte Carlo.

Anna portrayed her husband as a physically abusive man who also spent time chasing other women, an irony in that it would later be said that she was bisexual and had other lovers—male and female. Whatever the truth of Anna's claims, which she made as the case dragged on, the sensational headlines hurt Genovese's standing in the mob. His personal life became something of a soap opera that others in the Mafia never had to endure. The bad press and notoriety came at a time when the public had already been captivated by revelations about the mob from the 1951 U.S. congressional hearings chaired by Senator Estes Kefauver. The allegations in L'Affaire Genovese only further fueled interest in salacious gossip about the Mafia.

Anna later dropped her divorce action but lived apart from her husband after winning a monthly award for financial support. While his marriage was hopelessly shattered, Genovese nevertheless stayed a step ahead of the law. In the 1951 congressional hearings, Genovese earned only a handful of mentions in the testimony. Instead, the Senate turned its attention to Costello, who agreed to testify before Kefauver's committee. Costello's appearance turned out to be a disaster. While he believed he had nothing to hide, Costello came across as shifty, evasive, and untruthful. His raspy voice made him sound like the stereotypical gangster. What's more, while the public saw only his hands on the television broadcasts of the hearings, Costello's guilty conscience about something seemed to come across as his fingers fidgeted and he rubbed his sweating palms.

Costello's Kefauver committee appearance not only hurt him with the public but also made him vulnerable in the world of organized crime. His demeanor had been that of a wounded man, and Costello found himself not only having to do damage control in public but also bracing for the wrath of federal investigators. Convicted of obstructing and lying to Congress, Costello was sent away for eighteen months in prison in 1952, thus making Genovese the top acting boss on the street for the old Luciano family.

Genovese, although himself hurt by the public accusations his wife had been making against him, still managed to fend off prosecutors. Public hearings into labor racketeering and dockland corruption burnished Genovese's image as a major crime boss in New York City. But still he seemed to elude the law, even as he met with criminal associates openly on Kenmare Street in Little Italy. Genovese also took out troublesome crime family members like Willie Moretti and Peter Franse, who was rumored to have bedded Anna while her husband was abroad during World War Two.

Then, in May 1957, Genovese went after Costello and set in motion the attempted assassination as Costello entered the lobby of his apartment building on Central Park West after a night out with friends. The shooting of Costello only grazed his head, and the old crime boss fully recovered. But Costello got the message, and in a truce with Genovese, he agreed to "retire" from the mob, leaving leadership of the family in Genovese's hands.

But history would show that Genovese's reign as the boss would run into trouble almost immediately. In November, some six months after the attempt on the life of Costello, Genovese and scores of other mob bosses were detained after they all assembled at the Apalachin, New York, home of mobster Joseph Barbara. The conclave was ostensibly an opportunity for the gangsters to show respect for the sickly Barbara and share some good food. But Mafia turncoat Joseph Valachi later revealed that Genovese had called everyone together to anoint him as boss of the family. Other business at the summit was said to have included the murder two months earlier of crime boss Albert Anastasia and what the American mob should do about the lucrative and dangerous narcotics trade.

But the meeting broke up as the cops became suspicious of the gathering. Genovese and many of the other Mafia bosses would then spend over two years fighting legal proceedings over the meeting after federal officials claimed the barbecue was nothing more than a cover for a nefarious conspiratorial meeting of mob bosses. Ultimately, Genovese wouldn't be indicted over Apalachin, and others who were charged would see their convictions thrown out by an appeals court. But the damage had been done. If Genovese had engineered the summit as a sort of coronation for himself, as Valachi said, it had backfired badly, causing major trouble between himself and the other Mafiosi.

Genovese also made a major miscalculation over narcotics, something the mob ostensibly had a ban against but which unofficially had turned into a big moneymaker for a number of Mafiosi. Federal investigators with the Federal Bureau of Narcotics (FBN), the forerunner of the Drug Enforcement Administration, were well aware of the Mafia's involvement with narcotics, mainly heroin, and had targeted hundreds of its members in various investigations. The biggest catch would turn out to be Genovese, who was arrested in July 1958 along with nearly three dozen others on charges they were part of a major global heroin smuggling ring. For federal prosecutors in Manhattan, Genovese was "the Right Man," sitting at the top of a trafficking network between Europe, the Caribbean, and the United States.

Some legal experts would insist that Genovese was framed, that somebody of his stature in the mob wouldn't dirty his hands with involvement in drugs, at least not directly. The idea is plausible. But the evidence against Genovese, while circumstantial and based largely on the testimony of one witness, was enough to convict him in April 1959. The resulting sentence garnered Genovese a term of fifteen years in a federal penitentiary.

While incarcerated, Genovese still ran the crime family that came to hear his name. But as time went on, Genovese found it more difficult to control things and the Mafiosi back in New York planned for his succession. Then, in a major development that shook the Mafia to the core and in which Genovese appeared to be a catalyst, his old associate, Valachi, a killer from the Bronx who never really got that high up in the mob hierarchy but could talk up a storm nonetheless, turned into a government witness. It was Valachi who in 1963 broke the fabled Mafia code of silence—omerta—and held the nation entranced as he detailed in public hearings before Congress the secrets of La Cosa Nostra, as Italian organized crime was known on the inside.

Valachi had been a close associate of Genovese and portrayed him as the key figure in the mob, a man who ordered multiple murders and commanded a criminal empire, in much the way Anna Genovese had said. Valachi's testimony and the secrets he revealed in confidential debriefings provided fodder for law enforcement agencies all over the country, although in the end there was only one significant prosecution that resulted, that involving Carmine Persico. Even Genovese, already spending his old age in prison, remained unscathed by Valachi's stories.

But Valachi did a different kind of damage to Genovese. The mob knew that Valachi had been part of Genovese's borgata, his Mafia "family," and his turning into a government witness only added to the sullied reputation Don Vito had suffered. Valachi added more salt to Genovese's wounds when he penned a best-selling book with author Peter Maas called The Valachi Papers. If the mob hadn't watched Valachi on television, his book gave them the whole story, never missing a chance to mention Genovese's name. Plagued by heart disease and other ailments, including cancer, Genovese steadily slipped into infirmity, spending his prison days going to Catholic services, reading, and hoping for a legal miracle that would get him out of prison.

On February 14, 1969, decades of smoking and not taking care of himself caught up with Genovese. He died from complications of a heart ailment in the federal prison hospital in Springfield, Missouri. He was 71 years old, and as he had waited the approach of his scheduled release date, Genovese had busied himself with his Catholic faith, studying the religion in his cell and helping the prison chaplain with services.

Despite all of the misfortune and bad luck Genovese faced with his life within La Cosa Nostra, he was one of the few bosses who was important enough to become the namesake of a crime family. Today in New York City, the Genovese family and the Gambino family still have most of whatever Mafia clout remains. The other three groups—the Lucchese, Bonanno, and Colombo families—have been more severely hurt by prosecutions, turncoats, and competition from other ethnic crime groups.

While other mob bosses have been the subjects of recent biographical treatments, Genovese has not. The one exception is the 1959 book by the old *Journal-American* reporter Dom Frasca, who, along with his editor, wrote *King of Crime*, a book long out of print and now going for close to $1,000 on the Internet. Frasca's book was the state of the art for the time, written as it was before Genovese was convicted in the heroin case. The tone of *King of Crime* was sympathetic, and Frasca apparently enjoyed some special access to Genovese, likely because his relative may have been Cosmo "Gus" Frasca, an associate of the crime boss and would be a figure in a major homicide case. If for nothing else, *King of Crime* contained some remarkable candid photos of Genovese in domestic scenes—cooking pasta, doing yard work, and lounging around his Atlantic Highlands house as he lived the life of a bachelor. (Estranged wife Anna was living elsewhere.) The images portray a grandfatherly Genovese in his dotage.

Frasca interviewed Genovese in the company of his lawyer at the mobster's home and got some terrific quotes, even if the crime boss said nothing incriminating. Frasca was no slouch as a reporter, winning accolades from government officials for his work. But some of the material in *King of Crime* is suspect. For a start, there are facts and dates recited by Frasca that are incorrect. But the big issue is that Frasca quotes long conversations Genovese had over the years with others with no indication of how authentic the quotes are or what the sources may have been. At one point, Frasca portrays a conversation Genovese had with his parents, both of whom were dead by the 1930s, long before the book was written. One federal judge who reviewed a feature story Frasca did about Genovese for a magazine wrote in a ruling that the writer's account contained "highly fictionalized" versions of actual events that took place in court, with some journalistic "embellishments."

If Frasca made up quotes, he wouldn't have been the first true crime writer to have done so. Still, while realizing that there are problems with *King of Crime*, the book is useful as a source since much of the factual material—dates, places, courts—is correct. Where *King of Crime* is cited in *The Deadly Don*, I give it proper cautions so that readers can make up their minds about accepting the material as credible or not.

Bits and pieces of stories about Genovese and his life have appeared in biographies of other gangsters, and he has been the subject of the occasional television documentary. Very little film footage exists of him, and his voice is only preserved for posterity in a few short newsreel clips, notably from around the time of the 1958 Senate hearings regarding organized crime. But since Genovese was such a historical figure in the world of crime and since the passage of time has provided access to additional historical material about him, the idea for *The Deadly Don: Vito Genovese, Mafia Boss* was spawned.

Like any key figure in La Cosa Nostra, Genovese has been the subject of a few legends and fables. For instance, he was said to have arranged the murder of Anna's first husband, a lowly thug and burglar named Gerardo Vernotico, so that he could clear the field and marry her. But my research for *The Deadly Don* indicates that the story of spousal murder is very likely false. Vernotico was already divorced from Anna when a group of thugs, with no known connection to Genovese, strangled him. Anna, it seems, was already pregnant and gave birth three months after she and Genovese tied the knot.

Genovese has also been described as the man who engineered the brazen assassination in 1943 of journalist Carlo Tresca on a Manhattan Street as a favor to Mussolini. But given the way Italian history was evolving at that point—Mussolini was on the run and had bigger problems to contend with—it is unlikely that he needed the help of Genovese or anyone else to take out Tresca. The real threat may have come from other mobsters in New York whom Tresca had angered.

As noted earlier, some insist that Genovese was framed in the big 1959 drug trial. But the evidence, although very circumstantial and without the benefits of wiretaps or other recordings, showed to an appeals courts that Genovese played a role in organizing the syndicate. That is not to say the case didn't have some strange elements. A federal agent showed up at Genovese's home during the drug trial and told him that the government was only going after him for publicity. Then, the key government witness, a fellow named Nelson Silva Cantellops, recanted his testimony during a meeting with defense attorneys and a Catholic priest, only to later disavow his recantation. Cantellops would be beaten up in prison and might have suffered worse if it wasn't for Governor Nelson Rockefeller pardoning him. But Cantellops couldn't stay out of trouble, dying in a knife fight in a Bronx bar in July 1965.

As I have done with my other Mafia books, the approach for *The Deadly Don* was to immerse myself into the life of Genovese. This required a great deal of paper chasing through court files, both federal and state. Genovese's criminal record until the big 1959 trial involved a series of arrests and indictments in the 1920s and 1930s, including offenses ranging from weapons possession to counterfeiting and murder. Searching for those records was a challenge, but thanks to the help of some persistent court clerks and researchers at the National Archives and Records Administration, I was steered in the right direction. The result was a mass of documentation, some never before made available, that helped flesh out the story of Genovese in *The Deadly Don*.

There are several important research finds that allowed *The Deadly Don* to advance the story on Genovese and reveal new information. Perhaps one of the most important finds was the discovery of declassified papers on Genovese in the National Archives that reveal the story of his life and death behind bars. Another unique find was a private deposition Genovese gave in September 1954 when the U.S. government began proceedings to strip him of his American citizenship, which he had been granted in 1935. Within the pages of the transcript, Genovese talked about his early life and various arrests, giving his version of events and trying to make himself look like the aggrieved party. While the deposition didn't reveal the details of Genovese's various arrests, when it was coupled with newspaper articles of the time, a more complete picture emerged. The deposition, along with Genovese's court testimony in the denaturalization trial, helped trace his family life, both before and after the tempestuous Anna came on the scene.

The New York City Municipal Archives also helped fill in the mundane facts of Genovese's life, including his first marriage to Donata, a tragic figure who died from tuberculosis at the age of 28. Donata Genovese had a daughter with Genovese named Nancy. But in a twist, state court records hint at a little drama in the family, showing that Donata had a child with another man, a little girl named Lucy, whose story seems lost to history. One person interviewed for this book suggested that the way Genovese cared for Donata while she was ill indicated that he wanted to hasten her death. But Donata was a revered person in the community, and the treatment she received for tuberculosis in the final month of her life, involving a stay in a luxury apartment overlooking sunny and airy Prospect Park, was often the norm for the illness.

Later in life, Genovese's story left more of a trail of documentation. His travails in the waning days of World War Two were well documented, as was his narrow escape from the Brooklyn murder prosecution. The Apalachin meeting in 1957 filled numerous court files and police reports, all of which Genovese figured in prominently. There are also reams of paper in the federal court files surrounding the 1958 federal narcotics case and the subsequent trial in 1959. Genovese's prison record is also contained in a special file at the National Archives, and of course, the records of his denaturalization were also resurrected from a federal court in Philadelphia.

Aside from the transcripts I uncovered, Genovese didn't leave a great deal of his own written or spoken words. Even his will was only two pages long. But by doing a sort of archeological dig, an author can find enough in court records, affidavits, prison records, archival documents, and other materials to present a more complete biography. Genovese also testified in New Jersey state court in the matrimonial case with Anna in an effort to defend himself from her claims that he was a brute who abused her. In terms of video images, Genovese appeared in some scenes captured at the 1958 con-

gressional hearings in which all he did was repeatedly invoke the
Fifth Amendment in refusing to testify, which is just as well since he
was indicted on the drug charge within days of appearing on Capitol
Hill. News crews did meet up with Genovese outside the hearings,
but all that remain accessible are about fifteen seconds of film in
which he denies being part of the Mafia.

But the public record, along with voluminous newspaper and
magazine stories, does help provide a picture of Genovese and his
murderous rise through La Cosa Nostra that had never been compiled before. He was not a flashy character like John Gotti would be
decades late. Costello and Luciano to a degree were fodder in their
day for the gossip columnists and writers like Damon Runyon. But
Genovese wasn't part of that nightlife scene, although he did have a
hand as a secret owner of gay nightclubs in Greenwich Village and
there were some reports that in his early years he ran some prostitutes. There was scant mention of Don Vito in the gossips. The clubs
were more Anna's places and helped burnish her own reputation in
the Manhattan demimonde.

Two of Genovese's children are alive at this writing: Nancy and
Philip. Efforts were made to contact them and give them an opportunity to talk about their father. There was no response from them. A
few other relatives of Genovese did provide me with some personal
insight into the grandfatherly figure known as "Ba Ba" and helped
round out the portrayal of him in this book. Apart from Nancy and
Philip and their offspring, the family tree of Genovese relatives gets
a bit muddled. Some of Genovese's grandchildren trace their lineage through his second marriage to Anna and her daughter Marie,
who some claim was actually Vito's secret love child with Anna before they were married. The uncertainty is created by the fact that
sworn statements given over the years by Genovese stated that
Marie was his adopted child, which would make her children Genovese's step-grandchildren. In any case, while Genovese was known
as the King of Crime, he also doted on his grandchildren, whatever
their lineage, and acted as a man who loved children, said one relative. Such are the contradictions found in a man who was so feared
by many.

The story of Genovese as told in *The Deadly Don* is rooted in the Mafia, pure and simple. Yet it is a story broad in historical sweep, touching Prohibition, World War Two, and the tumultuous 1950s, with their personal scandals that hurt him. Genovese proved to be a survivor until the FBI and the FBN caught up with him. After he was incarcerated, men whom Genovese had handpicked to lead his family carried on operations in the street.

When he died in 1969, Genovese appeared to have been virtually penniless, at least as far as any personal fortune. But his name lives on in a crime family legacy that bears his name. Genovese's successors in the modern era—notably Vincent Gigante—kept things going in times of turmoil and setbacks. But the family still bears the name Genovese today. *The Deadly Don* reveals the story of the man who created the legacy.

Chapter One

CAPTAIN JOHN KLUBER HAD NEVER SEEN anything like it in all his years with the New York City Police Department (NYPD).

Certainly, his neighbors in the 109th Precinct had not witnessed such a spectacular home funeral for a person as young as Donata Genovese. She was only 28 years old when death took her. Funerals like the one Kluber was watching in his duties as the precinct captain were usually reserved for government big shots or gangsters, like what had been seen a few years earlier for Frankie Yale. But Yale was in Brooklyn. Richmond Hill in the peaceful borough of Queens in New York City hadn't seen such rites, especially for a woman so young. Even the *New York Times* took note with a story.

Donata Genovese had died on September 17, 1931, after suffering for just over a month from what her doctor called a virulent form of tuberculosis. She had one child with her husband as far as the neighbors knew, an 8-year-old girl named Nancy. It took a few days to arrange, but as was customary, the wake for the young mother was handled by Mulberry Street undertaker Paul Guidetti inside the two-story house on 101st Avenue. She had lived there with her husband, a man named Vito Genovese, who was described as an Italian businessman of some stature who owned some restaurants in Manhattan and imported olive oil and Italian cheeses out of his Vito Genovese Trading Company, located in Manhattan at 184 Thompson Street. Vito's father, Felice or Philip, and brother Michael also lived in the home. Vito's mother, Nunziata, had died a few years earlier.

Kluber couldn't have anticipated the pageantry he witnessed on the avenue outside the Genovese house. It was over the top, and the police captain and the rest of the cops in his detail had to make sure the cars and passersby could navigate the spectacle. Floral tributes kept coming and coming, so many that they spilled out of the dwelling and onto the street, covering the front, back, and side yards. They were big pieces and small pieces, some as tall as ten feet. There were so many flowers that a group of six young men were constantly arranging them in any space they could find. One of the men jotted down the names of those who sent displays in a little notebook, the better that Vito Genovese, clearly a man of some position in the community, knew who showed him respect. In his world, respect was something very important.

One newspaper reporter estimated the displays cost $10,000. Another reported $30,000 as the price tag. Neighbors sent flowers. Donata's husband's business associates sent them. But mostly, it was remembered that the bulk of the flowers came from the poor Italians in Ozone Park she had helped. It seems that the Depression was hitting the laborers from Italy particularly hard, and everyone remembered that Donata Genovese took it upon herself to help them survive.

"She had been doing philanthropic work for some time for the families of the unemployed Italians in the city," was how the *Standard Union* newspaper of Brooklyn described her. Donata's beneficence was aimed at many of her husband's employees, and when she died there was what was described as "general mourning" in Ozone Park.

As generous as Donata Genovese was, her charity work may very well have caused her demise. Tuberculosis in 1931 in New York City was a disease of the poor. With the Depression in full bloom, the city was seeing a rise in hospital admissions for respiratory cases that one official told the *New York Times* was due to "lowered resistance induced by the unemployment situation." Influenza, pneumonia, and tuberculosis were the main maladies. Death rates in Manhattan from tuberculosis had increased so that the borough was doing worse than other big cities.

Donata's death certificate noted that she died from "acute miliary tuberculosis." This variation of the disease can cause small lesions—resembling millet seeds, hence the name—that spread outside the lung to other organs. Medical journals note that risk factors for contracting miliary tuberculosis include contact with people who live in unsanitary conditions and have poor nutrition, likely those suffering from unemployment. While there is no way of knowing for certain, since Donata Genovese was in close contact with the poor and downtrodden, it is possible she became susceptible to the sickness from her ministering to the unemployed Italians who later flocked to her funeral.

Some in the crowd at the house on 101st Avenue were also no doubt attracted by rumors that philanthropist Donata's husband, Vito, was friends with Al Capone from Chicago. Maybe that is where some of the charitable money came from: the mob. One newspaper, citing the cops, said Genovese was one of Capone's "chief lieutenants," something that was quickly denied by the officers on the scene. In any case, this was the Prohibition era, and some of the public congregating outside the Genovese house were looking to catch a glimpse of Scarface, who reportedly did show up to pay his respects to the Genovese family.

There would later be other suggestions that Genovese didn't care properly for the infirm Donata. But back in the 1920s and 1930s, the treatment for tuberculosis was to have a person convalesce in a sunny, airy place. In fact, for the last weeks of her life, Donata was in a luxury apartment building on Ocean Avenue in Brooklyn that overlooked Prospect Park and had a sunny exposure. Sunlight and fresh air were the preferred treatments for tuberculosis, although the miliary variety of the illness had a high mortality rate no matter what was done at a time when there was no widespread drug therapy.

The morning of September 21, 1931, Captain Kluber and the rest of the police detail cordoned off 101st Avenue so that the funeral procession of two hundred "motor coaches" wouldn't have trouble navigating the throng of ten thousand people outside the Genovese house. Vito Genovese had only requested a dozen cars from the funeral director, but that didn't stop others from joining the long motorcade. The funeral procession didn't have far to go since the solemn requiem mass was to be at the Church of the Nativity of the Blessed Lady only about three blocks away. The streets off Rockaway Boulevard, where the church was situated, were filled of course with people and cars. Even rooftops provided vantage points for the curious.

Reverend Herbert Wuerts officiated at the mass, and when it was over, the body of Donata Genovese was borne to a waiting hearse for what would become a last journey through the streets of the city. With Vito Genovese in the family car—there is no official record left to show who was with him, although it was very likely his daughter Nancy was—the procession, which was more like a parade, turned north towards Manhattan.

Donata Genovese's final ride was no short jaunt. From the church, the funeral procession wound its way some eleven miles as the crow flies to Manhattan Island over the East River. Once in Manhattan, local cops took over and escorted the procession as it made its way through Broome, Lafayette, and Mulberry Streets, which so happened to be the spine of the Italian community. Then, the hearse and accompanying vehicles—estimated to be between forty-three to fifty-eight cars in all at this point—circled the ornate baroque-style NYPD headquarters building on Centre Street.

This circuitous part of the journey had a certain symbolism for Vito Genovese, and it would be understandable if he had mixed emotions as the cars motored past the headquarters building. Vito Genovese may have been a respected businessman like the newspapers said. But the detectives inside 240 Centre Street knew him for a variety of reasons—none of them good. It all came down to the fact that Vito Genovese, restauranteur and cheese merchant though he may have been, was an aspiring member of the growing confederation of Italian gangsters who were beginning to thrive in New York and run its criminal underworld.

By the time Vito Genovese arrived in New York Harbor on May 23, 1913, the Italian migration had already spawned a disparate criminal culture. The most troubling element was the so-called Black Hand, a loose amalgam of extortionists who preyed on the fears and gullible nature of their mainly Southern Italian compatriots. Various groups of shakedown artists used wild and vicious schemes involving kidnappings, anonymous threats, and bombings, the latter carried out if the intended victims disregarded demands for payment. Often the plots worked, but eventually the cops started their own "Italian Squad" led by the legendary Lieutenant Joseph Petrosino.

There was no evidence that Vito Genovese took part in any Black Hand activity, although he was later said to have developed with his friends their own protection racket in which they extorted payments from businessmen in Queens and Manhattan. Genovese became a young man at a time when Italian crime groups saw the potential in Prohibition for making big money in bootlegging and smuggling. He threw his lot in with other *paisans* who recognized Prohibition as the beginning of a boom time for the Italian criminals in Manhattan, Brooklyn, and just about everywhere in the city. When necessary, they had no problem working with Jewish and Irish gangsters.

It was soon after Prohibition got underway that Vito Genovese's involvement in bootlegging brought him to the attention of the cops on Centre Street, and they started the fill up the file they had on him at police headquarters. It became clear that Genovese had ties to bootlegging when he became a suspect in a vexing Brooklyn automobile homicide in Prospect Park in May 1924. Genovese and another man, reputed drug dealer Umberto Lombardi of Thompson Street in Manhattan, were charged with homicide and spent at least a night in a Brooklyn jail. Cops said that both men had criminal records. But after spending a night in jail, both Genovese and Lombardi saw the charges dropped.

Nevertheless, Genovese continued to get into trouble, and it was clear that he was turning into a bona fide gangster by the company he kept and the things he did. He was charged in another homicide case in November 1925, but cops again dropped the case.

Then, if there was ever any doubt about the kind of company Genovese was keeping, it became clear that he had made some enemies one night in July 1926. As Genovese would tell the police, a short distance away from the family home—then on 102nd Avenue in Richmond Hill—he was shot from behind in the neck. Wounded, Genovese was able to crawl back to the vestibule of his home and, according to an account in the *Brooklyn Times Union*, was found by his father "prostrate on the steps in a pool of blood." Genovese's wife said she had no idea who would want to harm her spouse, who was taken to Jamaica Hospital. Cops believed the assailant had lain in wait to ambush Genovese, but they never reported any arrest in the shooting.

Genovese, having survived a murder attempt and able to weasel his way out of two murder cases, took to regularly carrying guns. But the one thing Genovese never got caught at was bootlegging, even though he frequented the open-air curbside booze market in Manhattan where gangsters and suppliers of whiskey and other alcoholic beverages made deals for shipments expected to come into town on the smuggling ships arriving off Long Island. Given all his hassles with the law, it would be understandable if Genovese smirked as his limousine drove through Little Italy.

For Donata Genovese, the funeral journey to Manhattan represented a visit to some of the Italian neighborhoods that had meaning to her in her short, charitable life. It was customary for funeral processions to make these final passes through old haunts before the final leg to the cemetery. With the procession over, Donata's casket was taken to St. John Cemetery in Middle Village, Queens, an esteemed Roman Catholic burial ground where Vito Genovese had years earlier purchased a large outdoor underground family vault. This was a gravesite capped by a large stone that could be moved to allow access to place caskets in underground niches. His mother was already residing within for her eternal rest.

Donata's casket placed in the ground was described in the newspapers as being silver and valued at an estimated $40,000 to $50,000, an exorbitant sum by any standard. Even Frankie Yale's casket was reported to have cost only $15,000. The rumors about the opulence of the funeral seemed to pile up. But the truth was that undertaker Guidetti's final bill for the funeral listed the casket as costing only $575, and that included a "box" within which the casket was placed. After the mourners had left the cemetery, a workman sealed the box shut. He charged $10.

It took Vito Genovese close to three years to wind up his dead wife's affairs, such as they were. Donata had purchased the house on 101st Avenue for $13,000 in 1928, and at the time of her death, the home's market value had dropped a bit to $12,000. There was also rental income of about $900 in the year and a half before she died. With outstanding mortgages remaining on the property amounting to about $7,500, the Genovese family home would net only about $4,500 for Vito Genovese and the couple's daughter, Nancy.

Along with the house, Donata Genovese left two bank accounts. A checking account amounted to just over $152 dollars. A second account was more curious. It was a trust account at a local bank in Ozone Park for $92 for the benefit of Lucy Napolitano. An obscure notation in the Surrogate's Court file in Queens indicated that Lucy was in fact the daughter of Donata and a man identified only as "C. Napolitano." No age was given in the papers for Lucy. Was she born before Donata married Vito Genovese in 1924, or was she conceived sometime after the marriage? History has provided us with no answers. But whoever Lucy was, she would have been related as a half sister to Nancy, the daughter Donata had with Genovese.

While Donata didn't leave her family much, Vito Genovese wasn't hurting for cash. After his wife's death, records show that he moved with Nancy to 29 Washington Square Park, an apartment building in Manhattan that also had an address of 43 Fifth Avenue The neighborhood was one of those quiet enclaves that faced Washington Square Park, with its landmark arch. The Manhattan base of operations for Genovese kept him in close connection with his peers in the Italian mob scene, which was in the midst of a state of some violent change. It was a life that Genovese had been destined to be part of ever since he stepped off the slow boat from Naples.

Chapter Two

LIKE MANY OF HIS COMPATRIOTS in the gangster life, Vito Genovese was born in Italy, on November 21, 1897, to be precise. His birthplace was the town of Risigliano, about ten miles outside of the city of Naples. To the south of the city, dominating the history of the area and the psyche of its residents, was Mount Vesuvius, one of Europe's most active volcanoes and one that had erupted numerous times over the centuries. Neapolitans had long ago come to terms with Vesuvius, its giant cone dominating history and their lives ever since the eruption in 79 AD, one of the most powerful of all times, which wiped out the ancient city of Pompeii.

Vesuvius has always been considered one of the most dangerous volcanoes in the world, particularly since it is less than six miles from Naples, a city today of over three million. In 1913, when Vito Genovese emigrated to the United States, the motivation for him and his family to leave Italy may have had something to do with concern about Vesuvius: the volcano was active that year, its cone filling with magma that occasionally spilled out. But another eruption of concern on the Continent was the growing unease and conflict among nations. World War One wouldn't start until 1914, but Genovese's family couldn't help see that trouble was brewing.

It was May 23, 1913, that Genovese arrived in the Port of New

York aboard the SS *Taormina* after what was about a two week trip from Naples. His father, Felice, sometimes called "Phillipo," had arrived in New York in 1905, leaving the rest of the family back in the Naples area. This fractured migration was common among Italian families. The father would travel first, get settled in America, and then send for the rest of the family, sometimes over a period of years.

By the time young Vito was getting ready to sail for New York, Felice worked as a laborer on various construction projects developing about that time in the city. The *Taormina* was a one-smokestack vessel that couldn't make very good travel time. Records aren't clear if the 16-year-old Genovese traveled with his mother, Nunziata, and his brothers Michael and Carmine. Writer Dom Frasca claimed that Nunziata arrived in 1917, so that would have put her several years behind her son in her travels. But federal immigration records showed that Nunziata arrived in the U.S. around 1920 and died a short time later, in 1923. Genovese would also say at one point that he had a sister, but her name has never surfaced in police records or immigration files. He did have a female cousin who lived in Queens.

By April 15, 1917, Genovese got into his first legal scrape at the age of 19 when he was arrested on a gun possession charge in Manhattan. Genovese's lawyer told him to plead guilty, which he did. The resulting sentence from the court was sixty days in a local jail. With World War One in full swing around that time and the U.S. military heavily involved in Europe, the gun conviction didn't stop the local Selective Service official from trying to get Genovese into the army.

"They said, 'Italy and the United State are allies,'" Genovese recounted years later. "'Do you want to go and serve in the Italian Army or do you want to serve in the United States Army,' and I answered and I chose to serve in the United States Army, and that is how I was drafted."

At that point in his life, Genovese had not applied for American citizenship and believed that by serving in the American military he would have a path to becoming a citizen, which turned out not to be true. In any case, Genovese reported to a military camp on Long Island—probably the old facility in Yaphank made famous by songwriter Irving Berlin when he was in the army—for a preinduction physical. But as luck would have it, the Armistice was signed and took effect on November 11, 1918, and Genovese didn't have to serve.

The brief taste of jail Genovese had in 1917 didn't deter him from getting into more trouble, even though according to Frasca his stint behind bars had caused a rift between the young man and his mother and father. On April 22, 1918, just about a year after his first arrest, Genovese was picked up on a charge of felonious assault in Queens, accused of shooting someone. After surrendering to police with his lawyer present, Genovese was taken to court, where the victim took one look at him and said that the young Italian man wasn't the assailant. The judge threw the case out.

Frasca also reported in *King of Crime* that Genovese was at this time as a young man, to put it bluntly, a pimp, claiming he was given control of a brothel on the Lower East Side near police headquarters—then on Mulberry Street—by Charles "Lucky" Luciano. The clientele of this brothel allegedly included politicians and police brass. This claim that Genovese was a sex trafficker had not been publicized before Frasca's book, although Frasca claimed that the Manhattan district attorney's office had evidence from a woman who said she worked for Genovese. The woman, who was identified only by the name "Rita" in Frasca's account, was described as a 19-year-old "ravishing redhead" whom Genovese became smitten with in 1924, the year she started working in the sex business. Frasca said that Genovese essentially dated Rita, but that means he would have done so two years after setting up a married household in 1922 with Donata.

No records have surfaced to show Genovese was ever investigated in this period in connection with prostitution, and Frasca cites no identifiable source for his claim. As previously noted, some parts of the prostitution tale appear suspect, namely that Genovese met Rita in 1924 and then stopped seeing her to marry Donata. But the marriage to Donata had already taken place in 1922 and not after 1924, as Frasca's narrative indicated.

Even if he did dabble in prostitution, Genovese stayed out of trouble—at least as far as the NYPD was concerned—for almost six years, until he again was picked up on a gun charge in Manhattan. What appears interesting in that case was that it indicated that Genovese, now almost 27 years old, was in the thick of the world of the bootleggers. This was the best of career paths for a young, aspiring criminal. It was the best way to make money. A small newspaper story about that April 1924 arrest mentioned Genovese and codefendant Umberto Lombardi, his cohort in a mysterious Prospect Park auto accident a few months later, as being apparently involved in bootlegging. The location of the arrest on Kenmare and Mott Streets was adjacent to the curbside liquor exchange that had sprouted up near police headquarters. Genovese gave an address in upstate Albany, New York. Why he did that was never explained, and records show the judge threw out that case as well. Both Genovese and Lombardi were described as being "well-dressed" and cringing near the wall.

A month after the gun arrest, any doubt that Genovese was tied in with the gangster set was put to rest on May 13, 1924, when he was involved in a bizarre and serious auto accident in Prospect Park in Brooklyn that left one man dead and Genovese seriously injured. Years later, Genovese recounted what happened.

"There were four of us in my car. We went to Coney Island to have a little fun, to have a dinner," he said. "Coming home, I don't recall the exact time, maybe 11 or 12 o'clock . . . I was sitting alongside the driver and there were two other fellows in the back seat. We were driving on the street, Prospect Park, and it was raining. All of a sudden the car skidded and hit a tree. I got thrown off the car about 25, 30 feet."

The impact with the ground gave Genovese a dislocated shoulder, three broken ribs, and bruises all over his body. This was in the age before seatbelts. Another passenger didn't fare so well.

"One of the other fellows in the back hit the tree smack, and he died right there, got killed right there," Genovese explained.

One of the other passengers was also thrown to the ground, while the driver appears to have fled, according to Genovese's account.

But the NYPD had a different explanation for reporters about what had actually happened. To the cops, it wasn't a boys' night out for the group on Coney Island's famous boardwalk. Rather, detectives said that Genovese's car was being pursued when it smacked into the tree. It didn't just skid. Why was Genovese being pursued? The *Brooklyn Daily Eagle* account reported that the police believed mob violence had possibly been at the root of the chase.

"Police have intimated that the Prospect Park accident was the flowing up on a shooting affair in Manhattan on the evening before and that the dead man and his two companions had fled to Brooklyn," the *Eagle* reported. "On the ground near the wrecked car was a revolver and a stiletto." Another newspaper said it was likely the car was running away from an earlier bootlegging feud in Coney Island.

Apart from the weapons found outside the car, another mystery in the case surrounded the identity of the dead man. Initially, he was identified as "Carmine Russo" of Ozone Park, Queens, the neighborhood where Genovese was living. But then other members of the Russo family came forward and said that the deceased wasn't Carmine, who police said was the listed owner of the car.

Genovese and the other injured man, identified in the newspapers as 23-year-old "Umbarto" Lombardi of Thompson Street in Manhattan, a venue Genovese had become familiar with and where he would later have offices, were both charged with vehicular homicide. Cops likely filed the charges as a ploy to force either man to tell the truth about what happened. But nothing changed. No one talked. Later, Genovese said it made no sense to charge him because he wasn't even driving. When the case went to court, the homicide charges were dismissed.

The Prospect Park car chase and crash, reports of shootings, and the gun arrest by the old bootlegging market signaled that Genovese was no choirboy and was steadily becoming enmeshed in the gangster life. He was only in his twenties, but so were some of the other young toughs like Charles "Lucky" Luciano and Frank Costello, men whose careers and fortunes would shadow Genovese for all his days.

Bootlegging was of course the main business of the up-and-coming mobsters of the day, and there was plenty of evidence mounting that Genovese was involved, even if he was never convicted of any Prohibition-related crimes. He kept getting arrested for gun charges, and in October 1925 was again grabbed by cops on a homicide rap. This time, the deceased was a known street thug named Ciro "Jerry the Wolf" Scotti, 26 years old, who a few years earlier turned up as a suspect in the killing of a policeman in the upstate town of Binghamton. It was the night of October 18 that Scotti, who Long Island police said had an interest in an illegal speakeasy in the city of Long Beach, was shot and killed in Astoria; police said that Scotti was fired on by four men in an automobile. Four years earlier, at the age of 22, Scotti had also been shot at near the Queensboro Bridge. Police picked up Genovese, and in November 1925 he was arraigned on murder charges related to the slaying of Scotti, but in the end, they had to cut him loose—again.

Genovese was clearly living something of a charmed life so far as his arrest record went. He had not been unscathed since he did spend sixty days in a jail and would later spend another month in a cell for yet another weapons charge. But given the kind of company Genovese was keeping, it made sense for him to walk around with some protection. The night of July 5, 1926, Genovese apparently had nothing to protect himself with, and it almost cost him with his life.

According to the NYPD account, Genovese's father, Felice, found his son unconscious in the hallway of the family home at 5873 102nd Street in the Woodhaven section of Queens at about

5:00 A.M. with a gunshot wound to the neck. A trail of blood led from the house to a spot about a half a block away where Genovese had been shot. Police told the *Queens Leader-Observer* newspaper that Genovese "spent his remaining strength in banging on the front door to summon aid."

Although Genovese's wife told the police she couldn't understand why anyone would want to shoot her husband, the *Leader-Observer* subhead on the story read "Police Claim Bootleg Feud Responsible for Attack." Another report was more pointed, saying the attack on Genovese was "believed to be connected intimately with bootlegging and other illegal activities that have been engaged in by a band of Italians."

The shooting of Genovese, police noted, was "remarkably similar" to an attack on his 38-year-old friend Arnello Albertini a few weeks earlier. Albertini was also ambushed early one morning in May and shot from behind with a shotgun that was found later wrapped in burlap. Genovese was lucky. He was taken to a nearby hospital, where he recovered from his wound, but he didn't say much to the police. Albertini died, having being hit in his back, neck, and spine with buckshot. The way both men were attacked "strengthens the belief that both men were victims of a feud between bootlegging factions or between secret societies," the *Richmond Hill Record* newspaper reported.

Although most accounts of Genovese's life never dealt in detail with his early criminal past, it was clear from this search through history that Genovese was in the bootlegging business, which meant he was in the orbit of one of most important and powerful crime bosses of the period, Joseph "Joe the Boss" Masseria. A round-faced man with narrow eyes, Masseria ran a crime syndicate that specialized in bootlegging, and with the assassination of rival Salvatore D'Aquila in 1928, he became the *big* boss of the Italian mob. Masseria was a pudgy man known for his gargantuan eating habits. He had dodged assassination attempts aimed at himself over the years and had pulled together a group of acolytes that in the history of organized crime was very impressive: Al Capone, Frank Costello, Charles Luciano, Frankie Yale (originally Iole), Gaetano Reina, and of course Genovese.

With the likes of Costello and Luciano involved in rum-running and able to rely on subordinates like Genovese, Masseria's position in the fragmented Italian underworld in this pre-Mafia period was strong. The bootlegging racket was particularly lucrative, with Costello able to wisely integrate his operation, which included smuggling boats, warehouses, ship-to-shore radio stations, and the occasional seaplane used to meet the ships out at Rum Row, the area off the East Coast of the U.S. where smuggling ships waited to be off-loaded. Costello also spread money around in bribes to cops and Coast Guard officials and saw the wisdom of working collaboratively with Jewish gangsters like Meyer Lansky and Arnold Rothstein as well as big Irish bootleggers like the sportsman William "Big Bill" Dwyer, who ultimately became known as "King of the Bootleggers," an honorific many would share.

New York City in particular, with an estimated thirty thousand speakeasies, was a major bootlegging market, and well through the 1920s and into the 1930s. Costello and Dwyer themselves were raking in tens of millions of dollars a year from moving illegal booze, and they had ready buyers for their product all over the city. Costello had a number of secret hiding places all over the city, notably the historic Blackwell Mansion in Queens, where his relatives filled the place with thousands of cases of liquor secreted in hidden compartments. Dwyer also had warehouses at his disposal, and from the profits he made, he plowed some of the money into the purchase of sports organizations, such as hockey teams in Canada, horse racing tracks, and a football team he named the Brooklyn Dodgers, not to be confused with the baseball team, which also played at the same Ebbets Field in Brooklyn.

Genovese didn't make as big a name for himself in Prohibition as others in the Masseria combination did, notably Dwyer, Costello, and Luciano. It is just as well that he kept himself under the radar. Costello and Dwyer got indicted together on federal bootlegging charges in 1927; Costello ultimately had the case dismissed, but Dwyer got convicted and had to serve two years in prison and was socked with big back tax bills, which ultimately sent him to the poor house. But there is evidence that Genovese was doing well financially and allegedly was branching out into another kind of racket: counterfeiting.

Vito Genovese's alleged link to fake currency is one of those overlooked aspects of his life. But thanks to the National Archives and Records Administration, a unique case in which he was involved was found through a diligent search of the records. It was 1930, and as one newspaper said, "American currency was being flattered by a great deal of sincere imitation around the world." Clever forgers of the period were passing $100 bills so expertly done that even bankers were fooled. As a result, the American government called together international conferences to deal with the flood of fake papers, notably currency, bonds, letters of credit, and checks.

Back in Washington, DC, the big worry was about fake gold certificates being produced with face values of over a million dollars at a time. From about 1879 until about 1934, gold certificates were used in the United States government as a form of alternative currency. Technically, they represented an amount of gold and were embossed with a dollar value, similar to regular currency. As explained by the Investopedia.com website, gold certificates "were essentially a parallel currency and were technically exchangeable as such, although they were not often used in routine transactions." These certificates were in use until President Franklin D. Roosevelt uncoupled the dollar from the gold standard. Now, the currency certificates are only of value to collectors.

But in 1930, the currency paper was still legal tender, and Secret Service agents were alarmed by the quality of counterfeit $10, $20, and $50 gold certificates showing up out of Brooklyn and Manhattan. The certificates seemed expertly done by criminals with access to some very good printing presses and plates. Investigators apparently felt the need to act quickly. Surveillance from a nearby building traced some of the suspects to an apartment on Eighty-fifth Street in Brooklyn. Shortly after midnight on May 28, 1930, seven Secret Service agents, guns drawn, rushed the building and entered the apartment. Investigators were not disappointed. Three men were found working a giant lithographic press, and from the looks of things they had been in the process of cranking out bogus certificates with a face value of $1 million, some of which still had the ink wet. There was enough special paper at the location to print an additional $4 million in certificates. The printing press was said by investigators to have been one of the largest ever seen in such an operation, weighing some 3,500 pounds. It would eventually have to be dismantled before it could be removed from the building.

The three men arrested at the apartment were identified as Pericles Mannerini, who was the alleged ringleader, Joseph de Negris, who supplied the money for the operation, and Mattio "the Doctor" Mattera, who was identified as the expert engraver and lithographer whose skills were so vital to the forgery ring. But it soon became clear that those three suspects weren't the only ones the Secret Service was focused on. In July 1930, a federal grand jury in Brooklyn indicted not only the initial three men arrested but also five others, including Genovese.

The newspaper reports about Genovese showed how he had risen in stature in the mob when investigators described him to the *New York Times* as a "wealthy gang leader" from the West Side of Manhattan. Until then, Genovese had pretty much kept away from the big headlines as being a mobster. True, he had his close calls with murder cases, but he wasn't described as anyone terribly important among the Italian criminals who merited more ink in the tabloids. The counterfeiting case started to change that perception.

It also seemed that Genovese was succeeding as a businessman, both legitimate and otherwise, in ways that were making him very affluent. One federal prosecutor said Genovese had a summer home on Long Island—where wasn't specified—and a winter residence in Manhattan, apparently referring to the apartment off Washington Square Park. Later in life, Genovese did describe his home in Manhattan as being a "winter" residence. Since Queens was geographically on Long Island, the prosecutor might have conflated the house in Woodhaven, technically owned by the late Donata, as a summer home.

The one problem for the federal investigators was that Genovese, as prominent as he might have been to the ring and as well heeled as he was with real estate, simply couldn't be found. The twelve-count indictment returned in the case named Genovese in six of the counts, including the important conspiracy count. But just a day after the bench warrant was issued for Genovese's arrest, federal marshals said that "after a due and diligent search," in Brooklyn, Queens, and the rest of Long Island, they couldn't find him. They also couldn't find two of the other defendants.

Nevertheless, federal authorities were able to proceed against the other defendants in the case and quickly secured guilty pleas from Mannerini, de Negris, and Mattera, the ones caught red-handed with the printing press. A fourth defendant, Joseph Piscopo of Brooklyn, also pleaded guilty. In November of 1930, under conditions of tight courtroom security, a Brooklyn federal judge sentenced them to varying terms of prison ranging from a little over two years to eight years.

About a month after the sentencing, prosecutors came one more time into court, tail between their legs and asked that the case against Genovese and the other men never arrested be dismissed, a request the court granted.

Obviously, without Genovese ever being arrested and with there apparently being no corroborating evidence against him, the prosecution's case against him for counterfeiting was very tenuous. One defendant, Mattera, turned into a cooperating witness, and when he was sentenced, he was sent to prison so he could be protected. But the available court records don't show if Mattera in any way implicated Genovese.

So, what could have been Genovese's involvement in the gold certificate case? He may have provided money for the conspiracy. Another possibility is that since Genovese had an interest in the waste paper industry, with a firm on Thompson Street, he might have been able through his contacts to provide the conspirators with access to high-quality paper needed for the printing. But with the case against him dismissed, Genovese was free from any legal constraints, a good thing for his friends in the mob who were going to count him in on something very big in connection with Joe the Boss.

The problem with Joseph Masseria is that he kept young Turks like Luciano and Genovese on a short leash and they believed he was holding them back in the rackets. There were plenty of other criminal enterprises besides bootlegging where an ambitious young gangster could make his mark. Basically, the Italian hoods became adept at setting up cartels in prosaic trades like ice delivery, grapes used for production of wine, and coal. The industries were organized by a few big players who divided up territory and set prices. One of them was the Bronx-based Gaetano Reina, who specialized in the ice business and was part of Masseria's crime group.

But Masseria, ever greedy, wanted Reina to give up some of his ice business profits, something that apparently was not done. The result was predictable. The night of February 26, 1930, Reina was shotgunned to death as he left the Sheridan Avenue apartment building of a girlfriend. Reina did carry a handgun, but he didn't use it to defend himself. Cops found hundreds of dollars in cash on his body, so robbery wasn't a motive. Masseria also antagonized some of his subordinates by sanctioning the murder of Reina, a move that seemed motivated by pure greed.

Masseria's move against Reina was a bad one. The killing of Reina unsettled many in the Masseria faction, including the dead man's brother-in-law, Joseph Valachi, a low-level Bronx gangster who would carve out his own special place in history decades later as a Mafia turncoat. Luciano, Genovese, and Costello, as well as others like Joseph Bonanno, now all saw the treachery Masseria was capable of and saw that he was not a man to be trusted. They secretly maneuvered themselves in an alignment with Masseria's main rival, a fellow Sicilian immigrant named Salvatore Maranzano.

While Masseria impressed many as being a "greaseball," a derogatory slang term for a certain type of uncouth Italian immigrant male, Maranzano had an air of respectability about him. He was said at one point to have considered studying for the priesthood, but he turned to the Sicilian Mafia instead to make a living. Maranzano fled Sicily around 1925 during an anti-Mafia campaign being waged by Mussolini, about which more will be discussed in chapter seven. Once in Brooklyn, Maranzano parlayed his money into the business of the day for emerging Italian gangsters—bootlegging.

In the months after the murder of Reina, Maranzano's faction steadily increased its power, assassinating Masseria allies and damaging his rackets. Genovese, Luciano, and Costello saw the way the tide was turning, and in a clandestine meeting said to have taken place on Broome Street, they decided that Joe "the Boss" had to go. It was then, according to an account later given by Bonanno, that Luciano met with Maranzano and both men agreed that once Masseria was killed, Luciano would take over his rackets.

Unaware that many of his top young associates had switched allegiance to Maranzano, Masseria went about his business, including making time for his favorite activity—eating. It was April 15, 1931, that Masseria and Luciano—some accounts also have Genovese included as accompanying them for the repast—traveled to Coney Island. Their destination was the Nuova Villa Tammaro, a seafood restaurant on Fifteenth Avenue, about four blocks from the Boardwalk. After Masseria's entourage arrived, the owner, Gerardo Scarpato, sent his mother-in-law, Anna Tammaro, out to the market for some fish to serve the guest.

It was about 3:30 P.M. that Masseria, Luciano, and the others at the table finished eating. Masseria and Luciano began a game of cards, and after one hand, Luciano left the table to go to the bathroom. At that point, two or three men entered the restaurant and started shooting at Masseria. A total of twelve rounds were fired, five of which struck Masseria in vital organs, killing him. The assailants then fled in a waiting auto. When Luciano came back, he saw the carnage and Masseria's body on the floor.

In his account of the shooting published years later, Valachi said the assassins were Joseph "Joe Stretch" Stracci and Frank Livorsi, with Ciro Terranova driving the getaway car. Valachi also indicated that Genovese was an accomplice, although it may be that he was present for the meal and then left just before the shooting started. After the cops arrived, Luciano, who wasn't armed, told them he couldn't understand who wanted to do Joe "the Boss" any harm. One iconic crime scene photograph that was later published showed a bloody Masseria on the floor with a playing card between his fingers, although it is now suspected that the image was a set-up after he was already dead.

The killing of Masseria never resulted in any arrests. In a strange postscript to the event, Gerardo Scarpato met his own grisly end. The restauranteur went away for about a year. After he returned, he was found dead in a car in Brooklyn, hog-tied and stuffed in a burlap bag.

After the murder of Masseria, Luciano let it be known that he was the head of the dead man's crime clan. He made it clear that Genovese was his second-in-command, so to speak, and Costello another close advisor. But, as he had arranged earlier, Luciano had agreed that Maranzano would be the main Italian crime boss in New York now that Masseria was dead. A gangster who seemed more cultured than the others, Maranzano had his own idea as to how he wanted the mob to be organized.

"I didn't know until later that he was a nut about Julius Caesar and even had a room in the house filled with nothing but books about him," remembered Valachi. "That is how he got the idea for the organization."

Most crime historians report that Maranzano spelled out his plan for the crime families at a meeting of criminals in a big social hall by Washington Avenue in the Bronx. Valachi said that Maranzano took for himself the title of *capo di tutti capi*, or "boss of all bosses," and that everyone was going to be divided up into families, with each group having a boss, underboss, and lieutenants or *caporegimes*. It was the basic structure of the American Mafia families that more or less has persisted to this day. Maranzano also spelled out rules and the penalties for violations and said that the troubles of the past should be forgotten and buried.

New York was split into the Five Families. Luciano was one of the bosses and had as his underboss Genovese, a position that was a testament to his political prowess in such a violent world and his reputation as a killer and operative in the organization. The other bosses at the time were Thomas Gagliano, Vincent Mangano, Joseph Bonanno, and Joseph Profaci.

While peace should have been the new reality for the Five Families, it was not to be. Maranzano's Julius Caesar complex, as well as his paranoia, was alienating him from his fellow gangsters. Valachi recalled Maranzano telling him that "we have to go to the mattress again," an indication that he was thinking about mob warfare again after just having settled the score with Masseria. Maranzano even turned against Luciano and Genovese, the two men who helped propel him to the top of the Five Families. According to one account, Jewish gangsters became suspicious that Maranzano was trying to muscle in on their turf in the garment industry, and according to another version of the story, they convinced Luciano that the big boss had to be killed.

According to Valachi, Thomas "Three Finger Brown" Lucchese, at that time a major mobster, also suspected that Maranzano was hijacking Luciano's bootlegging trucks and flat-out said that he was planning to slay Luciano and Genovese. Things were getting very unstable in what was supposed to be a stable mob environment. The plan was to have Luciano and Genovese slaughtered after they showed up at a meeting inside Maranzano's office suite at 230 Park Avenue in Manhattan. But with word leaking out about Maranzano's plan, Luciano got the jump on things to save himself and Genovese by hiring a group of Jewish gangsters to carry out the murder. Luciano had long been close with Jews like Meyer Lansky and Dutch Schultz, so it wasn't hard for him to convince Lansky to take out a contract to kill Maranzano.

The assassination of Maranzano at the hands of Lansky's men is another part of mob lore that has been told many times. It was midafternoon on September 10, 1931, not even five months after Masseria had been killed in Coney Island, that Maranzano was gunned down and stabbed inside his offices. Cops reported that the assailants were posing as police officers.

The police rounded up a number of Italian men as suspects—the Jews involved weren't touched—and said they believed that Maranzano's death might have been related to immigrant smuggling activities. The case went nowhere.

With Maranzano out of the way, Luciano quickly convinced the other bosses of the Mafia families to join him in a "Commission," or overriding ruling body that would set policy for the crime families, settle disputes, and sanction murders when needed. The heads of the Five Families sat on the Commission as a Mafia court of last resort. It was something that would last for decades.

As Valachi would later relate in his biography, Genovese himself was well aware of why Maranzano had to die.

"He went on to explain to me how Maranzano was hijacking Charlie Lucky's alcohol trucks and I don't know what else. Vito went on to say 'If the old man had his way, he would have had us all at each other's throats.' "

Genovese also explained how conscious he and Luciano were about who to trust. Since Valachi was essentially part of Maranzano's camp, no one felt they could talk to him. Valachi admitted that had Genovese told him about the plot against Maranzano, he would have tipped off the doomed boss. By not bringing Valachi into the loop, Genovese and Luciano essentially saved Valachi from having to make the decision to be a double-crosser. No one would have wanted a proven turncoat in the midst of things.

Vito Genovese had come through what came to be known as the Castellammarese War, after Maranzano's Sicilian birthplace of Castellammare del Golfo, in very good shape. He had been on the winning side, and his friend Luciano was truly the first among equals among the Mafia bosses. True, Genovese had lost his wife and had a daughter to raise. But he was doing well on a number of fronts, his bootlegging had thrived, and he had some legitimate businesses like a waste paper company to show lawful income. He also had been lucky to survive the violence that was a constant in the life of a gangster. As the Mafia world settled into a more normal pattern, Genovese's personal life was on the verge of having a big change.

Chapter Three

BY THE EARLY TWENTIETH CENTURY, Greenwich Village was a New York City neighborhood that beat to its own drummer. The area had in the nineteenth century been the location of a prison and gradually became known as a low-rent district that attracted the bohemian culture, gay life, artists, and a fair number of Italian immigrants. Unlike other parts of Manhattan, the Village retained a patchwork of angled streets that gave it a special European feel.

As a young man, Vito Genovese was familiar with the Village because so many of his gangster friends frequented the area. It was close to the curbside bootleg liquor exchange on Kenmare Street and the docks on the Hudson River, as well as the growing Italian neighborhood of Little Italy to the east on Houston Street. The physical intimacy of the Village made it a good place for the criminal class to live and thrive among the artists and progressive thinkers who gave the place its special cultural stamp.

The southern section of the Village, the area below Washington Square Park, became known as a focal point for the Italian immigrant life. Churches like Our Lady of Pompeii on Bleecker Street and St. Anthony of Padua on Sullivan Street sprouted up, sometimes with assistance from the more well-heeled Catholics from outside the area, and became beacons in the lives of the southern Italians who settled in the affordable tenement housing they found.

Among the Italian immigrant families that gravitated to Greenwich Village was the Petillo clan, which by 1920 had taken an apartment at 115 West Houston Street, between Thompson and Sullivan Streets. Annello Petillo, a poolroom proprietor, and his wife, Concetta, lived in the building with the couple's five children: four sons and a daughter, all born in the United States. The daughter was the oldest, having been born in 1905. Her name was Anna.

With a fine-boned face and dark, Mediterranean features, Anna Petillo was a young woman who turned the heads of men and women with her glamorous looks. She would later be described as "lush," exuding a sensuality that was common among many of the young Italian women in the neighborhood. A photograph said to be of a young Anna showed a woman with wide eyes, a graceful nose, and hair done in the finger-wave style popular in the 1920s. As was expected of the girls of her age, Anna was destined to marry young. Her choice of spouse at the age of 19 was a 21-year-old man from an Italian immigrant family from Elizabeth, New Jersey, named Gerardo Vernotico, also sometimes known as Gerald and John. On the marriage license issued on March 3, 1924, Vernotico listed his occupation as a carpenter/builder.

The first marriage license for Anna and Gerardo Vernotico appears to have been issued for a civil ceremony at the New York City municipal building at One Centre Street. A year later, on or about September 26, 1925, the couple decided to have a clergyman perform a ceremony at an apartment at 157 Thompson Street. About two years later, the couple had taken up residence at 387 Sixth Avenue, and Anna gave birth to a daughter, Maria, also known in life as Rose Marie.

Although Vernotico professed to being a carpenter, he was fast becoming a petty criminal in Greenwich Village, one with some distinction as it turned out. In December of 1928, police in the Village became aware of numerous burglaries plaguing the area around Sixth Avenue and placed the neighborhood under surveillance. It wasn't long before cops busted Vernotico and an associate after they appeared to act suspiciously. The officers found on the pair jewelry and other items that appeared to have been stolen a few days earlier from the home of a woman on nearby Waverly Place.

The stolen property amounted to about $1,000 in value. But the real item of interest was a map found on Vernotico that listed addresses in the Village with notations about where the cops were posted and when. One note stated, "Cop on corner from twelve to one." The map earned Vernotico and his buddy the sobriquet in the newspapers as the "map burglars." Vernotico, whose age was erroneously reported as 21, and Joseph Gordelia, 17, were held for a preliminary hearing, but no record could be found for a disposition of the case.

Carpentry work apparently wasn't bringing in enough cash to pay the bills because less than three years later, in June 1931, Vernotico again made the newspapers. Cops in the Bath Beach section of Brooklyn grabbed Vernotico, listed now as being 28 years old, on charges that he and three others held up a barbershop on Memorial Day. Vernotico denied the charges, and records on the disposition of the case were unavailable.

Anna Vernotico must have been beside herself with anger and uncertainty about her domestic situation. She had a young daughter to worry about, and on top of things, her spouse was getting in and out of trouble. He also had a reputation for having a wandering eye for other women. His arrests were a sign that he was a small player in the gangster life, or so it seemed. While he was in jail for missing court appearances, Vernotico wasn't making any money. It took just over half of a year after the Brooklyn arrest for Anna to find out just how dead-end life was in her marriage. Around December 1931, Anna filed for divorce on the grounds of adultery, claiming Gerardo was living with another woman. Anna had started to look elsewhere for a relationship, and as things would have it, she found it in Vito Genovese, who, as it turned out, was a cousin on her mother's side of the family.

Genovese was no stranger to Greenwich Village life. Some of his closest gang associates were based in the area. The most important was Anthony "Tony Bender" Strollo, a self-proclaimed real estate broker in Manhattan who had connections with the New Jersey waterfront and was part of the Luciano crime family. Strollo at that point in his life in the early 1930s had a relatively minor criminal record of a gun possession arrest. Like Genovese, Strollo hung out on Mulberry Street at the Luna Restaurant.

It remains uncertain if Genovese ever crossed paths with Gerardo Vernotico, although it is likely that he did. The prevailing wisdom in Mafia lore is that Genovese, at this point in his life a widower, became captivated with Vernotico's wife, Anna, and eventually had her husband killed so he could marry her. The true story is more complicated than that and makes it doubtful that Genovese murdered Anna's first husband.

It was in the afternoon of March 17, 1932, that Vernotico and one Anthony Lonzo were found dead on the roof a six-story tenement building located at 124–126 Thompson Street, at the corner with Prince Street, a short distance from where Vernotico was living. Both men had suffered. Cops determined they had been beaten brutally. When a building janitor found them, they had sash cord nooses around their necks and the hands of one of them and the legs of the other were bound as well. Detectives followed a trail of blood over two adjacent rooftops to 161 Prince Street, where the source of the blood trail was found in a dingy, two-bedroom apartment on the third floor. The place was unfurnished except for some packing cases.

Cops also found some ashes and burned paper strewn around the floor of the apartment, something the investigators thought indicated Vernotico and Lonzo had been tortured. A bloody iron bar was also found in the room. Newspaper headlines blared "Mobsters Garrote 2 Victims on Roof." The question was, why did both men die so savagely?

The initial theory of detectives was that both men had tried to muscle in on the "alky racket" in the neighborhood, meaning bootlegging operations. They thought that the assailants had lured Vernotico and Lonzo to the empty apartment, where they were beaten, and then dragged them to the rooftop to be finished off. The only clue was that the building janitor said a "short dark man" had rented the place two months earlier and had as recently as a few days before the murder paid the rent. Some tenants of the rooftop murder building heard a scuffle early in the morning the day the bodies were found. Another tantalizing bit of evidence was a pair of woman's underwear found under one of the bodies.

The conventional wisdom in Mafia lore is that Vito Genovese, captivated by Anna Vernotico and eager to have a clear field with her, assassinated her husband. With Vernotico out of the way, Genovese and Anna would have been free to marry, which they did some two weeks after the murders, on March 30, 1932, city records show. Genovese's friend Strollo and his wife, Edna Goldenberg, showed up as witnesses at the city clerk's office. But there is plenty of evidence that undercuts that fabled story. For a start, Vernotico's death certificate noted that he was "divorced" in the line where the deceased's marital status was asked. Anna herself would tell congressional investigators later that she was granted a divorce decree on January 13, 1932, a full three months before her spouse's death. If the marriage of Vernotico and Anna had already been dissolved, there really wouldn't have been a need for Genovese to have the husband killed—for the simple reason that Anna was free and available, so to speak.

The haste with which Genovese and Anna were later married could have also been explained by the fact that she was already pregnant. Records that Genovese later filed when he became an American citizen described how Anna gave birth to a son, Philip, on June 30, 1932, about three months after Vernotico was killed and she married Genovese. Given the normal pregnancy duration of nine months, Anna would have conceived Philip around October 1931, a time when her first husband was allegedly living with another woman. In any case, Anna had a child with someone, and given the fractured state of her first marriage, she must have hooked up with Genovese, her distant cousin, at least in the fall of 1931 and probably much sooner.

Another indication that the tale that Genovese had Vernotico killed was a mob fiction comes from the fact that cops had focused on a 20-year-old denizen of the East Village known as Philip Picitello as a suspect in the rooftop double murder. He was labeled as a suspect in a *Daily News* story from September 1932, and the newspaper also reported that Picitello had been accused of kidnapping Vernotico's friend Patsy Pucci and placing him on a train about two months after the double homicide, with the warning never to come back to New York or else he would be killed. Pucci was later found in Ohio, and he told detectives about the threat from Picitello, who himself was later shot outside the St. Vladimir Ukrainian Church in New York City. All of this indicates that Vernotico was dealing in the low end of the criminal world and not a bother to Genovese.

After their marriage, Genovese and Anna now had a blended family as far as children were concerned. He had Nancy with his first wife, Donata, she had Rose Marie with Vernotico, and the two of them were parents to Philip. After the wedding, the couple, with three children in tow, lived in the apartment on Washington Square Park, where the six or seven rooms were enough. Living downstairs in the same building was Eleanor Roosevelt, the wife of the soon-to-be president.

Genovese did his mob business and legitimate business in Manhattan and when needed in the other boroughs. New York City was where he was making his fortune and his reputation in the underworld. But maybe because of his roots in Italy, Genovese felt that his family should have a place outside of the metropolis. It seemed like the right thing to do for the children. So in 1934, Genovese purchased a large house in the area of Middletown Village in Monmouth County, New Jersey, the Garden State.

"The Jersey home was supposed to be a summer home, and I bought it for that purpose," Genovese later recalled. "The children should be out in the country, and I maintained the apartment in New York in 1934."

Genovese was off by a couple of years about when he took the apartment in Manhattan: court records showed he moved in by

1932. The two youngest children, Rose Marie and Philip, stayed in New Jersey during the summer months and part of the winter. During the school months, Nancy went to Catholic elementary school in Manhattan, staying with her grandmother, Anna's mother, in an apartment in Greenwich Village on Thompson Street.

New Jersey wasn't unfamiliar territory for Genovese since his associate Tony Bender lived out in Palisades Park. Police records also show that in the years before he bought the New Jersey house Genovese got arrested there twice: once in 1925 for being a disorderly person and again in 1931 for carrying a concealed weapon. In both cases, the charges were dismissed.

The house in New Jersey was a place that was unusual for a New York City gangster to acquire. First of all, it was some distance from Manhattan, at least two hours by car over the George Washington Bridge, perhaps a little less through the Holland Tunnel or the Lincoln Tunnel. If mob activity required someone's presence for a meeting, travel could take time. Another thing was the sheer size of the place and its location in a part of New Jersey that at that time wasn't known for being a major magnet for Italian immigrants.

In the years before Genovese was born, Middletown Village was largely farmland, much of which was largely taken over by the local sheriffs in the late 1890s for taxes. A large tract in particular went through a succession of owners until Edward and Teresa R. Dangler snapped it up and built a large colonial revival mansion on a hilltop. When Genovese bought the twelve-room house on Red Hill from the Danglers, he went on an ambitious redesign of the landscaping and tinkered with some of the rooms in the house itself.

Genovese, it seems, wanted to reconfigure the land so that it resembled what one garden historian noted was a "pseudo-Italian style reminiscent of Naples, Italy, where he had been born." Genovese is said to have given a free hand to the landscape planner, but with only one condition, that there be created a small rock version of Mount Vesuvius. The garden, described as a mix of terraced landscaping, a low stone wall, and a masonry pagoda, was something that became the talk of the area. Aside from the garden and mansion, there were two tennis courts, a three-hole golf course, a swimming pool, and a greenhouse. Genovese was living large and clearly was making the money to afford it.

The Red Hill mansion, with its striking view to the east towards distant New York Harbor, was just one indication of how well Genovese was faring. Two years earlier, he and Anna had decided to take a three-month trip to Europe. Mob historians claim that the journey was a reconnaissance of sorts to allow Genovese the chance to plan an escape back to Italy if he ever needed it, along with a visit to banks to open secret depository accounts. He said it was strictly a pleasure trip. Whatever the real reason, Genovese and Anna traveled in a style that underscored their improved station in life. While Genovese's first voyage across the Atlantic in 1913 was aboard the relatively slow moving and cramped SS *Taormina*, with a mostly third-class passenger complement, the 1933 trip he made with his wife was aboard the SS *Conte de Savoia*, a luxury vessel that for a time reputedly held the westbound speed record across the Atlantic.

In *King of Crime*, Frasca quotes Genovese as telling his wife and Mafia friends that they were now living grandly and dressing like higher society.

Frasca wrote: "'We go in style, eh?' he boasted to an assortment of hoodlums who crammed the state room before the ship sailed. He caressed a silk shirt."

According to Frasca, Genovese added, "No holes in the pants this time."

The era of traveling in style on sumptuous ocean liners is something that is only a memory now, retold in history books and old travel brochures. Yet the *Conte de Savoia* was symbolic of first-class affluence, which Genovese now had. A family photograph depicted Anna and Genovese lounging in chairs on what appears to be the ship, and the couple looked a bit like Fred Astaire and Ginger Rogers: Genovese wearing a flat, Ben Hogan–style cap and Anna in a beanie with a pom-pom on top. The vessel had a swimming pool and plush interiors with prized dining facilities. Some of the lounges had marble paneling, and the first-class dining room was on two

levels. The vessel was a favorite of celebrities, and Douglas Fair-
banks could be counted as one of its passengers in 1933. It could
travel at a top speed of twenty-eight knots, had special gyro stabiliz-
ers to help cut down on the roll on rough seas, and likely got Genovese and Anna to the Mediterranean in about seven days before
eventually reaching its destination in Italy.

Upon his return to New York in 1933, Genovese was facing a
changed climate in the mob. Actually, things were afoot as early as
1931, when it became clear just how far out of favor Prohibition had
fallen. As time when on, the nation's great attempt to legislate tem-
perance was becoming more of a problem. Large swaths of the
American public hated Prohibition, and that became clear when the
Wickersham Commission, established by President Herbert Hoover
in 1929, finally issued a report in 1931 with some devastating con-
clusions. Prohibition was a disaster in terms of public acceptance,
and enforcing it was next to impossible. Criminals, bootleggers, and
smugglers had corrupted law enforcement officials at all levels. The
commission did conclude that Prohibition was worth keeping, but
one member of the panel, in a separate opinion, said it should be
done away with.

With the election of President Franklin D. Roosevelt in 1932,
Prohibition was steadily undercut. Roosevelt, who was backed by
Democratic bosses in New York like Costello, first revised the law
to allow the production of beer with 4 percent alcohol by volume, as
well as certain kinds of wines. The proposed Twenty-First Amendment, which called for the repeal of Prohibition, started to win approval of a number of states, then on December 5, 1933, Utah
ratified the amendment, and with that Prohibition came to an end on
the federal level.

The end to Prohibition forced the Mafia to diversify. Some gangsters went into legal liquor distribution, while others like Costello
branched out into the slot machine business. Gambling was still lucrative, as was labor racketeering, particularly in the garment industry. Prohibition had created a great deal of wealth for the mob, and
the money attracted desperate politicians, especially those Democ-

rats tied to Tammany Hall, where mob cash and gangster reputations gave some Mafiosi like Costello a great deal of influence.

As previously noted, Genovese had developed a paper and scrap paper business headquartered on Thompson Street in Greenwich Village, and it made him quite wealthy. Eventually, over time, Genovese would use his connections from bootlegging to set up nightclubs in the area, always using someone else as the outfront owner while he stayed in the shadows. This was a pattern of doing business that suited the mob well and allowed Mafiosi to bury their illegal gains in seemingly legitimate enterprises. As time went on, Anna would play a significant role in the clubs, something that would cause her husband big problems. More about that in chapter fifteen.

Yet Genovese was still a gangster, and even with his air of respectability and affluence, he couldn't help but fall back into his old street ways. It was in 1934 that Genovese and his close associate Michele Miranda, also known as Mike and Michael, a onetime Coney Island pickpocket who had also been born in Italy within the shadow of Mount Vesuvius, bilked a merchant out of $160,000 in a two-stage scam involving a crooked card game and a fake machine that supposedly made currency. The merchant did make a fuss but likely just ate his losses. Instead, the trouble for Genovese and Miranda came in the form of Ferdinand "the Shadow" Boccia (also spelled Bocchia), who had brought the victim to Genovese and began pestering him for his $35,000 share of the scam's proceeds. Modern fans of the Mafia genre might liken Boccia's nagging to what Marty Krugman did to try and get a share of the fabled 1978 Lufthansa heist at John F. Kennedy International Airport. The constant demands by Krugman of heist mastermind James Burke for a cut of the robbery led to Krugman's disappearance.

Genovese and Miranda needed to get rid of the pesky Boccia, who it seems was desperately trying to get back in their good graces by bringing them the scam victim in the first place. Boccia was doing them the favor as a kind of penance for holding up a liquor store run by a friend of Genovese. Boccia's accomplice in the rob-

bery was a street criminal named William Gallo. To finish off Boccia, Genovese and Miranda planned to have Gallo and his friend
Ernest "the Hawk" Rupolo kill Boccia.

It was in September 1934 that police reported Boccia was shot
dead inside a Brooklyn coffee shop known as the Circolo Christofo
Club and Café. Initial police reports said that a total of four men
were accomplices in the murder. After about a month, police arrested two low-level 21-year-old hoods for the homicide: John Sebastiano and Alfred Lofredo, both of Brooklyn. There was no
mention of Rupolo in early reports of the killing.

But in this biography *The Valachi Papers*, Valachi said the entire
murder plot against Boccia was a comedy of errors mixed in with a
double-cross. Boccia was killed, but according to Valachi, Genovese and Miranda decided that they had to have Rupolo also kill
Gallo, the other man involved in the Boccia homicide. Rupolo was
paid $175 to do the deed. But it wasn't a simple task. Rupolo was a
tender 22 years old and had a police record that went back at least to
the time he was 17 years old. If Rupolo had to declare an occupation, it would be that of a hired assassin who relished his reputation
in the gangster world as a "good boy," someone dependable to carry
out assignments. Although he had one obvious deficit, which was
that he had only one eye, having lost the sight in the other after
someone had tried to shoot him some years earlier.

The original plan of Genovese, Valachi recounted, was for Rupolo to kill Gallo. Then, Rupolo was to be assassinated by 19-year-
old Rosario Palmieri, another street tough. With Rupolo and Gallo
dead, the people who could link Genovese and Miranda to the earlier Boccia hit would be gone.

The plan sounded a bit complicated, and Genovese still could
be implicated in a double homicide if things didn't work out as
planned. Nevertheless, on the night of September 19, 1934, Rupolo
and Palmieri accompanied Gallo to dinner at the home of Rupolo's
girlfriend, where whiskey flowed freely at the table, and then they
planned to go see a movie. During a drive along Fourteenth Avenue
in the Bensonhurst section of Brooklyn things started to go haywire.

As Rupolo would later tell investigators, he pulled out a pistol and shoved it to Gallo's head and pulled the trigger three times. The gun didn't go off, and a shocked Gallo turned to Rupolo and asked, "What the hell are you doing?" Rupolo replied, "Nothing, I am only kidding with you; the gun ain't loaded."

In fact, the gun was loaded but mechanically defective and in need of lubrication. So Rupolo excused himself and said he was going to drop off the gun at the home of a friend. But that excuse was merely a ruse. Rupolo went to a friend's home and slathered the gun and its firing mechanism with oil, before going outside again. Once outside, Rupolo and Palmieri continued their drive with Gallo. Then, early on the morning of September 20, 1934, in front of 6603 Thirteenth Avenue in Bensonhurst, both turned on the unsuspecting Gallo, firing about a dozen rounds, four of which hit him.

"Oh Ma!" Gallo exclaimed as he was shot. He had been hit in the neck, head, and back. Rupolo and Palmieri dumped the wounded man on the street and fled.

The gunfire didn't kill Gallo, perhaps because Rupolo didn't have the greatest of eyesight. Rupolo also screwed up in another way. Miranda had earlier said that he wanted Gallo to be doused in gasoline after he was shot and set afire. Rupolo just didn't want to carry out that part of the plan.

After sleeping things off, Rupolo went to see Miranda in Little Italy and got an earful from his boss, who berated him for screwing up the hit.

"Why didn't you shoot him in the head like we did to that other bastard?" one of Miranda's associates yelled.

Miranda then ordered Rupolo to take Palmieri and go on a trip to Springfield, Massachusetts, apparently to wait until things cooled down. But as Rupolo later recalled to police, Palmieri became suspicious that they were both being set up to be killed, and he fled. Rupolo stayed about twelve days in New England and then returned to New York. But the case had not cooled down.

It took about two weeks for detectives to focus in on Rupolo and Palmieri, pulling both men in for questioning. Despite the fact that both denied knowing who shot Gallo, a grand jury charged Rupolo and Palmieri with assault. During a preliminary hearing in the case, Magistrate William O'Dwyer questioned a reluctant Gallo, who finally admitted that Rupolo and Palmieri were the ones who shot him.

O'Dwyer sensed that Gallo was afraid of someone aside from the two assailants and said so in open court. O'Dwyer also added that if federal agents were handling these kinds of cases they would "blow your brains, that's all."

With hindsight and the passage of several years, Genovese's involvement as the mastermind of the plot would become apparent. But at the time that Rupolo and Palmieri were found guilty of assault in December 1934, the cops only had speculation that Gallo was targeted by gangsters "whose enmity he had incurred" and that Rupolo and Palmieri had been hired for the job.

Rupolo and Palmieri were indeed branded as "killers who commit murder for hire" when they were sentenced to prison terms of twelve to twenty years for first-degree assault. The sentences gave them a lot of time to think about their predicament. While spending his youthful days in prison and realizing that he was going to spend a good portion of his adulthood behind bars, Rupolo did some serious thinking about a way to help himself. But it would take him a few years to figure out how.

There was some initial suspicion by police that Genovese and Miranda were involved in the Boccia hit. In November, some two months after Boccia was killed, Miranda was charged in connection with the homicide. Genovese recalled that he was hauled in by cops for what he described as a homicide case around the time that his father, Felice, passed away.

"My father died November 8, and he died in my house, 43 Fifth Avenue, and we took the body to Long Island to my sister's house because my father spent part of his life there and we felt we would have the funeral at my sister's house," Genovese would recall years later. (The sister wasn't identified, but Genovese could have been referring to a woman named Lucy Genovese who lived in Queens and would later be identified as a "cousin.")

"While my father was laid out somebody came to my house, I don't remember if it was an officer of the law, somebody who said, 'The Captain wants to see you, the police captain wants to see you,'" Genovese said.

"Well, I got my father laid out, tell the captain as soon as I bury my father I will walk in," Genovese told the officer.

After the funeral of his father, Genovese said he was physically ill and feeling remorseful over the loss of his parent, so it took about three weeks for him to haul himself to the precinct to see the captain.

Genovese recalled that he surrendered and was booked on what he indicated was a homicide charge and kept in a holding cell overnight. The next day, according to Genovese, he was brought to court, where the district attorney had a man waiting to see if he could identify him. Prosecutors apparently thought they had a witness who could put Genovese at the crime scene.

"The man looked at me for a few seconds," Genovese later remembered. "He said, 'No, that is not the man,' and the judge said 'Dismissed.'"

Clearly, either the witness genuinely couldn't identify Genovese or was too frightened. In any case, Genovese avoided another prosecution, at least for the time being. Miranda also lucked out when the homicide charge against him was also dismissed.

Seemingly insulated from the Boccia murder, Genovese and Miranda went about their lives. Miranda dabbling in car sales and gambling, while Genovese was getting richer in the paper business as well as the rackets he was skillfully negotiating. The house in New Jersey occupied Genovese's attention, and he opened up his wallet to satisfy the whims and desires of Anna to construct a place where they could raise the three children. The terraced gardens became a local horticultural attraction, and money was spent lavishly on furnishings. The upstairs bathroom was remodeled, and an annex also constructed.

Genovese may have thought that his New Jersey home would insulate him from becoming the focus of law enforcement in New York City. But times had definitely changed. While Costello and Luciano had in the early 1930s gained influence over politicians and police with cash, the political winds soon changed against them.

Chapter Four

OF ALL NEW YORK CITY'S MAYORS, Fiorello LaGuardia has remained one of the most well-known and colorful. A short, fireplug of a man with a high-pitched voice and tousled black hair, LaGuardia, the son of an Italian father and Jewish mother, was born in Trieste, an area bordering Italy and what was the old kingdom of Yugoslavia. After serving as a midlevel diplomat for the State Department in Europe, LaGuardia returned to the United States just before World War One started and finished up law school.

Turning to politics, LaGuardia was a Republican early in his career and represented East Harlem in Congress during the 1920s. As LaGuardia biographer Alyn Brodsky noted, the newly minted congressman had greatly impressed New York County's party chairman Samuel S. Koenig. The district LaGuardia represented was north of a Democratic bastion run by Albert Marinelli, a Tammany operative who typified the worst of the hard-knocks electoral machinations in the city.

Brodsky described Marinelli as lording over a "cadre of professional bullies, goons and criminals of every stripe." The Marinelli crowd perfected their ballot-box-stuffing tactics well. "They voted more times in any election than many people vote in a lifetime, and they made sure the Republicans realized that so much as a walk through the district, even accidentally, might well result in serious bodily harm."

Nevertheless, LaGuardia tried to run for New York City mayor in 1929, going up against the Tammany Hall–backed incumbent Jimmy Walker. LaGuardia tried to make campaign hay out a questionable land deal that Jewish gangster Arnold Rothstein, Costello's old friend and financier, had arranged in Queens, but the issue just didn't sway the electorate, and he lost by a half a million votes.

Walker eventually was forced from office by scandal, and in 1932, LaGuardia put together another run at the mayoralty through a coalition of Republicans and independents, socialists, Jews, and Italians. A Tammany-backed Democratic candidate was also the favorite of President Franklin D. Roosevelt, but even with that support, it seemed like LaGuardia was on track to win. Tammany, sensing defeat in the election, "set out to steal it."

Tammany's tactic was to use its usual bit of bribery and enlist the help of notable racketeers like Dutch Schultz and Joe Adonis, the latter a confederate of Genovese who was also known by his real name, Giuseppe Doto. Violence seemed to be the strong undercurrent of the day.

"Election Day, November 7, was a day of shooting matches, fist fights, black eyes, cracked skulls, police arrests and even one reported shooting, as a record number of New Yorkers for a municipal election turned out," recalled Brodsky.

Marinelli showed up at polling places with what Brodsky described as "two hundred of his underworld playmates sporting identical pearl gray fedoras and hobnailed shoes and proceeded to dissuade Fusion . . . voters with a show of lead pipes and brass knuckles."

But the violence and intimidation by the Tammany and Mafia goons was not enough to swing the result. LaGuardia, dubbed the "Little Flower" (his first name meant that in Italian), won by a margin of more than 250,000 votes over Joseph McKee, who ran on the Recover ticket, and slightly more over John O'Brien, the Tammany-backed Democrat.

The action of the Mafia characters and the Tammany operatives made it crystal clear to LaGuardia who his enemies where. This reality colored the tone of the next several years as LaGuardia set out to mold the city his way. For Genovese, Luciano, Costello, and the rest of the mob in New York, that meant that they would find themselves haunted and harassed by a mayor who would enjoy great popularity and saw his election as a mandate to do whatever he wanted, even if he had to bend the law.

LaGuardia was a progressive who was suspicious of government overreach, which he sometimes saw in the enforcement of Prohibition, a policy he believed to be disastrous. But in terms of the racketeers in the city, he would give them no quarter, calling them two-bit punks and chiselers. One story emerged about how on election day he had confronted a Tammany poll watcher and ripped off his badge, telling him to go away.

LaGuardia loathed gambling, a mainstay of the Mafia, because he believed it ruined families and put children on the path to immoral lives. No sooner had LaGuardia taken office then he started after the Mafia by targeting the slot machines of Costello and others. The machines had proliferated around the city, with the gangsters often trying to get around the law by dispensing slugs that could be used to buy cigarettes or candy mints. But the courts ultimately backed the police, and under LaGuardia's campaign, hundreds of Costello's slot machines were seized. The mayor then made a big show of smashing some of them with sledgehammers and having them taken out to sea and dumped.

Costello felt the particular wrath of LaGuardia, and the mayor would go on to say that the racket had been eliminated from the city. But the fact was that other forms of gambling were providing the Mafia and other crime groups with a stable source of income. Prostitution was another racket, and soon LaGuardia would encourage an ambitious lawyer named Thomas Dewey to go after those behind the brothels when local prosecutors proved either reluctant or unable to do so.

Meanwhile, Genovese, who stayed away from prostitution and other crimes that were getting law enforcement's attention, decided it was time to become an American citizen, something he had put off for way too long. Initially, Genovese believed that he gained citizenship from his father's citizenship, something known as deriva-

tive citizenship. Such a belief was apparently behind Genovese's reluctance to follow up on his earlier effort to start the citizenship
process until he learned—upon returning from the pleasure voyage
to Italy in 1933—that his father wasn't a citizen.

As soon as Genovese got back to the United States from Italy, he
filed papers to become a citizen. There were a couple of documents
required to begin the process. One was a certificate of arrival that
showed that Genovese first entered the United States on May 23,
1913, when he disembarked from the SS *Taormina* in New York.
This particular document had affixed to it a passport-style photo of
Genovese, which depicted a young man with chiseled features dom-
inated by a high forehead and dressed in shirt, jacket, and tie. His
signature was on the left side of the image. The form, issued by the
Naturalization Service of the U.S. Department of Labor, a bore the
signature of Charles Weiser, a clerk with the U.S. District Court in
Manhattan, and was dated March 14, 1933.

A second document prepared that same day was Genovese's dec-
laration of intention to become a citizen. The document, to which
was also affixed Genovese's photo, gave more details about him,
describing him as being five feet, seven inches tall and 158 pounds.
He had a scar on the right side of his face. The form details his place
and date of birth, the name of his wife, Annie, and the fact that his
first wife, Donata, the mother of Nancy, died in 1931. Genovese
noted on the form that he and Annie lived at 178 Thompson Street,
right in the West Village and adjacent to his offices, although he also
had an apartment on Washington Square Park.

Genovese's formal petition for naturalization or citizenship, an
altogether different document, wasn't completed and signed by him
until December 19, 1935. The document related most of the same
information on the earlier forms, repeating the birth dates of his two
children. Nancy on May 23, 1923, and Philip on June 30, 1932,
some three months after his marriage to Anna.

The petition, which was witnessed by lawyer Michael R. Matteo
of Queens and printer and sometimes boxer Rocco D'Allessandro
of Brooklyn, had a couple of errors. The date of death for Donata
was listed as 1930, instead of the true date of 1931. The marriage to

Anna was also incorrect, the true date according to the marriage certificate being March 30, 1932. Those mistakes were relatively inconsequential. After the filing of the petition and before he could be sworn in as a citizen, Genovese had to go through an interview process in which he was questioned about whether he had any criminal record. He responded—after being told by the examiner not to worry about misdemeanor arrests—in the negative. Genovese's words would be a time bomb in his life, as events later showed.

Papers filed with the National Archives show that Genovese finally became a citizen on November 25, 1936. He swore the oath of allegiance to the United States and, as was customary, renounced allegiance to his ancestral homeland and its king, Victor Emmanuel III of Italy.

As Genovese was formally embracing the country, some of those in it where doing their best to make him feel very unwanted. Progressives and anticrime zealots like LaGuardia and Dewey were in the midst of their push against the mob. It was Dewey who was taking things to another level. The young prosecutor focused on Tammany Hall, and he did it in a way in which he was able to enlist the important support of a key accomplice, Governor Herbert Lehman.

Chapter Five

FOR DECADES, THE TAMMANY HALL political machine had controlled the law enforcement establishment in New York City, approving the appointments of judges and police brass and giving the imprimatur to those running for the positions of district attorneys and city magistrates. Those candidates aspiring to those jobs were often associated with Tammany, essentially pledging allegiance to the Democratic machine and thus being susceptible to the influence of mobsters.

William C. Dodge, after serving for a few years in the New York State Senate, became an assistant district attorney in Manhattan in 1924 and then was appointed a city magistrate by Mayor Jimmy Walker in 1927. Dodge had a good political mentor in James "Jimmy" Hines, a Tammany boss who was close to mobsters like Dutch Schultz, also known by his real name, Arthur Flegenheimer, and Frank Costello. When the time came, Hines, a number of political historians have said, gave approval for Dodge to run in November 1933 on the Tammany ticket as Manhattan district attorney.

After winning the election handily, Dodge began an investigation of the gambling racket in the city at about the time that LaGuardia was pushing city officials to go after all of organized crime's money-making ventures: slot machines, prostitution, labor extortion, and cartels in food markets and the artichoke industry. Dodge did get some indictments, but they seemed to be inconsequential. No big racketeers like Schultz, who was the big numbers operator in town, were charged, and the grand jury that had been convened felt stymied; the jurors even going so far as to complain in open court in May 1935 about the lack of resources they were receiving to do the investigation.

It is unusual for grand jurors to take public stances, and when Dodge was confronted by that he agreed to have a special prosecutor appointed. The first appointee was a Republican, H. H. Corbin, but his selection met with disapproval from the grand jurors, who at this point were considered a "runaway" panel, seemingly answering to no one. Corbin refused to take the job, and the grand jury was disbanded in June, after having caused so much trouble.

It then became Governor Lehman's job to take Dodge off the job of supervising the grand jury and to select a special prosecutor. From a list of four possible candidates, he picked the young Republican lawyer in Manhattan named Thomas Dewey for the job. Dewey's appointment turned out to be a watershed moment in criminal justice and for the Mafia. Emboldened by LaGuardia and with a mandate from Albany, Dewey launched into a probe of prostitution and gambling, considered the lifeblood rackets.

Much has been written about Dewey's racket busting in this period, so it will not be gone into here in too much detail. But he picked up where the first, frustrated Dodge grand jury had left off and started to follow the chain of dealings among city prostitutes and those who controlled the business. Essentially, by the early 1930s, a group of low-level gangsters began to force bookers, those who provided madams with girls for prostitution, to join a combination in which some of the bookers turned over a portion of their earnings to the thugs. The madams were compelled to use bookers affiliated with the gangsters and in return got the protection of the mob and use of syndicate resources if lawyers had to be hired.

Initially, Dewey's tactic of targeting the cartel worked, with the arrests of some of the low-level gangsters. But others appeared to take their place, and Dewey switched to a new strategy, one aimed at forcing the prostitutes and madams to talk in-depth about the gangsters involved. The tactic was to ask judges to set high bails so that the women couldn't make the amounts and had to stay in jail, away from the influence and coercion of the mob toughs involved. This high-bail system amounted to a subtle form of coercion of its own and was one of the strategies later questioned by some about the way Dewey went about business.

In any case, the women did talk and Dewey got a new round of indictments in February 1936. A month later, one of those arrested, a former cop named David Miller, started to cooperate with Dewey. Miller's information was fragmented at first, but eventually, he gave investigators enough to indicate that Luciano was linked to the prostitution racket.

Dewey's grand jury eventually indicted Luciano on charges that he was taking money from the racket. But Luciano, with his numerous police and political sources, got wind of the charges and fled to Hot Springs, Arkansas, a place that was a gambling mecca with plenty of nightlife and pretty women. Hot Springs was the bastion of Owney Madden, another fabled New York mobster who had fled the Big Apple in the face of legal problems of his own to set up shop in the southern city with the help of its pliant politicians. Costello had also used Hot Springs as a favorite vacation spot and went there often with his wife, Loretta.

But Luciano wasn't safe from Dewey's clutches in Hot Springs. The New York prosecutor started extradition proceedings, and nothing Luciano could do—even a reported bribe attempt of $50,000 to the Arkansas attorney general—stopped Dewey. In April 1936, New York City detectives served Luciano with an arrest warrant and took him into custody.

"You! You are a hell of an Italian," an angry and flummoxed Luciano told the arresting detective.

"Sure I am," was the detective's reply. "I am a hell of an Italian."

Luciano arrived back in New York on April 17. His trial began two months later in June and was a headline-grabbing event. Dewey told the jury that Luciano took over the prostitution racket in 1933 by driving others out of the business and forcing them to join his syndicate or get out of town. The vice racket pulled in $12 million a year, which is over $200 million in contemporary dollar value adjusted for inflation.

Scores of witnesses were called, including prostitutes. As far as being credible, some of the women had problems. Some had drug abuse issues and were seeking leniency by testifying. But some did say that they recalled seeing Luciano in person or heard that he was boss of the combination. Luciano himself testified, but if he thought he might be doing himself a favor by taking the stand, he was very much mistaken. Under a withering cross-examination by Dewey, Luciano admitted he had peddled narcotics as a young man and had been involved in bootlegging. Luciano also acknowledged knowing gangsters like the late Joseph Masseria, garment district labor racketeer Louis "Lepke" Buchalter, and Benjamin "Bugsy" Siegel.

The result was inevitable. After only six hours of deliberations, the jury convicted Luciano and eight codefendants of compulsory prostitution. It was a solid win for Dewey, and he put out a statement saying Luciano was "the greatest gangster in America," who controlled narcotics, policy (illegal numbers lottery), loansharking, the garment industry, and the Italian lottery.

For LaGuardia, the conviction of Luciano signaled the end for "Public Enemy No. 1" and would be the beginning of a long series of racket-busting cases. The mayor couldn't help being political when he said Dewey's work reversed years of failure by Democratic district attorneys to take on the rackets and stop the growth of organized crime. The Luciano conviction was also a devastating moment for the crime boss, although like a cat, he would have more than one life to live as a Mafia chief. When it came time for sentencing, Judge Philip J. McCook gave Luciano a sentence of thirty to fifty years. Luciano's eyes flickered when he heard the time he would get, but otherwise he seemed composed. He appealed his conviction, but that went nowhere for him.

Over the years, it would be said that Luciano got a raw deal, that the prostitutes who testified against him were fed details of their testimony or just lied. Frank Hogan, who had been one of Dewey's top assistants and who later became the longest serving district attorney for Manhattan, said that under modern rules of criminal procedure and the law, Luciano might not have been convicted.

Well, what could have been in the best of worlds wasn't the real-

ity Luciano faced. He remained boss of his family even when he
went away to serve his time in the Clinton Correctional Center in
upstate Dannemora, New York. But practically speaking, he had to
rely on a good street boss to take care of things on the outside. For
that, Luciano actually had two capable people to look after things,
Frank Costello and Vito Genovese. Both men would become new
targets for Dewey.

Chapter Six

WITH THE CONVICTION OF LUCIANO, Dewey, again with LaGuardia cheering him on, set his sights on eviscerating Tammany Hall, the organization that he and the mayor saw as the real problem in the fight against the mob. It would be a campaign that had many targets, including Vito Genovese.

But as it turned out, Dewey wasn't planning to go after Genovese for any particular crimes or rackets. Genovese had a history of being able to duck prosecution and had kept his hands clean, using others to do his dirty work. He was relatively high up in the Mafia food chain and used stealth to get things done. Dewey, as it turned out, didn't have an easy time building his cases against the mob with evidence. Instead, he went after Genovese and others indirectly, shaming them in the court of public opinion and in the process neutralizing Tammany operatives like Jimmy Hines by indicting and convicting him for taking part in a protection racket as a way to protect gamblers like Dutch Schultz

Hines was a rather easy target for Dewey to build in court. The prosecutor's next move took a different tactic, a highly publicized denouncement of the Mafia and its connection with one particular Tammany boss, Albert Marinelli. A close associate of Luciano, Marinelli, with mob help, won election as the first Italian-American district leader of Tammany. His closeness to Luciano was no secret. Both had traveled together to the 1932 Democratic Convention, to which Costello had also traveled with Hines for the nomination of Franklin Delano Roosevelt as president.

Working out of offices at 225 Lafayette Street, Marinelli was close to the Little Italy base of important Mafiosi. He became a power in Tammany and was appointed the New York county clerk, a major patronage-dispensing post in Manhattan. With such ties, Marinelli became a lush target for Dewey, who had been elected after his victory against Luciano to the job of district attorney in his own right.

It was early in December 1937 that Dewey sent a long, blistering document to Governor Lehman, accusing Marinelli of close association with forty-four heavy-duty gangsters, mostly Mafiosi and of course Italians. The allegations were a repeat of claims Dewey had made earlier in October during a speech and which Lehman had asked for the prosecutor to submit formally to him. Dewey's follow-up letter was characterized as a series of "sworn charges" alleging that Marinelli "is a political ally of thieves, pickpockets, dope peddlers and big-shot racketeers." Dewey essentially asked that the governor remove the county clerk from office.

Lehman didn't remove Marinelli but instead sent him a letter demanding that he answer Dewey's allegations within a week. In his letter to Lehman, Dewey listed twenty-one mobsters and associates, among them Genovese, whom the prosecutor described as "since the conviction of his associate Luciano, has been conducting his operations from the state of New Jersey."

Along with Genovese, Dewey listed in his rogues gallery Luciano associate Joe Adonis, fish market racketeer Joseph "Socks" Lanza, and imprisoned garment-trucking boss James Plumeri. Dewey said he generously kept the names of some men out of the papers because they appeared to have gone straight and he didn't want to set them back in life.

The publicity generated by Dewey put Marinelli on a downward spiral, and he not only resigned his job as county clerk but also found himself indicted in 1938 for harboring a fugitive, his own driver, who was facing federal charges. Ultimately, Marinelli was acquitted of the charges, but he had become a broken man and died in April 1948 at the age of 65, although some judges did attend is funeral at St. Patrick's Old Cathedral in Little Italy.

When Dewey announced Genovese's name, the mobster's picture became fodder for the tabloids, the first time he had been so publicly branded as a member of the mob. "Vito Genovese: Dewey calls him Luciano's successor and Marinelli pal," said the *Daily News* in a caption under Genovese's photo. Dewey might have been right about Genovese working out of New Jersey at some point, but by the time he put Genovese's name in the charges against Marinelli, his information was out of date. In fact, Genovese couldn't easily live in the New Jersey mansion because it had burned down several months earlier. It also appears that Genovese, feeling the heat generated by LaGuardia and Dewey, decided to go back to Italy, leaving Costello as the street boss of Luciano's crime family.

Dewey did try a more direct approach in going after Costello. Evidence in the prosecution of Hines gave Dewey an entrée into a probe of the liquor distribution business. Witnesses had told investigators that thugs would approach restaurant and bar owners and force them, under pain of physical injury if they refused, to take their liquor supplies from certain connected distributors. One of those companies was Alliance Distributors Inc., of 153 Fifth Avenue in Manhattan. Alliance was believed to have been connected with Costello, who received his mail at the company offices and was known to have frequented the place. In the 1950s, Costello would tell congressional investigators that he had tried to work out a deal with Alliance in which he would get five shillings per case—about one U.S. dollar at the time—but the whole deal fell through.

Dewey's interest in Alliance and Costello turned out to be small beer. The prosecutor indicted a company office manager named Lilen Sanger on charges that she lied about Costello and his ties to Alliance. However, Costello, the true target of the investigation, wasn't charged at all. With weak evidence, a three-judge panel acquitted Sanger. After that, Costello, who had moved some of his slot machine dealings to New Orleans, wasn't bothered again by Dewey. With Genovese on his way to a self-imposed exile in Italy, Costello was considered the effective street boss of Luciano's operations.

Genovese's return to Italy came at some point after he signed his naturalization papers in December 1936 while in Manhattan and February 1937, when his glorious mansion in New Jersey was destroyed in a mysterious fire. A couple driving home late on Red Hill Road, where the Genovese estate was situated, noticed flames coming out of the first floor windows of the home and telephoned the fire department. When the police arrived, they rescued what were described as "two valuable dogs" in the caretaker's house.

The blaze was fed by strong winds, and it became apparent that more fire units needed to be called in to handle a situation that was fast going out of control. Because the area was somewhat rural, fire-fighters had to waste more time stringing hoses a distance of three-quarters of a mile to the nearest hydrant. It took about two hours for the fire to be declared under control, but the damage resulted in almost a total loss. The house, its furnishings, paintings, and other works of art were calculated at a value of $80,000, some of it reportedly covered by insurance.

A caretaker, contractor D. A. Caruso of nearby Atlantic Highlands, told police that the oil furnace had been kept on to keep pipes from freezing and to supply a greenhouse Genovese had built. Caruso had been heavily involved in the renovation of the structure and reported that telephone installers, plumbers, and electricians had been working in the house in the days before the fire. Police later reported that the furnace had been causing some trouble earlier in the season.

Genovese, fire officials said, had been traveling in Europe with his wife at the time of blaze. This is the first indication in the United States that the Mafia boss was out of the country. Anna's mother had reportedly visited the home earlier with the couple's three children. Genovese's trip to Europe was described by police as a "vacation." The trip would turn out to be a long sojourn.

With three children to deal with back in New York, Anna returned to the United States while her husband stayed in Italy. According to Frasca in *King of Crime*, Genovese and his wife would meet up in Europe and she would carry him loads of cash, perhaps $100,000 at a time, to replenish his bank account. Anna claimed she did take care of some of Genovese's business and illicit dealings, notably the so-called Italian lottery in New York. Genovese wasn't exactly poor in Italy given that he went over with a reported $750,000 and a portfolio containing $2 million worth of letters of credit. Genovese also had the companionship in Italy of Michele Miranda, his old partner in crime in the Boccia murder, who had also gone back to his country of origin once the charges were dropped. Miranda was also feeling the heat that Dewey had generated all over the Mafia and figured it made sense to leave New York.

Although it is now impossible to document, Frasca and other writers have reported that while in Italy, Genovese availed himself of the services of a well-known and beautiful brothel owner known as Innocenza Monterisi. (One American military investigator did say he found Genovese with her business card.) Both Genovese and Miranda are said to have used Monterisi's services, and her business was known among the highest governmental officials, Italian gentry, and military leaders. The bordello was right across from Borghese Gardens in Rome on the Via Veneto. But it was more than whoring that kept Genovese occupied in Italy. The country had changed radically politically, and by all rights it shouldn't have been the safe haven it turned out to be for a Mafia boss like Genovese.

Chapter Seven

It was in May 1925 that Benito Mussolini, three years after his Partito Nazionale Fascista, or the Fascist Party of Italy, had essentially taken over the broken Italian government, revealed his plan for dealing with the Mafia. Italy—Sicily in particular—had been under the yoke of the Mafiosi for decades. The criminal brotherhoods had thrived in an Italy that, with its version of democracy, had been unable to deal with them—or any other pressing public issue—in any meaningful way. Then came Mussolini, Il Duce as he was known, strutting into the political firmament in 1922 by marching into Rome with his army of black shirt supporters and essentially bullying the government to appoint him as prime minister. It was a classic political shakedown.

For Italians, whatever Mussolini had wrought in their lives seemed to make things better. As historian John Dickie wrote in his book *Blood Brotherhoods*, the Fascists had done what had not been done before, "finally imposed order and discipline on an Italy debilitated for so long by politicking and corruption. The country now marched as one to the thumping beat of a totalitarian ideology: 'Everything within the state. Nothing against the state. Nothing outside the state.'"

The one particular task Mussolini had carved out was to go after the Mafia all over Sicily. In October 1925, Mussolini appointed Cesare Mori, a once obscure policeman from the northern part of the country, where he had been raised in an orphanage, to begin an anti-Mafia campaign the likes of which Italy had never seen before. With good reasons, Mori was known as the "Iron Prefect," and his effort was known as the Mori Operation.

As described by Dickie, one of Mori's most highly publicized actions was against the Mafia stronghold of Gangi, on the edge of the city of Palermo. Mori's forces cut off all communication with the town, and criminals were flushed out of their hideouts with what Dickey called "flagrant ruthlessness, their women and children were taken hostage, their goods sold off for pennies, their cattle butchered in the town square."

Similar roundups occurred throughout Sicily, and hundreds of arrests were tallied. By 1927, Mussolini was ready to declare victory over the Mafia and did so in an address to the government. Mori's iron-fisted tactics Mussolini likened to a doctor operating on a patient and removing a cancer. According to Dickie, Mussolini touted a litany of statistics to prove his point: thousands of suspected Mafiosi had been arrested and murders had declined nearly 58 percent in a three-year period, while cattle rustling had fallen 82 percent in the same period from 1923 to 1926. Il Duce was confident that at some point in Italian history people would be hard-pressed to even remember the Mafia.

Given such an official party line, it is hard to figure out why Genovese would think to find Italy a hospitable place for a Mafioso such as himself. The answer lay in the fact that politicians like Mussolini and his ilk in Italy were eager to make money from the rackets and to use the connections with the Americans when it suited them. Genovese had access to plenty of money, and he spread it around in a way to enhance the Fascist power. He also knew that a relationship with Mussolini could be reciprocal and allow him to operate with impunity. Genovese could get away with this because in the end it seemed that the Mafia power, while underground in Sicily and other parts of the country, still existed. It was like a chrysalis, waiting to be reborn when the time was ripe, no matter how long that might take.

It helped that Genovese was seen as a Fascist. In July 1938, according to Dickie, the daily newspaper *Il Mattino* (the Morning) published a short item stating that the "Fascist Vito Genovese, enlisted in the New York branch of the Fascist party and currently resident in Naples," had donated money to a local branch near the city to acquire land and build the local party headquarters as well as a "heliotherapy centre," a place where sunlight or artificial ultraviolet rays were used for therapeutic purposes. The contribution amounted to about $25,000.

While Genovese had brought money with him from New York when he fled and was getting his cash stockpile replenished by visits from Anna, he had to be doing something on a more regular basis to keep him in the kind of money he needed. As would later be developed by the FBN, Genovese appeared to have hooked up with the narcotics trade in Italy and became a player in that illicit business.

Possibly from his connection to Madam Monterisi but also because of letters of introduction he had received before he left, Genovese had an introduction to Mussolini's social and political circle. Genovese entertained both Mussolini and his son-in-law, Count Galeazzo Ciano, who also served as the foreign minister. Ciano, who politically would become a tragic figure a bit later in Italian history, is considered by some Italian law enforcement sources to have been a heroin customer of Genovese. So impressed with Genovese was Mussolini that he awarded him the title of Commendatore del Rei. Genovese was clearly on Mussolini's A-list, not a bad place to be with war clouds looming, so long as one remained on Il Duce's good side.

With the advent of World War Two, passenger ship travel between the United States and Europe was greatly restricted. Vessels were commandeered and appropriated for shipping troops and supplies after the U.S. entered the conflict in late 1941. Air travel, unless for official war business, was also out of the question. While some have claimed that Anna made trips to the Continent during the war to supply Genovese with cash, there is no evidence of that occurring. The only documented evidence to surface of Anna's visits to Genovese just before the war was his later claim to federal officials that during a visit she made to Italy in 1939, he gave her a power of attorney over his affairs, something he said she used to sell his assets out from under him. While not impossible, the transportation logistics at that time during the war in Europe would have made it impractical for a civilian to travel back and forth from New York City.

So how did Genovese continue to thrive in Fascist Italy during the war? As will be described further along in this narrative, Genovese built up a black market supply operation in war-torn Italy that provided him with a steady revenue stream. The supply network Genovese developed continued well into the period when the United States joined the Allied forces and they eventually drove out the German occupying forces, by which time Mussolini had been captured and executed. But it also appears that Genovese began to explore drug trafficking, reportedly with the help of Ciano. According to crime historian Salvatore Lupo, by the 1920s, morphine had already been traveling from Palermo in Sicily to the U.S. in crates of fruit. Genovese tried to obtain Ciano's help to develop additional smuggling facilities to get the drugs into Italy from Turkey, the country that was at that point a main cultivation area for the opium poppy.

Some crime historians also believe that Genovese provided a way for Mussolini to silence one of his most vocal critics in New York, the radical publisher and Italian émigré Carlo Tresca, publisher of the anti-Fascist newspaper *Il Martello* (the Hammer). Even five thousand miles away from Rome, Tresca apparently stoked Mussolini's anger. Tresca was also an anti-Communist who denounced the Soviet Union, so it appears he had enemies all around the political spectrum. The U.S. government at one point in the 1920s tried to deport him, but that was quashed by President Calvin Coolidge.

It was in 1943 that Tresca has his downfall. The evening of January 11, 1943, Tresca exited his office building at 2 West Fifteenth Street in Manhattan. With a trimmed beard and cape, Tresca was distinctive and not easy to miss. Witnesses said at around 9:40 P.M., a short, squat man got out of a dark sedan and fired three shots at close range at Tresca. The gunman didn't miss. A wounded Tresca staggered to the nearby corner of Fifteenth Street and Fifth Avenue, where he finally collapsed and died.

Over the years, a number of theories have arisen as to why the feisty firebrand was murdered. Some theorize that the Italian-American publisher Generoso Pope had Tresca killed because of virulent criticism he received from Tresca. Another is that Communists had targeted him. But among many Mafia experts, it is accepted more or less as gospel that Genovese, as a favor to Mussolini, had Tresca killed. The shooter is said to have been Carmine Galante, a violent New York gangster who was becoming an emerging player in the international heroin racket and would later be implicated with Genovese in the drug trade.

But in his 2010 book *Carlo Tresca: Portrait of A Rebel*, author Nunzio Pernicone describes facts and scenarios that work against the idea that Genovese took $500,000 to have Tresca killed. For a start, by late 1942, Mussolini was politically on the ropes in Italy and had more on his mind to deal with than a pesky newspaper editor in New York, noted Pernicone. Traction for the story that Genovese was involved stemmed from a story that appeared in the *Brooklyn Eagle* that reported how Ernest Rupolo, one of the killers of Boccia, alleged that the mob boss had arranged the Tresca hit, again with no substantiation. Tresca did allude in one article about dirty laundry in Genovese's closet such as narcotics, but that was in 1940, and Tresca never did write about drugs specifically, explained Pernicone. Why would Genovese risk going after Tresca in 1943 for something written in 1940? Pernicone asked rhetorically.

After examining the available evidence so many decades later, Pernicone believed that mob involvement in the Tresca killing was feasible but that it was more likely that the instigator was mobster Frank "Don Ciccio" Garofalo, a distinguished-looking Sicilian whom Tresca had publicly insulted at an Italian war bond dinner in 1942 at the Manhattan Club. Tresca had attended the dinner out of respect for a local businessman he knew but blurted out insults to Garofalo and other pro-Fascist Italians. Garofalo was born in the Mafia city of Castellammare del Golfo and eventually was linked to the Bonanno crime family. As it turned out years later, a biographical summary of Garofalo, also known as "Garofolo," said that he was "believed to have ordered the murder of Carlo Tresca at NYC in 1943." Nevertheless, the story that Genovese arranged the Tresca murder still persists in modern Mafia lore.

As close as Genovese was to Mussolini and his family, it certainly became apparent to the American by the summer of 1943 that his protector was in deep trouble with his own people. Initially, Mussolini had thrown his lot in with the Axis of Germany and Japan, sending Italian troops to North Africa and the Russian front, two major military areas. Italy itself was not resource rich, and its army had fared poorly in earlier campaigns in Africa. Nonetheless, Mussolini felt it imperative that the Italian military join with Germany on those two fronts. The results were disastrous. The Russian Army overwhelmed the Italian Army and destroyed it. In North Africa, the Axis campaign stalled with the Battle of El Alamein and then collapsed, with thousands of Italian troops taken prisoner.

The real damage for Mussolini was done with Operation Husky, the Allied invasion of Sicily, which began on July 9, 1943. It would take over a month for the combined Allied forces of the United States, Britain, and Canada to finally push the German and Italian forces out of Sicily. But the way the battle developed in the early going made it clear to the Italian people and their government that Mussolini was a failure. On July 25, 1943, just a bit over two weeks after General George S. Patton Jr. and the rest of the Allies landed on Sicily, the Grand Council of Fascism passed a vote of no confidence in Mussolini, and the next day King Victor Emmanuel III dismissed him as head of government and had him taken into custody.

In Sicily, Patton was smelling victory. In an open letter from Patton, dated August 1, 1943, the commander exhorted his soldiers and airmen of the Seventh Army to get ready for the push to the Italian mainland.

"Landed and supported by the Navy and Air Force, you have during twenty-one days of ceaseless battle and unremitting toil, killed and captured more than 87,000 enemy soldiers, you captured or destroyed 351 cannons, 172 tanks, 928 trucks and 190 airplanes—you are magnificent soldiers!" exclaimed Patton. "The end is certain and is very near. Messina is your next stop."

With Mussolini deposed and the Germany Army fighting a lost cause, Genovese, like the Old Man in *Catch-22,* had to change his stripes and align himself with the Americans. He did so in a way that would line his pockets but also lead to his loss of Italy as a refuge.

Chapter Eight

MUSSOLINI WAS RESCUED BY GERMAN FORCES in September 1943 in a raid carried out by paratroopers and Waffen-SS commandos. The action was personally ordered by Adolph Hitler, and after Mussolini was freed, he was installed as the head of a puppet Italian government in the northern part of Italy. Mussolini's son-in-law, Count Galeazzo Ciano, a friend of Genovese, had actually voted earlier for Mussolini's ouster, and when he attempted to flee Italy, he was captured and turned over to Mussolini, tried for treason, and executed in early 1944. With Mussolini in the north and Ciano dead, Genovese, Miranda, and any of their pals in the south around Naples had to deal with the reality of the Allied forces. Il Duce wasn't going to do them any good now.

Although Mussolini was ensconced in the north, the German Army still was operational in southern Italy. When the Allies initiated landings at Salerno and pushed to Naples, it was September 1943, the beginning of what would be months of costly fighting for all sides. This was the beginning of a period in which Genovese had to be careful. The German Army still occupied the city, but the American forces were bearing down. Assistance for the Allies came in the form of a rebellion by Italians residents and soldiers in Naples. Over a four-day period, in what became known as the Quattro Giornate di Napoli (Four Days of Naples), from September 27 to September 30, locals disrupted the Germans with attacks and ambushes, setting the stage for the Allied liberation of the city on the morning of October 1, 1943.

A relative of Genovese who spoke with me said that the expatriate American was part of the resistance movement. In the face of the Allied offensive, Genovese worked with partisans to harass the German units and commit sabotage in order to stymie the Nazi defense, said the relative. The partisan effort by the Italians has been well documented in the history of World War Two. But there is no confirmation or any other information to verify the claim that Genovese worked with the partisan movement, although given the fluid situation in Italy and his connections, it remains a possibility.

The civilian battling took hundreds of lives, and in the end, the German Army in retreat burned the archives of Naples and set explosives that detonated even after they had fled. Where was Vito Genovese in all of this? While there is the claim that he worked with the partisans, American investigators learned after the fighting that Genovese had a nicely appointed apartment in the town of Nola. He then proceeded to make the most of the changing situation. By the fall of 1943, right after the liberation of Naples, Genovese walked into the offices of the Allied Military Government of Occupied Territories (known as AMGOT) in Nola and let it be known that he would serve as an interpreter, without compensation—although with his drug and black market dealings, he didn't have to worry about money or expenses. Genovese "worked day and night and rendered most valuable assistance to the Allied Military Government" gushed one U.S. Army major in a letter of reference he provided Genovese, dated November 1943.

At this point, AMGOT needed all the help it could get from somebody like Genovese, who was fluent in Italian and English and was an American citizen, because the situation in Naples was dire. As well-intentioned as AMGOT was in trying to help the Neapolitans, the military faced problems of enormous scope.

While it was occupied by the Germans, Naples had been bombed by the Allies, and the citizens, after so much fighting and deprivation, were in a sorry state—Genovese excepted. A history of conditions prepared by U.S. Army's Office of Medical History said that Naples, a city of one million, "was in a state of utter confusion." The Serena Aqueduct, which provided the water supply for the city, had been blown up in bombing raids. Drinking water was found only in about sixty shallow and deep wells scattered near the port area. None of the wells had pumps, so residents had to carry water home in bottles, jugs, and anything they could find.

While people had enough water to drink, there wasn't enough for flushing toilets. Electricity was out, causing an inability for the sewage system to pump. Without power, hospitals found themselves "well-nigh paralyzed." Mounds of garbage blocked the streets, and over five hundred corpses decomposed in bombed-out homes, air raid shelters, and hospital morgues. Italians didn't like the idea of burying their dead without caskets or coffins, but wood was lacking. On top of that, the danger of venereal disease led to AMGOT placing all brothels off limits to the servicemen.

An epidemic of typhus erupted, followed by typhoid fever. AMGOT had its hands full in Naples, and somebody like Genovese proved to be very useful in communicating with the suffering populace. Yet, like First Lieutenant Milo Minderbinder, the opportunistic capitalist who ran his own thriving black market operation at the fictional airfield in *Catch-22*, Genovese saw his opportunities in the squalor of the war and took them.

Food during the war throughout southern Italy, especially Naples and Sicily, was in short supply. Part of the reason was that Mussolini's government had a habit of falsifying wheat harvest figures, inflating them in a propaganda move. Also, fertilizer was scarce, causing production problems for the growing seasons. Feeding the people in places like Sicily after the Allied invasion, said one secret AMGOT report, was going to be problematic.

The same report also put its finger on another problem: the black market. While Mussolini tried to minimize the black market issue in a place like Sicily after his highly publicized anti-Mafia campaign, the prevalence of the illegal commerce in foodstuffs throughout Italy was something the Allies didn't anticipate. It also indicated that the Mafia was back, signaling what one AMGOT official said was "a revival of the Mafia, which is believed to be stronger now than at any time since the Fascist regime took power."

Of course, with Vito Genovese in Italy and so close to Mussolini's clique, in one sense the Mafia never really left. After singing the praises of the American military and AMGOT, Genovese went about business as usual in a concerted way, exploiting the scarcity in basic foodstuffs and other staples like gasoline. He may not have been the only black marketeer in the Naples area, but he had a gang that knew how to deceive the military.

To be clear, Genovese wasn't the only Mafioso to work on "infiltrating" the military government after the Allies landed. In Sicily, one Nicola Gentile, a mobster born on the island in 1885 who later emigrated to Philadelphia, also decided to help the Allies. As recounted by Dickie in *Blood Brotherhood*, Gentile had spent much of his adult life traveling back and forth from the United States to Sicily, where he finally settled after jumping bail in a 1937 drug case in New Orleans. When AMGOT took control in Sicily, men like Gentile were able to easily convince military leaders to accept their help to deal with the intractable problems facing the new civil authority.

As Dickie related, "Amid an explosion of prison breakouts and armed robbery, AMGOT sought authority figures untainted by Mussolini's regime to help them deal with the anarchy. As 'middle-class villains,' Men of Honour are very good at creating the respectable façade that AMGOT was looking for."

Around Naples, Genovese was living a good life, with his own air of respectability, being chauffeured around and operating with seeming immunity from law enforcement. Wheat, flour, olive oil, and other essential items for cooking and survival were hot commodities, particularly in the face of the shortages that developed because of the war's disruption. As investigators would later determine, Genovese was able to recruit Italians and American and Canadian soldiers—some of whom were AWOL—to drive U.S. Army trucks stolen from the Naples docks. The vehicles were then driven to supply depots, where commodities like wheat, sugar, and olive oil were collected. The trucks then went out into the countryside, where private cars then arrived and transported the foodstuffs to nearby towns and villages for further distribution to a hungry populace. To cover his tracks, Genovese is said to have had the trucks destroyed by arson. If any of the trucks were ever stopped in the course of their smuggling trips, the drivers were to say "Genovese sent us."

Genovese, according to informants, had some safe-deposit boxes in Italy that he used to horde money, generally U.S. currency other than the colored invasion currency, which was marked with a yellow strip and other distinctive markings to show that it was issued for the payment of American soldiers. Given Genovese's travels around Europe, beginning in the 1930s, he had a number of relationships with banks in financial centers like Switzerland.

While Genovese was living well from the black market racket, it was just a matter of time before the American military became suspicious of him. Interest in Genovese was sparked by an informant's tip to an Army intelligence sergeant with the name of Orange Dickey, who in civilian life had been a baker in Altoona, Pennsylvania. Dickey had joined the Army in 1942 and was sent to the Mediterranean in 1943 and later sent to Italy in December of that year, just a few months after the Army had accepted Genovese's services as a translator.

Once in Italy, Dickey was appointed as an agent in the criminal investigation division of the army, the unit that, as its name implies, looks into possible criminal conduct impacting the military. Dickey's first assignment was to look into reports of black market activity in the area of Naples and the nearby town of Nola. As Dickey would later explain, Nola was a center for smuggling. While black market dealing started someplace else and was completed elsewhere, Nola seemed to be a temporary clearinghouse, although Dickey initially didn't know why.

"This was a very extensive operation," Dickey remembered of the Nola black market. The hot commodities flowing from Naples toward eastern Italy were sugar, blankets, clothing, and food, while smugglers brought into Naples staple foodstuffs that were desperately needed, like wheat, olive oil, and beans. The investigation found that army vehicles were used to transport the materials and later destroyed, set afire, sometimes within sight of Mount Vesuvius. The soldiers who had driven the trucks would then lay low in some rooming houses in Nola and wait for another assignment.

Earlier in the investigation, about forty Allied soldiers had been arrested for black market offenses, as well as about eight or nine Italian civilians, including one man who seemed to be a key to the activity in the Naples-Nola area. According to the Italian smuggler, a key man in the activities in the area was one "Vito Genovese," who had assured him that if he ever got arrested nothing would come of the case.

As Dickey probed deeper, he learned from other informants who were former officials with the Italian government under Mussolini that Genovese also had some clout with Il Duce. They recounted the stories about his funneling money for Fascist projects, including the government building in Nola, and how, for his efforts, Genovese was given the highest commendation that a person could receive, the Commendatore del Rei.

Among the informers Dickey talked to were some Americans who had either been deported back to Italy or returned voluntarily. Among them was one Julius Simonelli, who told Dickey that Genovese was a member of the Mafia. When he learned that, Dickey knew the investigation into the black market had taken on a greater meaning. Dickey kept pressing the investigation and at one point traveled to areas where he located a great many burned U.S. Army trucks. There were as many as forty trucks found in a hazelnut tree grove about five miles from Mount Vesuvius, which, as it turned out, was causing its own problems for the American military at this time.

It was March 18, 1944, that Vesuvius, after threatening and belching smoke and ash for days, finally erupted with what was described as "a sinister prolonged roar." The lava advanced from the crater, and the wind blew ash and smoke for many kilometers.

"It was a night without stars, but full of light" was how one eyewitness noted the strange darkness illuminated by the glowing lava. The lava engulfed much of nearby towns of San Giorgio a Cremano and San Sebastiano al Vesuvio. Italian civilians fled to seek the protection of the Allied forces. One commander even allowed Italians to march with religious statuary to the very edge of the lava to pray for the eruption to stop.

The eruption became a top priority for the American commanders, overriding all else, including criminal investigations into black marketeering. The ash fell like snow, sometimes as deep as three feet, and the military had to scrape the roads with plows to keep traffic going. U.S. Air Force bombers stabled at an airfield near Pompeii were hit with ash and rock, which damaged or destroyed an estimated eighty aircraft.

By late March, the eruption had subsided and Dickey could get his investigation back on track. It was early August when Dickey and his commander believed that they had enough to arrest Genovese on the black market offenses. But Genovese couldn't be found. It is possible he got wind of the army probe or temporarily sought refuge from the Vesuvius eruption. The forward edge of the frontline against the Germans had also moved farther northward at the time, so it is possible Genovese shifted his operations to follow the troop movements. In any case, Genovese was scarce and on the move.

Enter Humbert Costello, otherwise known as Humberto Consentino and Hubert Miri. Costello was a career criminal who didn't like snitches, especially those in the jailhouse, where he had spent much of his adult life. After he emigrated from Italy to the United States at the age of 8, Costello's life was a constant struggle against the law. As a youth, Costello wound up in a Missouri reform school, and when he got out, he was sentenced to four years in the state penitentiary for grand larceny.

Given his criminal credentials, Costello found himself a valued member of the gang of legendary St. Louis gangster Edward "Jelly Roll" Hogan Jr., who when he wasn't bootlegging and directing his crime crew was a political fixer of sorts in Missouri. Costello's skein of armed robberies and other larcenies, as well as his usefulness in gunfights with the rival Irish mob, earned him the reputation of being the "best bet" among Hogan's hired hands. But as useful as he was on the streets of St. Louis, Costello—he doesn't appear to have been related to the more prominent Frank Costello in New York—couldn't get away from a prison cell. In 1923, Costello was sentenced to twenty-five years for the $5,000 holdup of a jewelry store in St Louis in 1920. After being paroled after twelve years, Costello was promptly jailed in 1935 on a federal immigration deportation case following his conviction on two crimes of moral turpitude.

Costello fought his deportation case, and in one instance won a delay of deportation just minutes before he was to be put on a special "deportation train" for shipment east to catch a ship back to Italy. But finally in 1937, Costello had exhausted all his appeals, and on the night of April 10, he was bundled on to the special deportation train with just minutes to spare before its scheduled departure. In the company of a number of other deportees, mostly Italians, he was sent on to Chicago and then east to catch the boat to return to Italy. His only distinction aside from his reputation as a criminal was that Costello had spent most of his thirty-eight years behind bars.

During his days in the Missouri penal system, Costello was known as a "right-o," a convict who the newspapers said was unwilling to talk about the activities of his criminal brethren or enemies. In other words, Costello was what became known in Mafia parlance as a standup guy. "He also regarded as 'snitches' other convicts who won promotions to easier jobs through good behavior," was how the *St. Louis Globe-Democrat* described him.

So why then did Costello, in August 1944, some six years after he had returned to the Naples area following his deportation, agree to help Dickey in his attempt to find Vito Genovese? As Dickey would later recall, Costello was considered a good friend of Genovese, and as it turned out, he was living in an apartment in Nola directly beneath the one being renovated for Genovese. When asked, Costello told Dickey that Genovese would be occupying the dwelling, so the American military kept the building under surveillance.

Why Costello talked with Dickey was never clear. Perhaps Costello wanted to remain on good terms with the Americans during the fluid war situation as a way of currying favor for his own possible return to the United States. In any case, based on Dickey's account, Costello did give American investigators help that would lead to Genovese's arrest. But the capture wouldn't be easy. Genovese finally moved into the Nola apartment on August 25, 1944, and talked with Costello. It was then, according to one account, that Genovese, after conversing with Costello, decided suddenly to leave Nola. This suggested that Costello might have told Genovese that the military cops were asking questions about him.

It was on August 27, 1944, that Genovese stopped by the municipal building in Nola to get a travel permit that would allow him to travel outside the province of Naples. After Genovese drove away, his limousine parked in downtown Nola, and Dickey and his men pounced, taking Genovese into custody, searching the limousine, and finding a number of handguns inside. Genovese also was carrying a number of letters from American and British military officers saying that he been doing translation work for AMGOT.

A search of Genovese's apartment produced fresh evidence for investigators of just how well he was doing during his time in Italy. For a small-town boy like Dickey, Genovese was living high and his tastes were exquisite. The soldier may not have seen firsthand the women Genovese had access to from Madame Monterisi, but in a time of great deprivation for most Italians, his lifestyle exuded material excess. He had expensive custom-made clothing, lavish furnishings, and shoes, lots of shoes.

"I don't recall ever in my life having seen a man with so many pairs of shoes, or so many suits of clothing," Dickey would recall years later. "I have never seen anything like that in my life."

Genovese was taken by Dickey's men to a temporary jail in Nola and then quickly on to the AMGOT jail in Naples. Genovese's arrest should have led to his prosecution for black market activity. But instead, it began a strange odyssey that would take place over a period of two years and in the process sully the reputations of some top American military officials and politicians and further embellish Genovese's reputation for ducking trouble.

And what of Mussolini, who had been Genovese's protector in

the Fascist heydays? By April 1945, his puppet government would collapse. Trying to escape to Switzerland, Mussolini and his mistress, Clara Petacci, were captured by partisans and summarily executed on April 28, 1945. In one of the war's grisly Italian tableaus, the bodies of Mussolini and Petacci were strung up at a gas station in Milan for the world to see. Less than a month later, Genovese would find himself back in New York to await his fate.

Chapter Nine

ERNEST "THE HAWK" RUPOLO'S LIFE as a street thug doing the mob's bidding had not served him well. His contract work in the Boccia 1934 killing got him up to twenty years in prison. While Vito Genovese, Michele Miranda, and others were running around free in Europe—war torn though it might be—Rupolo was paroled after serving about eleven years in 1944. But he couldn't shake the old life and was living more or less hand-to-mouth.

In a way, Rupolo was like Humberto Costello. Both were sold on the idea as young men of keeping quiet about their criminal bosses. Costello got deported yet was able to live as a free man in Italy. But in the case of Rupolo, he was getting nothing for his silence. The measly $175 he got for the Boccia shooting was a pittance. The $200 for a second shooting got him more trouble. He was left high and dry by the mob. Nobody provided Rupolo with an attorney when he was advised to plead guilty. The mob had "let me down," he said. Rupolo clearly had enough.

It was the shooting of one Carl Sparacino, a 31-year-old from Brooklyn, that forced Rupolo to finally change his attitude for good about being a silent, stand-up guy. Sparacino, described as a long-shoreman and former dressmaker, was shot three times as he sat in his parked car on the night of April 17 in Brooklyn. Four days later, Rupolo and 20-year-old Ernest Filocomo were picked up by cops and held without bail. Rupolo had been paid $200 for the shooting of Sparacino, who earned the mob's wrath because he had the temerity to rip off some dice games.

Arrested for the shooting of Sparacino—who survived being shot in the face and neck—Rupolo was facing the prospect of being a two-time loser if convicted. Worse yet, Brooklyn Judge Samuel Leibowitz promised Rupolo a sentence of up to eighty years in prison if he didn't cooperate and tell prosecutors why he did the job and who was behind it. Rupolo wanted never to see the inside of a cell again and started talking, at first not about the Sparacino hit attempt but about what he knew about a $2,400 stickup that took place in March 1943. That was just a warm-up. When Rupolo finally came up for sentencing in August 1944 for pleading guilty in the Sparacino shooting, he had what one newspaper said was "a song or two left in him."

Actually, Rupolo's main aria had taken place earlier in the Brooklyn district attorney's office, and when he came to court, Leibowitz asked the prosecutors if Rupolo had been helpful. He most certainly had, said Brooklyn Assistant District Attorney Edward Heffernan.

"He has given us very valuable information," said Heffernan. "He has made disclosures that have wide ramifications, and I am satisfied he has been telling the truth."

Good, said the judge. Rupolo had learned his lesson well.

"You continue that way," Leibowitz told Rupolo. "Tell the truth completely and in every detail. If you do that you'll get full consideration from this court." Rupolo mumbled in assent and sentencing was put off, indefinitely. He was held in jail in the meantime for his own safety.

Soon, the world came to know that Rupolo had squealed on Genovese and others in the Boccia killing, leading to indictments on August 7, 1944. This was a big break for the prosecution, which had failed ten years earlier to charge Genovese and Miranda in the case. The timing of the news was fortuitous because Genovese was on the verge of being arrested in Italy as part of Dickey's black market investigation.

The NYPD didn't know where Genovese or any of the other suspects were at this point. So, on August 14, 1944, assistant chief inspector John J. Ryan put out a bulletin to all commands announcing that warrants had gone out for six arrests: Genovese, "Michael Mirandi," Gus Frasca, George Smurra, Peter DeFeo, and somebody known only as "Sally" (probably "Solly" Palmieri). Physical descriptions were given for each of them, their ages, and last known addresses. In the case of Genovese, he was described as being 36 years old, five feet, seven inches tall, and 160 pounds with black hair. His last known address was the apartment at 29 Washington Square Park in Manhattan, and he had a tendency to hang out in Little Italy. "Use caution," the bulletin said to alert the officers.

As it turned out, Rupolo's cooperation and the police bulletin came just as Genovese was cooling his heels in a Naples military jail, where American authorities were at least initially unaware of his impending problem in Brooklyn. As Dickey remembered, after Genovese's name was referred to the FBI because of his status as a U.S. citizen, a records check discovered the fresh Boccia murder charge in New York.

For reasons that were never made clear, Genovese was moved from the military holding facility to a civilian jail in Avellino for a few months and then to a civilian jail in Bari, on the east coast of Italy. He obviously was fairing a bit better there, but he still wasn't going to get out of custody any time soon.

Back in Brooklyn, the publicity about Rupolo's squealing hit the newspapers, along with the startling and embarrassing claim that Genovese had been working for AMGOT and its prime leader in the Naples area, Lieutenant Colonel Charles Poletti. A card-carrying Democrat and a lawyer in civilian life, Poletti had from 1939 to 1942 served as lieutenant governor of New York State under Governor Herbert Lehman. When Lehman resigned to take up a position with the U.S. Department of State, Poletti succeeded him as governor for the few months left in Lehman's term, the first Italian-American to hold that position in state history. It was during the brief period he served as governor that Poletti sparked a little bit of controversy in Albany when he decided to offer pardons to a number of criminals, including some labor racketeers and goons.

Poletti didn't win election on his own, and he left state government in 1942 to take a job with the office of the secretary of war and then took a military posting with the army to the Mediterranean Theater. Eventually, Poletti was appointed military governor to the liberated Allied areas of Italy as the Mussolini government collapsed and Germans began their long northward retreat up the boot of Italy. A fluent Italian speaker (his family had immigrated to the U.S. from Italy) Poletti won his share of the accolades and brickbats that came with the job of trying to sort out the problems of the Italian civilians.

In an interview with CBS correspondent Eric Sevareid, in early 1944, Poletti said that over time the Allied government had made progress besting the typhus epidemic, getting food supplies moving, and restoring electricity, water, and sanitation services. "The high cost of living and the black market remain our chief headaches," Poletti admitted in the interview. Another problem, according to Poletti, was that Italians had been so fearful and distrustful of the "racket" government under Fascism that they didn't know what to make of AMGOT. But with time, said Poletti hopefully, the Italians would operate their own democratic government.

Most of the American press seemed to favor the job Poletti was doing as commander of AMGOT. He also received awards and praise from the locals and eventually would get honored by Pope Pius XII. But Poletti was seen by some critics who were mired in their own politics as a questionable character, if not corrupt, because of the various pardons he had issued to what one newspaper called "labor sluggers and goons" who had been held in New York State prisons. The *Knickerbocker News* even went on to say in a reference to Poletti that it doubted a "governor who would pardon a labor terrorist can demonstrate Americanism successfully."

But any criticism of Poletti related to AMGOT was small stuff compared with the way the headlines back in Brooklyn were blaring about the Genovese case.

"Poletti Aide Nabbed in Rome For Boro Killing," blared the *Brooklyn Daily Eagle* in November 1944. The story said that Genovese, a "Brooklyn gangster of the Prohibition Era," had been working as an interpreter for Poletti. The controversy over just what Genovese's connection was to Poletti would rage on for years, almost leading to libel lawsuits as the former lieutenant governor tried to distance himself from Genovese and defend his reputation in the public arena.

Back in Italy, American officials tried to interrogate Genovese for intelligence, but to no avail. There had been suspicion that Genovese had been working as an agent for the Germans, a claim made by the late DEA agent Tom Tripodi in his book *Crusade: Undercover Against the Mafia and KGB*. Tripodi said that Genovese had even traveled on a few occasions to Germany during the war years, and Genovese's wife would later claim that her husband was entertained by German Air Marshal Hermann Goering at his estate in San Remo, Italy. But, Genovese didn't give up anything of substance in his talks while in custody. One intriguing find when American investigators raided Genovese's apartment was that of some radio apparatus capable of being hooked up to a transmitter, an item that was not found during the search. The fact that Genovese had access to this type of a radio indicated he had been making clandestine transmissions, to whom was unknown.

However, Genovese still had a great deal of clout outside the jailhouse walls, and people working on his behalf tried to arrange payoffs to either get him out or keep him from being moved around. At one point, Dickey said he heard that some of the guards were offered cash bribes to spring Genovese. Dickey, who was a 24-year-old soldier making about $210 a month in salary, said he personally was offered $250,000 to let Genovese out and on another occasion was offered payment to leave him in one particular jail in the town of Mario, apparently because criminal elements had better access to the facility.

The process of getting Genovese back to Brooklyn from Italy was an involved one, taking months of wrangling. Finally, on May 14, 1945, Dickey took custody of Genovese, and the two of them began an ocean voyage back to New York on the SS *James Lykes*, a 141-foot-long freighter built for the government for war service. It was a strange trip in one sense because Dickey and Genovese shared the same stateroom, with the army agent having given his gun over to the ship's captain for safekeeping.

At first, Genovese was violently opposed to being taken back to the U.S. and demanded access to an attorney. He flat-out didn't want to go back to Brooklyn. But eventually, Genovese's attitude softened, and he actually thanked Dickey was getting him on the boat.

"Kid, you are doing me the biggest favor anyone has ever done to me. You are taking me home, you are taking me back to the United States," said Genovese, according to Dickey's recollection.

Given the circumstances, Genovese proved to be a somewhat lively conversationalist, schooling Dickey on the ways that gambling and labor rackets worked, letting the military man know that there were certain ways things worked and that he was simply too young to know them.

"He would speak freely about many things, such as horse racing or policy or things of that nature," remembered Dickey later. "He told me how they could be fixed and how they would run a 'ringer' and so on, and he told me how policy operated and how it could be fixed."

During the voyage, Dickey got a good schooling in the fine points of some gambling rackets and heard from Genovese about his family back in the U.S. The mobster regaled Dickey with tales of his vacations to Hot Springs and Little Rock in Arkansas, two places that had in the prewar years become fashionable spa towns and gambling meccas for the Mafiosi in New York.

"I take the mineral baths, you know, and I come back feelin' like a new man," Costello said about his Hot Springs vacations.

Genovese may have done a lot of talking on the voyage, but one thing he made no mention of was the pending homicide case he faced in Brooklyn. The indictment for the Boccia homicide was one of six slayings cops were trying to link to Genovese, along with Miranda, DeFeo, Frasca, and Smurra, as well the man known only as "Sally," who was listed in the indictment as a John Doe.

All of the suspects had criminal records and were linked to Cosa Nostra families. But the oddity was that the newspaper accounts didn't refer to the Mafia or La Cosa Nostra but rather linked Genovese and the others to the "Unione Sicilione," an apparent reference to Unione Siciliane, an Italian fraternal organization that over the decades had became co-opted by mobsters like Al Capone but that by 1940 or so had really become irrelevant. Genovese and the other suspects were also claimed by police to be members of the Black Hawk gang, a group that had terrorized the Brooklyn waterfront and was believed to have orchestrated a number of murders, the most prominent being that of John Flaherty, president of the grain handlers union.

The use by police of old gang names like Union Siciliane and Black Hawk was an indication of how tentative and incomplete was the knowledge of investigators into the structure of the Mafia or what it was known as in the underworld. The term "Mafia" would take a few years to emerge in the U.S., although it had been a staple of common parlance in Italy. Part of the problem was that some in law enforcement, notably FBI director J. Edgar Hoover, didn't believe in the Mafia and instead eventually gave gangsters like Genovese and Costello the label of "Top Hoodlum" and carried them in a specially designated program for increased attention and surveillance.

Genovese and Dickey arrived back in New York harbor finally on June 1, 1945, about seven months after he had first been jailed in Italy. Given the gravity of the charges facing Genovese and his reputation in the underworld, Dickey and Genovese were given a surprisingly small escort at the pier. Two military security men picked them up and drove them to the Brooklyn district attorney's office in a military police car. Genovese was handcuffed to Dickey's wrist. It was that simple.

At the prosecutor's office in downtown Brooklyn, Dickey brought Genovese to Heffernan.

"And, so this is Vito?" Heffernan said as he sized up Genovese, remembered Dickey.

Upstairs, Heffernan turned Genovese over to detectives. The suspect Heffernan never expected to see back in the U.S. was now in hand.

A day later, Genovese appeared for arraignment in criminal court, and through his attorney, Hyman Barshay, who had defended gangster Louis Buchalter four years earlier, entered a plea of not guilty to the murder charges. Genovese was sent to the Thompson Street jail to await further court dates.

Genovese was only one of the defendants in the case, and while Brooklyn prosecutors had Smurra and Frasca in hand, Miranda was still in Italy. Prosecutors knew Miranda was overseas because Dickey had spoken to him. It seemed that other investigators had told Dickey that Miranda was indeed an associate of Genovese. While Dickey had spoken with Miranda, the military man wasn't aware of Miranda's status as a New York gangster or his alleged involvement in the Boccia homicide. "Just call me Mike," was how Miranda introduced himself. For the moment, Miranda could afford to be chummy.

Genovese might have been wanted for the Boccia murder and the justice system would deal with him, but the way his case was handled and the connections he had with the U.S. military while in Italy were fast becoming focal points for politicians and the news media.

The one thing Charles Poletti and Vito Genovese had in common was their Italian ancestry, but that was the only real similarity between them. With little guidance from his parents, Genovese had grown up to become a mobster, feeding the stereotype many Americans had about Italian immigrants. He hardly had any formal education but learned the lessons of the street on the Lower West Side of Manhattan. Poletti had been close to his Italian immigrant parents growing up in Vermont and had intended to run a bakery after high school, that is, until a teacher encouraged him to go to college. Genovese earned his early fortune in bootlegging, gambling, and perhaps prostitution. Poletti waited tables and washed dishes to help get through Harvard University on a scholarship.

Poletti valued learning and public service and found himself at the pinnacle of New York State government at the same time that Genovese was busy doing black market deals and serving as a banker and money launderer for Mussolini and his Fascist cabal. Given their disparate life stories, it is astonishing that in the history of organized crime the names of Poletti and Genovese became linked. Genovese would die a gangster, true to the oath the Mafioso took when they decided to stay with the life. Poletti, when he died at the age of 99, earned an obituary in the *New York Times* that avoided any mention of Genovese and extolled his life of public service. But while he was alive, Poletti was shattered by the way he was linked to the Mafia.

The initial stories about Genovese's arrest in Brooklyn claimed he had been working for Poletti as a translator, and once that story line started, it propagated through other media accounts and magazine articles. The reports angered Poletti, who asked lawyers to consider filing libel suits. For a start, Poletti told his lawyers that Genovese had been hired by an AMGOT officer in Nola in October 1943, right after the town was captured by the Allied Forces. The officer was a civil affairs officer and had the authority to hire and fire local people. Poletti didn't know the exact circumstances for the hiring of Genovese, but since Poletti was a fluent Italian speaker, he didn't need a translator.

Poletti also wasn't in the Naples area when Genovese was hired because in October 1943 he was the regional Allied commissioner for AMGOT based in Sicily. Poletti didn't transfer to the Naples province until February 1944. While Genovese may have worked as an interpreter in the Naples area at the same time that Poletti was stationed there, Poletti's reaction was "So what? I didn't hire him or keep him on the payroll."

What appears to have also made Poletti angry was the source of the information linking him to Genovese. His first suspicion was the NYPD, but he also wondered about LaGuardia and people in the Brooklyn district attorney's office. The latter office had been run by William O'Dwyer, a high-profile prosecutor who during the war had been appointed to the rank of brigadier general and was as-

signed to Italy to, as it turned out, ironically, work with Poletti in
AMGOT and help with the administration of the country as the Allied Forces advanced.

Despite all of his anger over what he saw as a smear campaign,
Poletti apparently didn't file any libel suit. In 1945 and beyond, the
main news about Poletti revolved around the accolades he received
over the transition of Italy from a military controlled area to some
form of democracy. Given the nature of war-torn Italy, getting the
country on its feet again didn't all go smoothly. But when Poletti finally left the military in 1946 to return to civilian life and his career
in the law and public service, he must have thought that he left the
Genovese controversy behind. Such was not the case.

After returning Genovese to Brooklyn, investigator Dickey gave
some testimony to the staff of acting District Attorney George J.
Beldock about events leading up to the capture of the mob boss in
Italy in August 1944. What Dickey had to say about Poletti made
the commander look like he was closer to Genovese than he had indicated. In his testimony, according to various accounts, Dickey
said that he learned from secondhand sources that a 1938 Packard
auto that Miranda had brought with him to Italy wound up being
given by Genovese to Poletti as a gift. Poletti never paid Genovese
a dime for the vehicle, said Dickey.

In addition, Dickey claimed that when he tried to see Poletti in
his office in Rome, presumably to talk with him about Genovese, he
found Poletti in his office with his arms folded on the top of his desk
and his head down, apparently asleep. When Dickey said he returned to try and speak with Poletti again, the commander was busy
in his office talking with people with liquor bottles on his desk, said
Dickey, adding that Poletti was "just more or less enjoying himself."

Dickey then recalled in his statement to Beldock that he ran into
General O'Dwyer, the former Brooklyn district attorney and political rival of Beldock, and mentioned that Brooklyn prosecutors were
interested in Genovese. Dickey said that he asked O'Dwyer what
Acting District Attorney Thomas Hughes intended to do about Genovese now that he was biding time in an Italian jail. O'Dwyer re-

sponded that the matter didn't concern him and that Dickey should contact Hughes.

Poletti wouldn't have known at the time that Dickey gave his statement to Beldock in September 1944 what was actually said. Dickey indicated that Poletti seemed to be on the take with Genovese, was using his office as a party place, and generally was too busy having fun to do any work. Meanwhile, O'Dwyer, whom Beldock opposed politically and wanted to embarrass in any way he could, was portrayed by Dickey as someone who was nonchalant about a criminal wanted back in Brooklyn.

In 1952, crime writer Ed Reid was preparing his true crime book titled *Mafia* and had a section in which Dickey's statement to Beldock was republished with large sections verbatim. Reid, a well-known crime writer who published many books in the genre, portrayed Dickey as a "loyal citizen" who brought Genovese back to the U.S. despite many obstacles. In a bit of hyperbole, Reid said the Dickey statement was in his opinion one of the "most significant documents to come out of World War II."

Poletti got a copy of Reid's book and went ballistic. As far as Poletti was concerned, the book portrayed him as an intimate of Genovese who sought to obstruct justice and was an incompetent officer. He contacted noted New York City attorney Morris Ernst to prepare a libel suit.

To Poletti, Reid's book had numerous errors and demonstrable falsehoods, particularly about Genovese. Among the key points pointed out by Poletti was that he was never military governor in Nola, where Genovese had set up shop, but rather military governor in Naples, and months later when Genovese was indicted, he had the same position in Rome. Poletti also said he never had a Packard as a staff car and was never given one by anyone. He acknowledged that the military governors could requisition any civilian vehicles by giving the owners a receipt.

Poletti claimed that some of the dates cited by Reid—particularly in 1944 when the military commander allegedly returned to the U.S. with Genovese—were demonstrably false based on his military personnel records. As far as Poletti was concerned, he never met Genovese in his entire life, never communicated with him, and had no responsibility nor took any action connected with Genovese's extradition to Brooklyn in 1945.

Poletti's lawyers contacted Reid's publishers in May 1953 and began several months of negotiations to clean up the book. In the end, according to correspondence examined by this author, a number of offending statements in Dickey's testimony were excised and references to Poletti in the text kept to a minimum.

Another battle Poletti had with the *New York Times* seemed to go a bit easier. In November 1952, the paper published a story about Genovese and in one paragraph reported that he had worked as an "interpreter for former Lieut. Gov. Charles Poletti, than head of Allied Military Government in Italy." That one phrase revived the old stories and incensed Poletti. A law professor friend, Maurice Neufeld, who had worked with Poletti in Italy, wrote a courteous letter to the newspaper, denying Genovese's ties and asking that the error be corrected. Poletti also wrote his own letter.

Sometimes it pays to be nice. Arthur Hays Sulzberger, the publisher of the *Times,* wrote back to "Charlie" and noted that the newspaper had printed a corrective article noting Poletti's denial of any ties to Genovese. Sulzberger admitted that he didn't know how the information got into the story, although he figured it was probably lifted from an earlier report in the newspaper morgue files. Sulzberger sent along a copy of the story. Case closed, at least for the time being.

Chapter Ten

WHEN HE FIRST APPEARED IN BROOKLYN CRIMINAL COURT in June 1945, Vito Genovese seemed concerned about his style of dress. Reporters described him as wearing a tan plaid suit jacket, tan trench coat, no tie, and no hat. Still, Genovese had a certain presence, and one detective was overheard saying that if he had some new clothes he would look like a movie gangster. But the clothes on Genovese's back were the same ones he had with him for the ten months he was jailed in Italy, and that wouldn't do for a man of his station. The defense attorney, Hyman Barshay, asked the court to allow Genovese some new threads. The judge granted the request.

It would be months before anything of substance happened in the Boccia murder case. But one thing that did happen occurred before Genovese returned Stateside and that was the loss of a man considered to be a key witness: Peter LaTempa. In the annals of organized crime, LaTempa was headed toward a life of obscurity. He was a nervous, unremarkable bachelor from Brooklyn with a tendency to take all sorts of medicine. Joseph Valachi said it was LaTempa who once tried to knife him while both were lodged in Sing Sing.

But LaTempa had the distinction on the night of September 19, 1934, to have witnessed the slaying of Boccia by Ernest "the Hawk" Rupolo and William Gallo. As noted, by 1944, Rupolo had decided to spill everything he knew about Genovese's role in the murder, and he convinced LaTempa to corroborate parts of the story. On the strength of that evidence, Genovese was indicted. What made LaTempa's evidence important was that some of what he said corroborated details of the incident, and because he wasn't a participant, prosecutors could use what he said without running afoul of the state rule against accomplices' evidence being used against a fellow coconspirator.

But on January 14, 1945, as LaTempa resided in a cell at a Brooklyn jail on Ashland Place, the government's star witness was found dead. The prosecutor, Edward Heffernan, said there was nothing suspicious about his death. But that was before an autopsy revealed that LaTempa had ingested enough sleeping tablets to, as city toxicologist Alexander Gettler said, "kill eight horses."

Of course, the rumor mill went into overdrive with suspicion that the long hand of Genovese, who was in a jail in Italy at the time, somehow played a role in LaTempa's demise. But there was never any proof that Genovese was able to penetrate Brooklyn jail security to get LaTempa to overdose. About a month earlier, LaTempa had tried to hang himself in his cell, so suicide was a possibility. The death could also have very well been an accidental overdose, although if LaTempa realized that Genovese would at some point return to face him at trial, then the witness might have thought it best to take his own life. We will never know.

Both Vito Genovese and the man who was the boss of the crime family, Charles "Lucky" Luciano, found themselves behind bars in 1945. Luciano was playing out a lengthy sentence in the 1936 prostitution case, while Genovese was dealing with the shadow of the Boccia indictment and a trial that had yet to happen. Genovese's wartime experience in Italy didn't save him from legal trouble once he was extradited. But in the case of Luciano, ironically, World War Two proved to be his salvation—of sorts.

The story of Luciano's involvement with the American military intelligence effort during the war is a story which has been told numerous times, so it need not be spelled out in detail here. But in 1942, U.S. Naval Intelligence reached out to some Mafia-connected men in New York, namely Joseph "Socks" Lanza and Meyer Lansky, for help in securing the waterfront from possible German sabotage. Lanza was a Mafia powerhouse on the docks and a likely person for officials to approach to see about help. The issue of dock security was paramount on the minds of military officials after a suspicious fire led to the destruction of the SS *Normandie*, a French cruise ship requisitioned as a troop carrier, while it was being refurbished at a pier on the Hudson River in February 1942.

While the idea of the government resorting to the Mafia for help might have seemed wild and even harebrained, Manhattan District Attorney Frank Hogan assigned a top aide, Murray Gurfein, to make some contacts to help push the idea along. Lanza was one of the first gangsters to be approached. Lanza had many contacts in the fish market and knew fishing boat captains and bargemen who plied the Atlantic Coast. Officials suspected that fishing boats might be helping German submarines recharge their batteries and replenish supplies as they sailed close to the U.S. mainland.

Lanza agreed to help, even though he wasn't promised any benefit by Hogan in any pending criminal cases. Lanza was able to get union cards for navy undercover agents so they could travel on fishing boats. Civilian employees of the navy also got cards so they could work with trucking companies that shipped fish from Long Island to the city fish markets.

But with Lanza's influence limited to the seafood industry, the mobster told officials that major Mafia help couldn't be counted on unless certain Mafiosi got the okay from Luciano in prison. Here the beginnings of some mob political intrigue comes into play. According to George Wolf, the attorney for Frank Costello, his client relished the idea of Luciano back in the mix so that he, Costello, could back away from his role as acting boss of the crime family. After all, Costello had some legitimate businesses and he needed to give up the title of Boss of All Bosses so he could tend to his companies, Wolf later explained.

Lanza emphasized that Luciano would be a big help in getting the important mobsters—Costello, Joe Adonis, Lansky—on board with the plan to help the navy. "The word of Luciano may give me the right of way," said Lanza. The approach to the imprisoned Luciano was made initially through Lansky, who cautioned officials that they had to be careful since some Italians still liked Mussolini; he may have been thinking about Genovese at that point. But in the case of Luciano, Lansky believed he would cooperate since his family members were largely in the U.S. and out of harms way in Italy. State officials agreed to transfer Luciano from the isolated Clinton Correctional Center in upstate Dannemora, New York, to Great Meadow Correctional Center, a maximum-security facility near Vermont, and then to a similar facility in Albany, which was much closer to Manhattan and all of Luciano's mob friends.

State records show that from May 1942 through August 1945, Luciano had a number of visits from mobsters, with Lanza and Lansky being the most frequent, although the records were incomplete and the mobsters had more visits than shown. Costello helped smooth the way in the plan and got Luciano to go along.

The other part of the intelligence plan was to locate longshoremen who had familiarity with Sicily and its geography. This would feed into the Allied plan for the 1943 invasion and allowed Naval Intelligence to gain friendly contacts in Sicily, among them local Mafia bosses. Operation Husky, the invasion, was able to use the help of Luciano and his friends, although the battle was costly in terms of casualties. For decades, scholars and organized crime experts would debate the true importance of Luciano's contribution to the war. It clearly had some importance, but it was the military might of the Allied forces, led in part by General Patton, that won the day. Still, the Sicily operation and whatever value Luciano gave it led to further disillusionment among Italians with Mussolini, Genovese's protector, and ironically led to Il Duce's ouster. So, in one sense, Luciano was helping force Genovese's decision to shift alliances and throw his lot in with the Allies, all of which would lead to his predicament in the Boccia case.

But the impact of the Luciano wartime saga didn't end with Mussolini's ouster. Thomas Dewey, the prosecutor who had convicted Luciano, became New York State's governor with the November 1942 election. Dewey was aware of Luciano's cooperation and advised his attorney to get different counsel to make a motion to the trial judge in the prosecution case for a reduction in the mob boss's sentence. Such a motion was filed in February 1943 by George Wolf with Judge Philip J. McCook, the trial judge. McCook seemed to take seriously the argument that Luciano had helped the military effort, although in his decision he skirted mentioning exactly what the assistance was.

McCook didn't reduce Luciano's sentence but instead said that if he continued to be a model prisoner and helped the government, he could apply in the future for clemency from the governor. Essentially, McCook was giving Luciano and Wolf a roadmap telling them what to do next. Dewey clearly had the power to help the very mob boss he had put away. It was an unexpected turn in Luciano's life.

Luciano had at least twenty more years to run on his sentence when the New York State parole board took up his case. Despite a lack of cooperation from Naval Intelligence about the mob boss's cooperation, on December 3, 1945, the board recommended Luciano's sentence be commuted for the sole purpose of deportation. Dewey mulled things over for a month, and finally, on January 3, 1946, commuted Luciano's sentence, noting that he had contributed to the war effort, although the value of his information was unclear. Luciano would be going back to Italy.

Years later, in his biography, done in collaboration with film producer Martin Gosch and writer Richard Hammer, Luciano claimed that Dewey had agreed to go easy on city racketeers. Luciano also alleged that he funneled $90,000 to one of Dewey's campaigns, presumably the 1944 presidential run that Dewey lost. Such statements are virtually impossible to verify today.

But what was clear was that Luciano was headed back to Italy. It was on February 2, 1946, that Luciano was transferred from Sing Sing to Ellis Island, where Costello and lawyer Moses Polakoff brought the mob boss his luggage and other personal items. There were reports that a group of mobsters held a going away party for Luciano, with good food and drink, but that was questioned by the U.S. immigration officials who had custody of him before he left. However, a congressional memo uncovered by the author revealed that an immigration guard at Bush Terminal in Brooklyn, where Luciano had been placed on the victory ship *Laura Keene*, stated that the mob boss indeed had visitors just before he sailed. Luciano went into the ship's dining room with a group of five or six men, whom the immigration officer didn't identify but who were believed to have included Costello and Albert Anastasia.

Once inside the dining room, Luciano appeared not to have any appetite for the veal cutlets, which were described as "very greasy." So Luciano's friends left the vessel for about an hour and came back with lobsters, spaghetti, and wine, said the official. Luciano didn't drink any wine because of an upset stomach, but he did eat spaghetti, and then the group, the official remembered, talked and reminisced for a few hours. On February 10, 1946, the *Laura Keene*, with Luciano aboard, started a two-week voyage to Genoa, carrying a cargo of flour. It would not be the last anyone would hear about Lucky Luciano.

Meanwhile, Luciano's changing fortunes were having a profound impact on Genovese. Since Luciano was gone from the U.S., his influence over crime family affairs, while still important, was greatly diminished. Luciano just didn't have the day-to-day handle on the rackets Stateside. As a result, Costello became the effective power on the street and in New York, serving as Luciano's acting boss. Genovese, incarcerated and awaiting trial after years of absence from New York, had little ability to challenge anyone for the leadership position. For Don Vitone, or "the Old Man," as Genovese was known, the future was very uncertain.

As Genovese awaited a trial date in the Boccia murder case, he was getting more publicity of the kind that he didn't need. It was November 1945 that "Hawk" Rupolo stirred things up when he decided to write a sensational letter to a Bronx judge. Since Rupolo was being housed as a material witness awaiting his sentencing in the Sparacino attempted murder case in a Bronx jail, he decided to send his explosive missive to a judge in that county. While the letter stayed secret for a while, when Rupolo was going to be sentenced a judge in Brooklyn decided to unseal it.

In the letter, Rupolo made a number of sensational claims. For a start, he said that the late Peter LaTempa died from poison, despite an official finding after his autopsy that he had taken an overdose of sleeping pills. There were more allegations, and Rupolo said that there were a lot of people who were worried about what secrets he could reveal.

"The people I talked on are very powerful, with money and connections," Rupolo said in his letter. He had information not only about Boccia's killing in 1934 but also a slew of other murders around town.

"They are worried about 15 unsolved killings and they are afraid Genovese will talk," said Rupolo, referring to the so-called Unione Siciliane.

The letter was read in court by Judge Samuel Leibowitz, the jurist who had told Rupolo earlier that if he cooperated he would get good consideration when he came before the judge for sentencing. What really seemed to agitate Leibowitz was the claim by Rupolo that four other inmates in the Bronx jail had conspired to put strychnine in the food or on the toothbrushes of both Rupolo and William Gallo, his cohort in the killing of Boccia. For the poisoning effort, the four men were to get a total of $10,000. Another witness told Leibowitz that in fact inmates were free to roam around the Bronx detention center and thus could carry out a poisoning or other crimes at will. Leibowitz was flabbergasted.

"This is a desperate situation, we cannot let gangsters, murderers and cutthroats mingle freely in jail," said Leibowitz. "Some method must be devised to protect these important state witnesses.

"This man is in my jurisdiction," Leibowitz continued. "It is up to me to sentence him. He is a self-confessed guilty defendant and I do not want to be responsible for his being murdered in jail. I will either sentence him today or we will have to make arrangement for his safe-keeping. We could send him to a hotel. I hope he does not jump from a window."

That last reference by Leibowitz was to the way gangster-informant Abe Reles fell from a window in the Half Moon Hotel in Coney Island early in the morning of November 12, 1941. Reles had become a government witness for a series of prosecutions of members of Murder Inc., an amalgam of Jewish and Italian gangsters in Brooklyn who had terrorized the city for years. However, he either fell or jumped from the hotel window, thereby ending his career as a witness.

Rupolo's sentencing was put off, but rather than gamble with his safety, he was sent to the federal house of detention, a facility of the U.S. Bureau of Prisons, where security was better than the local jail. But what of his claims that there was a $10,000 contract for some other inmates to poison him in jail? While the matter was referred to a Bronx grand jury, no charges were ever lodged.

During the months Genovese was cooling his heels in the Brooklyn jail awaiting trial, his case played second fiddle to political matters centered around the run up to the 1945 mayoral election and the election for Brooklyn district attorney. It was political gamesmanship at its finest, or worst, depending on your point of view.

The story actually began back in Italy in 1944 when Genovese was already in the custody of the U.S. Army and awaiting trial for black market activity. Once the army learned that Genovese was wanted back in the States for the Boccia murder, the military decided he should stand trial on the more serious homicide case. But as Orange Dickey would later recall, it took months for the military to get Genovese back to Brooklyn, and he suggested that Lieutenant Colonel Charles Poletti, who served as the Allied military governor, and Brigadier General William O'Dwyer, who had given up his former job as Brooklyn district attorney to take the military wartime post, had somehow dropped the ball, something that was never proved.

O'Dwyer said he had nothing to do with the Genovese deportation delay, but that didn't prevent some political rivals of the former prosecutor from using the situation as political ammunition. As 1945 ground on and Genovese remained in jail, the political landscape of New York City was facing some big elections. For a start, O'Dwyer, after returning from his military service in Italy, decided to officially resign as Brooklyn district attorney and run for mayor of New York City. That meant that the sitting governor, who happened to be the Genovese and Luciano nemesis Thomas Dewey, ap-

pointed a fellow Republican, George Beldock, to be interim prosecutor until the election in November.

Beldock was a staunch Republican and wanted desperately to be
elected Brooklyn district attorney in his own right, and he figured
he had to sully the reputation of O'Dwyer to show how poorly a Democrat had performed in the job. For that, Beldock dragged up the
way O'Dwyer had supposedly delayed the deportation of Genovese
and Michael Miranda from Italy in connection with the Boccia murder case. To make things sound even more suspicious, Beldock said
in a radio address that O'Dwyer had social relations with a number
of underworld figures, notably Frank Costello. In addition, Beldock
said that two of the triggermen in the Boccia murder had been law
clients of O'Dwyer when he had been in private practice.

Beldock's aspersions against O'Dwyer were big news. But lost in
all the hoopla was the fact that the assassins of Boccia—Rupolo and
Gallo—had by this time been convicted and were no longer law
clients of O'Dwyer. Still, Beldock said that it was O'Dwyer's
staffer Edward Heffernan who had drafted a letter in an attempt to
get Genovese extradited from Italy but never sent it for some unknown reason. Trying to make things seem even more suspicious,
Beldock noted that the late, lamented Peter LaTempa, who was to
have been a witness in the Boccia murder trial, had requested he be
moved to a safer jail the day before he was found dead in his cell.

All of those claims by Beldock seemed designed to make
O'Dwyer look at the least as incompetent and at the worst as in
league with the mob. Never mind that O'Dwyer had told army officials in 1944 to take the Genovese deportation matter up with his
successor in Brooklyn. The list of seemingly disparate events that
Beldock dwelt on seemed to be strung together for some sensational
impact on the public.

Beldock then went one step further. In the months leading up
to the mayoral election, Beldock convened a special grand jury—
actually two grand juries, as it turned out—to look into the "laxity
of enforcement" in the way O'Dwyer's office handled cases. Beldock said the mystery of the paralysis in the office was connected to
the way the cases of Genovese and Miranda were handled. Beldock

took a few shots at Miranda, saying he hung out in a West Side restaurant in Manhattan with Costello, Joe Adonis, and "other gentry of that stripe."

Miranda claimed to be a waiter in the restaurant, but he lived like landed gentry in a $75,000 showplace house in Forest Hills that was the object of wonder to neighbors, not only for its elegance but also for the group of men who showed up at all hours in black cars, said Beldock.

About a week before the election, the grand jury issued a "presentment," which wasn't an indictment but rather a statement of facts But after so much mud being thrown against the wall, the grand jury presentment found problems with O'Dwyer's tenure as district attorney but mentioned nothing about Genovese and Miranda. Rather, the panel issued a report that said O'Dwyer's people had stifled an investigation into the waterfront rackets five years earlier and had lax record keeping. A follow-up report criticized O'Dwyer's handling and ultimate dismissal of a probe into mobster Albert Anastasia, the king of the dockland rackets and a so-called high executioner of the underworld.

Democrats didn't let Beldock get away unscathed and warned that he would face the wrath of voters on election day for all of his smears of O'Dwyer. One ally of O'Dwyer noted that he couldn't be faulted for any delays in the extradition of Genovese and Miranda because of the uncertainty of the laws in Italy during the war. It was also well-known that O'Dwyer had gone after a number of members of the notorious Murder Inc.

When the voters had their say, they handed Beldock an overwhelming rejection, which wasn't surprising in such a Democratic city. Although he was backed by Dewey, Beldock lost resoundingly to the Democratic-American Labor candidate Miles F. McDonald. A Brooklyn lawyer who only a few months earlier had been appointed Brooklyn's U.S. attorney, McDonald pulled 416,203 votes to Beldock's 117,814. If Beldock thought he would damage O'Dwyer's campaign for mayor with all of the claims about closeness to gangsters and screwing up investigations, he was very much mistaken.

O'Dwyer became mayor after pulling in 1.1 million votes and beating Republican-Fusion candidate Jonah L. Goldstein by nearly 700,000 votes.

A few days after the election, with his tail between his legs, Beldock listened quietly as a Brooklyn judge, in convening a new grand jury, essentially gently rebuked him and warned against defaming people in a presentment who weren't actually indicted.

"I advise that in no presentment by the grand jury should there be disclosure, even if the name of a witness, or a quotation, paraphrase or summary of the testimony of any witness," said Judge Franklin Taylor. To report adversely against either a public official or a private citizen without finding an indictment against the person was unfair because there was no opportunity for defense, explained Taylor.

Beldock would have until the end of the year to present the findings of this new grand jury into allegations of laxity by O'Dwyer, and he said it would be a vigorous and conscientious investigation. But by then Beldock was simply a lame duck and whatever he might have found was consigned to the wastebasket of history.

McDonald was sworn in just before the end of 1945 and then took over the office and set out to make his own agenda. The existing docket of cases included the murder indictment against Genovese and the others, including Miranda. However, with only Genovese in custody, the upcoming trial in 1946 would have just him as the marquee defendant.

Chapter Eleven

THE TRIAL OF VITO GENOVESE for the murder of Ferdinand "the Shadow" Boccia was set to begin by the spring of 1946. But as usually happens, the need for an adjournment was raised because the Brooklyn district attorney's office didn't have another key defendant, Michael Miranda, in custody and had no idea about when he might finally be brought to justice. It was May 5, 1946, when the prosecutors, defense attorney Hyman Barshay, and Genovese trooped into the courtroom of Brooklyn Judge Samuel Leibowitz to do their first bit of legal wrangling.

Assistant District Attorney Julius Helfand asked Leibowitz for an additional sixty-day adjournment in the trial so that the government could get Miranda extradited from Italy. At the same time, Helfand couldn't resist undercutting the claim made by former prosecutor George J. Beldock that his fellow prosecutor William O'Dwyer had dropped the ball. In fact, Helfand told Leibowitz, the law of extradition with Italy during the war was a diplomatic muddle, making it impossible to bring the suspect back to Brooklyn.

"Although considerable criticism had been leveled at a prior administration [O'Dwyer] for failing to extradite Miranda, we found that his extradition was legally impossible at that time under existing treaties between the United States and the Kingdom of Italy and that these treaties could not be modified while a state of war existed," said Helfand.

With his client in jail, Barshay asked to have the trial start immediately, raising the possibility that Miranda in Italy might not be the same suspect named in the indictment. After a hushed conference at the bench with the attorneys, Leibowitz split the difference and adjourned the case for thirty days, with a trial date of June 6.

Leibowitz was not wasting any time in getting the trial started. When jury selection began on June 6, over one hundred potential jurors were brought in for questioning. After some initial weeding out of prospects, it took Leibowitz only eighty minutes to pick the jury, something the judge described as record time. Leibowitz showed how committed he was to starting things when he brushed aside another request by Helfand to delay things until the FBI reported back on efforts to extradite Miranda. Leibowitz didn't buy the reason, calling it "too nebulous."

"Every defendant, whether he is good or bad, has rights under the Constitution that cannot be frittered away. This defendant has been in jail for almost a year. The trial must proceed," Leibowitz ordered.

In any murder trial, there would always be evidence about the cause of death and the results of the autopsy. The examination would show that Boccia suffered fatal wounds the night of the attack and died as a result. There would be no surprise there.

But to make the case against Genovese, Helfand had one star witness: Ernest Rupolo. It would be Rupolo's testimony that would be crucial, and he would not disappoint. But lurking in the background like some three-hundred-pound mob goon was a thorny legal issue that prosecutors hated to confront—the New York State accomplice testimony rule. A staple of the law in New York for decades, the rule required that a defendant couldn't be convicted solely on the testimonial evidence alone of an accomplice to the crime. If the witness were a "material witness" and not an accomplice, well, that was different and the testimony could be used. Helfand had to hurdle that obstacle posed by the rule, and he believed he could by showing that Rupolo was a witness to the murder of Boccia and not an accomplice.

Rupolo's appearance on the witness stand was one of those singular moments in a criminal case, particularly a highly publicized trial with a high-value defendant like Genovese. The public was well aware of Rupolo's astonishing claims about poison plots that knocked off another witness, Peter LaTempa, and his allegations against Genovese. He had an unforgettable physical appearance, with his right eye patched, a full head of dark hair, a slightly slanted mouth, and a dour look. It was on June 7 that Rupolo finally appeared in court to confront Genovese, a man he once feared and whose fate he now held in his hands.

The *Daily News* called "Hawk" Rupolo "a thug as predatory as the bird he was named after." Judge Leibowitz needed to hear it all and conducted his own voir dire questioning of Rupolo, who didn't mince words about who he was.

What did Rupolo do for a living?, Leibowitz asked.

"Stabbing, killing, burglary or any other crime I got paid for," replied Rupolo, who seemed to freely perspire on the stand.

"Murder for money?"

"Yes sir."

Rupolo gave his address as the Bronx county jail, where he was being held for his protection and to await sentencing.

Why the eye patch, Rupolo was asked

Rupolo explained that he had lost the eye in a gunfight with a thug whom he pumped five bullets into.

The real meat of the testimony came when Rupolo related how he got the assignment to kill Boccia, who he said had demanded a $35,000 cut from Genovese, his share of what the mob boss got after duping a businessman in a rigged card game. The initial connection came from Gus Frasca, a Brooklyn gangster who introduced him to Mike Miranda.

"Frasca tells me you are a good boy, that you could do a good job," Miranda said, according to Rupolo.

"He also said to me the Shadow [Boccia] and [William] Gallo are no good," remembered Rupolo. According to Rupolo, Miranda said, "I want you to put Gallo and the Shadow on the spot, so they can be killed."

The problem with Gallo and Boccia was that they had stuck up the real estate broker Tony Bender in his office, where he had illegal alcohol stock, and took $5,800 from him.

What Miranda wanted to do was set up the two men so that others could then kill them. Boccia obviously had made a pest of himself demanding the money from Genovese. Both he and Gallo had also won the wrath of the downtown gangsters because of the rip-off of Bender. In the end, it didn't matter because the mob could kill anybody for the most trivial of reasons.

But Rupolo, perhaps to show how tough and useful he could be, said that he would rather do the homicidal deed himself.

"Miranda seemed disappointed," remembered Rupolo, "and told me to meet him in a restaurant on Mulberry Street, near Kenmare Street.

"I went over there and I met Miranda with Patsy Pavona and Vito Genovese," said Rupolo. "Miranda introduced Genovese to me as Don Virdone, in the Italian underworld that means 'The Great Man.'"

Rupolo might have mumbled his recollection because the newspaper reporters appear to have misunderstood the words as "Don Virdone" instead of "Don Vitone," which is what Genovese was known as.

"Glad to meet you," Rupolo said to Genovese, adding that they both shook hands. However, Rupolo was clear in the next part of his testimony that Genovese told him if he didn't want to put Gallo and Boccia "on the spot," then things would have to be done his way.

According to Rupolo, Genovese called Boccia a "cokie bastard," probably meaning he was a narcotics user, and said Gallo was a "pimp bastard."

Miranda then told Rupolo to go back to Brooklyn, lay low, and keep in touch with him, Frasca, and George Smurra. Miranda then took Rupolo to see the gangster Peter DeFeo at 221 Mulberry Street, where DeFeo told the Hawk to kill Gallo and said that Smurra, Frasca, and another man would kill Boccia. DeFeo then gave Rupolo $175, he said.

For a variety of reasons, Gallo and Boccia had earned a great deal of enmity from the mob. They were hated so much and their deaths were so eagerly awaited that Rupolo said he was told by Miranda that if necessary the pair had to be murdered even if the mobsters had to "cowboy" them, meaning shoot them wherever they were found, "even in the middle of Broadway."

Rupolo than testified how with the help of an old prison associate, Rosario Palmieri, also known as "Solly," he took Gallo to Coney Island on the evening of September 18, 1934, to wine and dine him while they waited to learn if Boccia had been killed. As Rupolo told investigators, he was to be paid $5,000 for the hit in total, and he planned to give Solly $1,000. After spending a night in a hotel and plying Gallo with whiskey, Solly went away to find out what had happened to Boccia. The Shadow had been killed, said Rupolo, so all three men then continued their carousing and drove around, at which point the Hawk said he pulled out a pistol, pointed it at Gallo, and pulled the trigger three times. The gun misfired each time, and when the shocked Gallo asked what the hell was going on, Rupolo told him, "I was only kidding."

After oiling the gun at a girlfriend's house, Rupolo explained that the three men continued on their drive to Bensonhurst. Why Gallo stayed in the car after Rupolo had pulled a gun out and pointed it at him is unclear. Perhaps he was too drunk to figure out what was going on. In any case, during the drive, Rupolo said he and his associate both pulled out handguns and fired a total of nine times at Gallo. Some shots missed, but Gallo dropped, and Rupolo thought he was dead.

The next day, Rupolo said, he met up with a "grouchy" Miranda, who told him that Gallo had survived. Miranda was also annoyed, remembered Rupolo, because he didn't pour gasoline on Gallo's body and set him afire. Smurra also yelled at him, saying, "Why didn't you shoot him in the head like we did to that other bastard?" recalled Rupolo. With the screwup, Rupolo didn't see the $5,000 fee. Palmieri got nothing. Still, Rupolo got to keep the $175 payment for the attempt as well as an additional $300 or so he had been paid before the errant hit.

Rupolo's testimony clearly put Genovese in the conspiracy to kill Boccia as well as Gallo, but there really wasn't much else to tie Don

Vitone into the plot except Rupolo's word. Peter LaTempa, who could have also been a witness in the case, was dead. So the prosecution was left with the problem that if Rupolo was seen by the court as part of the conspiracy—and not a material witness—the case would evaporate. The prosecution had produced the now-recovered Gallo as a material witness as well, but the court didn't think he gave enough evidence to connect Genovese to the crime. After all, Gallo wouldn't have known at the time he was shot that Genovese had wanted him dead and had ordered the hit.

Defense attorney Barshay knew the problem with the case and made a motion to Judge Leibowitz to dismiss the charges because of the accomplice testimony issue. If Barshay prevailed, Genovese would walk out of the courthouse a free man. Helfand, the prosecutor, argued that his office had made every effort to find evidence and witnesses who might connect Genovese to the Boccia murder but that those who could help either refused to testify or were dead. Leibowitz reluctantly agreed with the defense and on June 10, 1946, dismissed the murder charges because there was no corroborating evidence. But Leibowitz let Don Vitone have it.

"You are always just one step ahead of Sing Sing and the electric chair," Leibowitz told Genovese after the jury on the judge's instruction gave a directed verdict of acquittal. "You and your criminal henchmen have thwarted justice time and again by devious means, among which were the terrorizing of witnesses, kidnapping them, yes even murdering those who could give evidence against you. . . . I cannot speak for the jury but I believe that even if there was a shred of corroborating evidence you would have been condemned to the chair."

The *Daily News* said Leibowitz's excoriation of Genovese was "as savage a castigation of an acquitted witness as ever been heard in a New York court." Reporters in the courtroom said that Genovese seemed bored and impatient with the proceedings. He was dressed, as the *New York Times* reported, in a double-breasted blue suit, white shirt, and maroon tie, and smiled slightly as the judge blasted him.

"There were witnesses who refused to talk and tell what they knew of the crime because of their fear of Genovese and the other bosses of the underworld, knowing full well that to talk would mean their death," Helfand told Leibowitz.

As Helfand talked, Genovese seemed to stifle a yawn.

As if to underscore the darkness that shadowed the case, on the day Genovese walked out of the courthouse a free man, police in Bergen County, New Jersey, found the bullet-ridden body of Jerry Esposito, a 35-year old Brooklyn man, dumped in the town of Norwood in some brush by a road. Cops believed that Esposito, an ex-con who had been convicted in New York on weapons and assault and robbery charges, had been shot in a speeding car and then dumped from the vehicle. A preliminary check of ballistics led cops to believe he was shot by a revolver of foreign manufacture. Speculation immediately arose that Esposito had been wanted as a material witness in the Boccia murder case. But the next day, Helfand denied that the dead man was to have been a witness against Genovese.

Meanwhile, Rupolo, who had done his bit for the justice system by testifying against Genovese, got his reward. On July 15, just over a month after Genovese was freed, Rupolo appeared before Leibowitz for sentencing in the Sparacino assault case. Helfand asked the judge to give the defendant a break because there was hope he would be rehabilitated and become a "useful member of society."

"What assurance have I that you will go straight?" Leibowitz asked Rupolo.

With his good eye looking at the judge, Rupolo replied, "I'll go straight. I don't want any part of any underworld. They are all scum and double-crossers."

Leibowitz followed the request of Helfand for leniency and gave Rupolo a suspended sentence of five to ten years in the Sparacino assault case. The sentence meant that if Rupolo stayed out of trouble he wouldn't go to prison for the crime. The judge also said he would discuss with the parole board Rupolo's pending charge of parole violation for the Sparacino assault.

For a while anyway, it seemed like Rupolo had gotten the break he needed from the criminal justice system. If he kept quiet in jail, he could look forward to getting out in a year. But even in prison, trouble seemed to find Rupolo. A fellow inmate tried to stab him in his good eye with a pencil but missed. For his own protection, Rupolo was sent back to solitary.

Then, as luck would have it, the state parole board changed its policy, which meant that Rupolo would have to spend as many as eleven years behind bars on the Sparacino case. Since Governor Dewey wouldn't commute the sentence, the only way out was for Rupolo's indictment to be dismissed. Leibowitz had promised Rupolo that he wouldn't have to serve the eleven years, and the jurist meant to keep his word. To do otherwise would hurt future chances of gangsters becoming cooperating witnesses.

So, in September 1949, Rupolo was hauled back before Leibowitz to be resentenced, and the judge was going to do the right thing with some prompting by prosecutor Helfand.

"I had promised Rupolo that he would only have to serve a portion of the 11 years he still owed the state," noted Helfand. "We can't break promises to mobsters if we expect their cooperation. I ask dismissal of the indictment against this man."

Leibowitz did have some reluctance in springing Rupolo free because he knew that once the gang thug was away from the protection of the state, his lifespan was definitely limited. (Rupolo would be murdered by persons unknown in 1964.)

"The underworld neither forgives nor forgets. If I let you go, you will be murdered as sure you are standing here," said Leibowitz. "As an underworld squealer it even was necessary to keep you in solitary these last three years.

"What do you want me to do?" Leibowitz asked Rupolo.

"Let me go, Judge," Rupolo replied.

Leibowitz wanted to know if there was anywhere in the world that Rupolo could go to escape the mob and its wrath.

"I am willing to take my chances," said Rupolo.

"Very well," Leibowitz finally said. "You've been a murderer, a holdup man and a gorilla, but we must keep our word to you. Discharged,"

* * *

In Italy, Michael Miranda was watching events with great interest. He was aware that the case had fallen apart against Genovese in 1946 because of the witness corroboration rule. The way things stood, Miranda was in the same position as Genovese had been: aside from the accomplice testimony of Rupolo, there was no other evidence against him for Boccia's murder. He decided to take his chances.

In early September 1946, about three months after Genovese was freed, Miranda returned to the U.S. and walked into a Brooklyn police station to surrender. After some questioning by prosecutor Helfand, Miranda was taken to a Brooklyn courtroom, where he entered a plea of not guilty to the first-degree murder charge.

But after Miranda showed up, no other corroborating evidence against him appeared. As a result, in January 1947, Helfand went to court and asked Judge Leibowitz to dismiss the murder charge for lack of corroboration. Leibowitz agreed, and Miranda "briskly" walked out of court a free man after five months in jail. Two of the biggest names in the mob, both linked to a slaying that grabbed headlines for years, beat the rap. And what of the other three suspects—Smurra, Frasca, and DeFeo? All of them did a very good job of not being seen and eluding the police, for years as it turned out. Finally, in April 1947, both Frasca and Smurra turned themselves in to cops and pleaded not guilty to the charges. Their cases suffered the same fate as that of Miranda. DeFeo would remain elusive for years to come.

So, now a free man for the first time since coming back to U.S. soil, Genovese went back to living his life as a husband, father, businessman, and crime boss. This was 1946, and the nation and New York City were starting to come out of the austerity and shortages of the war years. There was money to be made.

When he fled to Italy, Genovese's family was staying in the Washington Square apartment building off Fifth Avenue in Manhattan after the mansion he had built in Middletown, New Jersey, had burned to the ground in a fire in early 1937. After getting out of jail in the Boccia case, Genovese sold what was left of the estate to builder Dominic Caruso, who in turn sold it to Gladys Cubbage for a price of $25,000. The only building left was a small house, but the landscaping and tennis courts still remained, although it was never clear if Genovese used them. Oh yes, Genovese's old replica of Mount Vesuvius was also part of the deal. Eventually, other owners donated the property to the Monmouth County Park System, which renamed it Deep Cut Gardens, whose landscape design and surviving replica of Vesuvius attract tens of thousands of visitors a year. It is also a favorite spot for wedding photography.

Genovese took whatever he might have received from the sale of the old property and other cash and put it all into a home in Atlantic Highlands on Ocean Boulevard, a home that overlooked Sandy Hook Bay and Sandy Hook, a thin bar of land that jutted out into the Atlantic It was a house not as large as the old mansion, but the view it offered was spectacular. From his new home, Genovese could survey his gangland territory to the east—New York City.

Chapter Twelve

AFTER WORLD WAR TWO, THE SITUATION for all the New York City Mafia families was essentially the same in terms of organization and structure. The Five Families ruled the landscape. Luciano's clan was the most important. The other families included those run by Joseph Profaci, Gaetano Gagliano, Vincent Mangano, and Joseph Bonanno.

Luciano was physically absent from the U.S., but his influence was still felt. As will be shown, Luciano was scheming to come back to the Western Hemisphere so that he could be close to the action. In the interim, Vito Genovese and his rival for power, Frank Costello, were engaged in what would prove to be a long struggle for control of Luciano's family.

But in the early going after Genovese beat the Boccia case, he and Costello seemed to be acting like old friends. George Wolf, the attorney who was representing Costello in many of his legal battles, remembered in his book *Frank Costello: Prime Minister of the Underworld* that the two mob bosses got along famously at this point. But Wolf was certain that Genovese grated under the fact that the Boccia situation had set him back in his effort to control the family and that Costello, the smooth guy from uptown, was someone he had to defer to.

"From what we know now he began almost from the minute he arrived to undermine Frank in every way he could," recounted Wolf. "But at first he had to move softly."

Mugshot of crime boss Vito Genovese taken around 1945 as he awaited trial
in Brooklyn for the 1934 murder of Ferdinand Boccia.
(National Archives and Records Administration)

Genovese as he appeared on his way to testify before a Congressional committee in 1958, during which he refused to talk and invoked the Fifth Amendment over 150 times *(Library of Congress)*

Genovese in a federal prison mugshot taken around 1964, a time when he still held out hope of getting his narcotics conviction overturned. *(National Archives and Records Administration)*

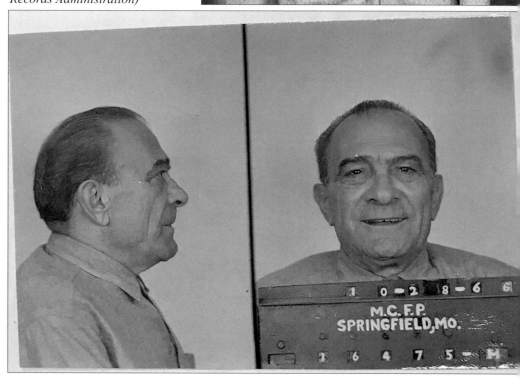

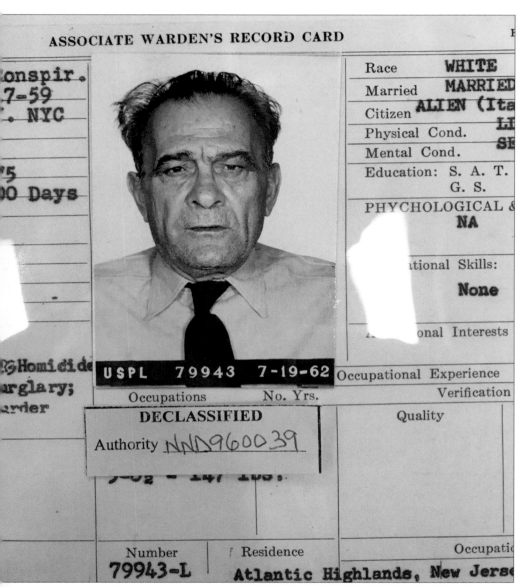

ASSOCIATE WARDEN'S RECORD CARD

onspir.
7-59
. NYC

5
00 Days

Homicide
urglary;
arder

Race	WHITE
Married	MARRIED
Citizen	ALIEN (Ita
Physical Cond.	LI
Mental Cond.	SI
Education: S. A. T. G. S.	

PHYCHOLOGICAL &
NA

ational Skills:
None

onal Interests

USPL 79943 7-19-62 Occupational Experience

| Occupations | No. Yrs. | Verification |

DECLASSIFIED
Authority NND960039

Quality

| Number | Residence | Occupati |
| 79943-L | Atlantic Highlands, New Jerse |

One of the first prison mugshots of Genovese, taken sometime in 1960, when he
started his 15-year sentence in a federal penitentiary for his narcotics conviction.
(National Archives and Records Administration)

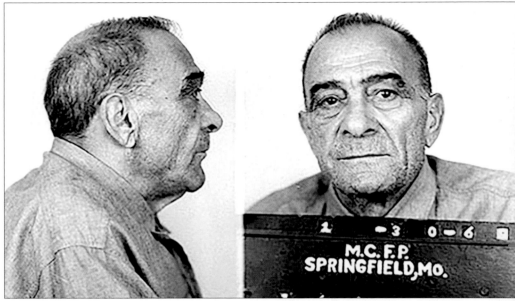

An aging Genovese while incarcerated at a federal prison hospital in Missouri.
As this photo shows, Genovese aged a great deal in prison, and his health
steadily deteriorated till his death in 1969. *(Library of Congress)*

Albert Anastasia, the "Lord High Executioner" of the Mafia, one of the more bloodthirsty
members of organized crime, rivaled Genovese in terms of ruthlessness until Anastasia
was assassinated in 1957. His murder in a barbershop was one of the events
that preceded the Apalachin meeting in upstate New York.
(National Archives and Records Administration)

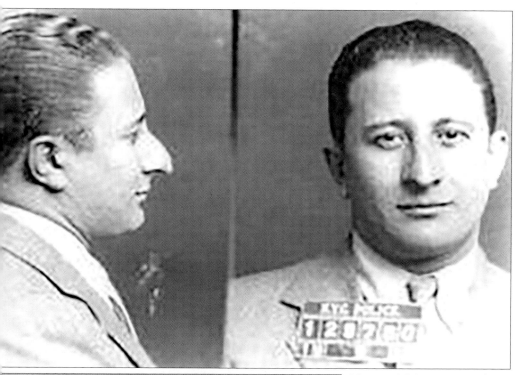

The youthful Carlo Gambino,
who went on to take over
the crime family of Anastasia
after his assassination.
(NYPD/Wikipedia)

Former New York State Lieutenant Governor Charles Poletti, who, as a U.S. military official in World War Two, was head of the Allied military government in Italy. Poletti's name came up as allegedly having employed Vito Genovese as a translator, something Poletti vigorously denied.
(Library of Congress)

Frank Costello, "Prime Minister" of the underworld, who for years had an uneasy relationship with Genovese as both men vied for power in the crime family Lucky Luciano had once ruled. Genovese engineered the May 1957 assassination attempt against Costello, an event which led to Costello's "retirement" from the mob.
(Library of Congress)

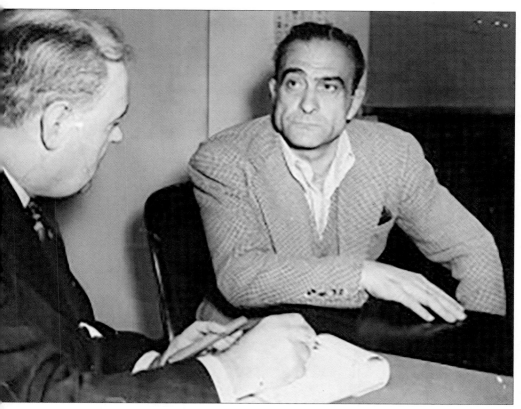

Genovese being questioned by a member of the Brooklyn District Attorneys Office
in 1945 after he was brought back from Italy to face murder charges
in the 1934 death of Ferdinand Boccia.
(Brooklyn Daily Eagle Photographs, 1945, PORT_0407,
Brooklyn Public Library Center for Brooklyn History)

The Genovese family grave and outdoor burial vault at St. John Cemetery in Middle Village, Queens. Vito Genovese was entombed here after his death in February 1969. His parents, first wife, Donata, second wife, Anna, and other family members are also buried at the site. *(Author's collection)*

The Genovese family grave. *(Author's collection)*

Meyer Lansky, the financial wizard credited with being the brains behind the power of the Mafia. Although a Jew, Lansky was accepted for his acumen and toughness by all the crime families. He had major interests in Cuba, Miami, and New York. Although he had been close with Lucky Luciano, he was not with Genovese. Lansky was instrumental in arranging for Luciano to cooperate with the American military in World War Two, something which ultimately got Luciano out of prison and deported in 1946 to Italy, where he died in 1962. *(Library of Congress)*

William O'Dwyer, former mayor of New York City. O'Dwyer had been the district attorney of Brooklyn and was aware of Genovese's indictment for the 1934 murder of Ferdinand Boccia. O'Dwyer also served as a member of the American military in World War Two and was criticized by his political opponents for not securing Genovese's extradition from Italy at the end of the war. *(Library of Congress)*

Anna Genovese, wife of Vito Genovese, as she appeared with her signature beehive hair style while waiting to testify in Trenton, New Jersey, in 1957. Anna had been estranged from Genovese since their very public and contentious marital lawsuit.
(AP photo)

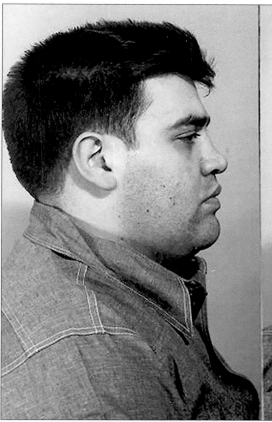
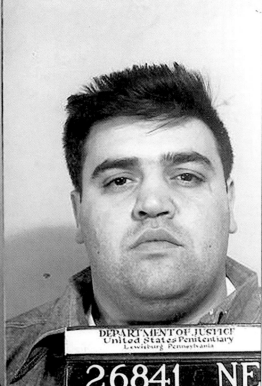

Vincent Gigante, a driver
and acolyte of mob boss
Genovese, in a prison mugshot
after he was sentenced for
his conviction in a federal
narcotics case, the one
that also led to the
conviction of Genovese.
(U.S. Bureau of Prisons)

Genovese, on the right,
waves as he leaves Manhattan
federal court after making bail
following his July 1958 arrest
on narcotics charges.
To the left of Genovese is
his attorney Wilfred L. Davis.
In the background is Al Gibson,
a deputy federal marshal.
(AP photo/Anthony Camerano)

Some of Genovese's friends in high places in Italy during World War Two. On the right is Count Galeazzo Ciano, Italy's prime minister and allegedly a Genovese drug customer. To the left of Ciano is Italian dictator Benito Mussolini, the father-in-law of Ciano, who gave Genovese a commendation for his financial support of the Fascist party. In the waning years of the war, Mussolini had Ciano executed. On the far left is British Prime Minister Neville Chamberlain. *(CC by SA 3.0 de Bundesarchives Bild)*

Genovese in a Brooklyn courtroom, circa 1945, to face murder charges in the 1934 death of Ferdinand Boccia. The case was dismissed after it was determined that the prosecution didn't have independent evidence linked Genovese to the crime. The prosecution's case rested heavily on the testimony of Ernest "The Hawk" Rupolo, but because he was deemed a co-conspirator, his words couldn't be used, under the law, as the main evidence against Genovese. *(Brooklyn Daily Eagle Photographs, 1946, PORT_0408, Brooklyn Public Library Center for Brooklyn History)*

John Ormento, one of the Mafia's main narcotics traffickers in the 1950s, who played a key role in the drug conspiracy in which Vito Genovese was snared. Ormento was himself convicted separately of drug trafficking and sent to prison. *(U.S. Drug Enforcement Administration)*

VITO'S GARDEN: After Genovese bought an estate in rural New Jersey in 1935, he spared no expense to make it reminiscent of his old home near Naples. He hired a local landscaper to plant hemlock trees imported from Europe and surround them with stonework and paths, and he had a replica of the volcano Mount Vesuvius made for the garden. Some say the model volcano belched smoke at one time, and it remains an attraction at Deep Cut State Park, located on the site of the Genovese homestead. The large house burned down in 1937. Around that time, Genovese and his wife, Anna, were traveling in Italy, where he had decided to live, as investigators were closing in on him for the murder of Ferdinand Boccia. *(Author's collection)*

VITO'S AMPHITHEATER: Genovese and his wife used the estate as a place
to receive visitors. He had a local contractor fashion a stone amphitheater,
where, it was reported, the couple entertained guests from New York City, who might
have included mobsters like Albert Anastasia, Frank Costello, and Willie Moretti.
(Author's collection)

Michael Genovese, the younger brother of Vito, seen in this 1960s photo
trying to avoid press photographers by looking up at an elevator sign, after testifying
at a New York State hearing on loan sharking. Michael, while close to his brother,
was considered by law enforcement to be a messenger for Vito.

(Newsday LLC)

Genovese died in prison on February 13, 1969. Pall bearers carrying the casket
containing the body of Vito Genovese from St. Agnes Catholic Church
in Atlantic Highlands, New Jersey, following the funeral mass.
(Newsday LLC)

Costello was the smooth operator who had the respect of many of the lieutenants in his family and the other families, in part because of his moneymaking ability and his political connections, which were substantial. Costello also was someone who disdained violence and preferred negotiations to fighting. As Peter Maas said in *The Valachi Papers*, Genovese could only count on the support of Miranda and Strollo, two friends from the Lower West Side days.

"Privately, according to Valachi, he raged at the position he found himself in," Maas wrote about Genovese.

Valachi recalled one meeting in which Genovese, feeling somewhat marginalized and frozen out of some rackets, snapped at his old friend Tony Bender.

"You told me to lay low," Bender replied, according to Maas's account.

"I didn't tell you to let them bury you!" replied an angry Genovese.

Genovese never had a proper welcome when he first arrived back in the United States: he was taken straight to a jail cell. But after walking out of the courtroom a free man in the murder case, his gangster friends decided he was due a big welcome. It was in late June, barely two weeks after the dismissal of the criminal case, that Genovese's mob cronies held a welcome-back dinner of sorts at the Hotel Diplomat in Manhattan on Forty-third Street. Joseph Profaci and Albert Anastasia attended, as did Santo Volpe, a mob boss from Pennsylvania, a center of garment manufacturing, an industry for which Genovese had some control. "Welcome Back, Vito" was the theme. Based on an informant's report, Genovese struck a theme of caution and stressed the need to keep a hand in legitimate businesses.

Anastasia and Genovese were rivals of a sort for the reputation of being the top gangster in New York, apart from Costello. Anastasia reportedly showed respect to Genovese at the banquet but suggested that he didn't necessarily agree with Don Vitone's cautious position. And what of Costello? He didn't attend, and his absence was the most glaring omission from the list of attendees. That certainly spoke volumes.

The years immediately after the war, and Genovese's escape from justice, saw the emergence of key players in the Mafia who would wield major power in the gangster life of the city. Among them was Anastasia, the "Mad Hatter," and "Lord High Executioner," who had a reputation for ferocity few could exceed. Like Genovese, Anastasia chose to live in New Jersey in a walled and gated mansion in Fort Lee, overlooking the Hudson River. In a few short years, Anastasia and Genovese would come into conflict, but in this period, they tolerated each other since they were part of different family alignments. Besides, the Mafia was soon to turn its attention to the Caribbean and that bastion of rackets, Cuba.

A mere ninety miles from Florida, Cuba had long been a business center and playground for the Mafia. The relationship had existed for decades. Over the years, there have been a number of accounts about the way the mob was able to essentially take over the island with the help of corrupt and pliant government officials. At one extreme is the book *The Mafia in Havana: A Caribbean Mob Story*, written from a perspective sympathetic to the government of Fidel Castro by Cuban journalist Enrique Cirules. A more politically independent view can be found in *Havana Nocturne* by American true crime writer T. J. English. Both are works that are valuable in their own way and represent a great deal of research. Cirules in particular had access to Cuban government archives and articles from old scandal-sheet Cuban newspapers from the pre-Castro era. But there are also original U.S. government materials found in the National Archives and Records Administration from which additional perspective can be gained. The museum and library of the Drug Enforcement Administration also has historical material that helps flesh out the story, one in which some mob folklore has been embroidered in the telling.

As described by Cirules, American mob activity began to appear in Cuba during Prohibition as the island saw rum-running from its shores. There is no surprise there. The Caribbean basin was a major source of alcohol such as rum and also a transshipping point to places like "Rum Row," the area off the Eastern Seaboard of the U.S. where smuggling ships congregated just outside the territorial limits as they awaited rendezvous with other vessels that would take the product to customers.

But what had been little appreciated until later was the role that Meyer Lansky played in opening up Cuba for the mob. Although an immigrant Jew from old Czarist Russia and thus not eligible for membership in the Mafia, Lansky became the mob's financial minister, and in Cuba, he became a central figure in the opening up of legitimate gambling in Havana and was said to have been an advisor to Cuban politicians of all stripes.

"Lansky was a man of practical intelligence, ingenious and persuasive, who preferred to operate from the shadows," said Cirules. "He had been a great friend of Lucky Luciano since childhood. They went to the same school, and as adolescents became involved in criminal organizations in New York."

Cirules, citing some unpublished Cuban materials, indicated that Lansky was busy setting up hotels and casinos in Havana soon after Masseria and Maranzano were done away with by Luciano in 1931. His activity is said to have continued well into the 1940s. Robert Lacey, in his biography of Lansky titled *Little Man: Meyer Lansky and the Gangster Life*, doesn't go that far but said that Lansky was very comfortable in Cuba, having gone to Havana to secretly get married to his second wife, Thelma "Teddy" Schwartz, in 1948. They traveled around after the nuptials for a couple of months.

But recently released FBI files on Lansky show that when he applied for a U.S. passport in 1949, he indicated that he had lived in Cuba from December 1938 until March 1939 and then again from December 1939 until March 1941. So it seemed that Lansky was actively residing in Cuba during the pre–World War Two years and was quite obviously making political and financial connections that would serve him and the U.S. mob well. This was underscored by one FBI memo in which it was stated that he spent a lot of time in Cuba and had been connected with racetrack and casino operations in Havana since 1938. Lansky also did a great deal of traveling abroad, ostensibly for pleasure, although one trip he took to Italy raised speculation that he had traveled to meet with the exiled Luciano.

In Cuba, Lansky was into the hotel and gambling industries, and he eventually would set up a residence in Florida, which allowed him easy access to Havana to supervise his operations. He freely admitted over the years being associated with some of the top Mafia members, including some of the so-called Top Hoodlums, as FBI director J. Edgar Hoover called them: Frank Costello, Bugsy Siegel, Joe Adonis, Frank Erickson, and Longie Zwillman. But Vito Genovese was not among the men Lansky would talk about, including to the FBI. This was the first indication that Lansky and Genovese didn't have a close or trusting relationship, certainly of the kind "the Little Man" had with some of the other Italians and Jews in the underworld. Cuba became important to Genovese because it was a place that, soon after he beat the rap in the Boccia case, was the focus of one of the major mob meetings of the twentieth century. No one expected that when Luciano went packing back to Italy, he was going to go quietly and not return to somewhere close to his old haunts in the U.S. Granted, he wouldn't try the risky approach of actually coming back home. But he decided to go to a place that would prove to be most hospitable thanks to Lansky's connections: Cuba.

Before there was the fabled Mafia summit of 1957—which will be dealt with a little later in this story, in chapter 19—there was Havana. After a circuitous trip, assisted by pliant government officials in Italy, Brazil, and Cuba, Luciano wound up in Cuba in early October 1946. Cirules said it was Lansky, the king of Havana, who told Luciano in a cryptic message delivered in Italy that a meeting was to happen: "December, Hotel Nacional."

Lansky had an interest in the Nacional, so he knew it would be the perfect place for Luciano to stay and meet his old friends from the Mafia world in the U.S. Luciano arrived by plane from Brazil at the airport in Camagüey in the eastern part of Cuba. Limousines were awaiting him and whisked him to Havana, where lunch and a suite at the Nacional were set up.

"When I got to the room the bellhop opened up the curtains on the big windows and I looked out. I could see almost the whole city. I think it was the palm trees that got me. Every place you looked there were palms trees and it made me feel like I was back in Miami," Luciano would remember in his biography. "I realized somethin' else, the water was just as pretty as the Bay of Naples, but it was only 90 miles from the United States. That meant I was practically back in America."

Of course, Luciano was not going to America, rather some of America was coming to him in December. The setting of the Nacional was appropriate for the meeting, with its old style décor and luxurious furnishings. The president of Cuba, Ramón Grau San Martín, reportedly had his own private elevator set aside for Luciano's use.

The first to arrive in Havana was Vito Genovese. Free of his own legal shackles, Genovese had wanted to have some time with Luciano before the official start of the meeting. He wanted to make his own power play. Luciano had a firm recollection of what happened between the two of them.

"It was a couple of days before I was expectin' anybody, about the 20th December, when Vito called me at my house. It was a private number and he got it from Lansky," recalled Luciano.

Genovese told Luciano that he came down early to enjoy the sun and surf. Luciano wasn't buying it.

"Now I know that little prick well enough to know he didn't come to Havana to get a suntan. That wasn't the way he operated. I knew he had somethin' in mind," said Luciano.

As Luciano remembered it, Genovese told him matter-of-factly, "Charlie, I think you ought to quit—I mean retire. You'll have all the dough you can ever need. I give you my personal word on that."

Genovese was proposing to buy out Luciano and take over as de facto boss, running things back in New York, although Luciano would think he was still the boss of everything. The power play was to be expected. Genovese felt invulnerable, and given Luciano's predicament—no ability to easily run things in New York—the offer made sense on the one hand. Genovese knew he had to deal with Costello—who was due to show up in a few days—so he figured a preemptive strike before any big meeting would work to his advantage.

Luciano, who had an intense dislike of Genovese, was livid but said he kept his composure. The "guinea son of a bitch," as Luciano called Genovese, using a derogatory term for Italians, was making a gutsy move but doing it with no one else around. Keeping his calm, Luciano said that he told Genovese in no uncertain terms that long ago it was decided there would be no so-called boss of bosses in the mob but that if that changed, he himself would take the title. "Right now you work for me," said Luciano, "and I ain't in the mood to retire."

In a firm way, Genovese had been read the riot act and knew that he couldn't try to usurp Luciano: that certainly wasn't going to happen at the meeting. In a few days, the other guests started to show up. It was the top of the Top Hoodlum world, and there was a lot for them to talk about. Lists later compiled by federal investigators and found in later reports of the meeting showed an impressive assembly of gangsters. The New York contingent included not only Genovese but also Joe Adonis, Albert Anastasia, Joseph Bonanno, Anthony "Little Augie" Pisano, Costello and his friend Phil Kastel, Thomas Lucchese, Vincent Mangano, Mike Miranda, Willie Moretti, and Joseph Profaci. From Chicago came the Fischetti brothers (Charles and Rocco), while Carlos Marcello, Lansky, and Santo Trafficante represented the southeastern U.S. Cousins Stefano and Giuseppe Magliocco from upstate New York also attended. Luciano's lawyer Moses Polakoff also showed up, according to some accounts, as well as a young singer out of New York and New Jersey—Frank Sinatra.

The list of guests read like a pantheon, if there ever was such a thing, of the American Mafia. They dined like kings of the Caribbean. Cuban specialties like crab or queen conch enchiladas, roast breast of flamingo, tortoise soup, and other delicacies were served, along with some venison provided by a government official from Camagüey who owned livestock, according to Cirules. Aged rum and Montecristo cigars topped off the dining. Select women from the big hotels—the Tropicana, Montmartre, and Sans Souci— were available for parties, reported Cirules.

If the menu was top-shelf, the agenda of the conclave was of major importance. Some of it was very serious. Bugsy Siegel, who wasn't listed as being present in Havana, had pulled off a grandiose scheme of investing mob money in Las Vegas to build the Fla- mingo, which he believed would be a major entertainment venue in the nascent city in the desert. Cost overruns and suspicion that Siegel had siphoned some of the money for himself made mob in- vestors angry, and they said as much to Luciano. Things also weren't helped when the highly touted opening of the Flamingo was a bust after foggy weather kept major entertainers from flying into Las Vegas. The hotel was said to have lost $500,000 on the opening night alone.

Costello was on the hook because he had put together some of the investors for the Flamingo, and even though he had put some of his own money in, he was the object of intense criticism. Costello had to come up with a return on the investment or else, according to his attorney, George Wolf, Costello's safety couldn't be guaranteed. Some in the mob wanted Costello's head. Luciano told Costello in Havana that he had to recoup the cash or else he "couldn't hold them back," according to Wolf.

There was another wrinkle in the Flamingo affair, and it involved both Costello and Genovese. Luciano, according to the account at- tributed to him in *The Last Testament*, had told Genovese that he wasn't going to be in line as the boss so long as he, Luciano, was around. But Wolf, in his biography of Costello, related that Luciano told his client that he had to give up his seat on the ruling Mafia Commission to Genovese until the Flamingo money came back to investors. Once Costello got the cash back, then he could take over the Commission position, said Luciano, according to Wolf. So, if Wolf's account is true, Luciano was using Genovese as a temporary surrogate, who was to be replaced by Costello.

Costello survived the Flamingo money problem and apparently recouped what the investors had put up. Genovese also remained as the second fiddle in the crime family and would for a few more years. But Siegel ran out of time. The night of June 20, 1947, six months after the Havana meeting, Siegel was shot dead in the Beverly Hills home of his girlfriend, Virginia Hill. An assassin fired a carbine through the living room window as Siegel sat on a couch reading the *Los Angeles Times*. The next day, newspapers showed a prostrate Siegel on the bloody couch, his left eye pierced by a bullet and the other eye blown out of its socket by another round, which was found over a dozen feet away. No one was ever arrested for the slaying.

After dining on exotic things like breast of flamingo and fillet of manatee and deciding that Siegel would have to die, the boys in Havana had to sort out some other major items on the meeting agenda. Federal Bureau of Narcotics agents could only surveil the comings and goings of the delegates and didn't have the capability at the time to penetrate the secret talks. But over time, it came out that one of the major issues to be hashed out was indeed that of narcotics.

Cuba had been a major drug transshipping point for the mob for years, and the U.S. gangsters well knew from experience that there was a great deal of money to be made from narcotics. At the meeting, according to Luciano's spin, he laid out that there was so much money to be made from all sorts of rackets that it was foolhardy to risk it all for a major drug investigation.

"I tried to make them understand that everything was different now that the war was over; we was businessmen runnin' businesses and givin' people what they wanted in a way that didn't hurt nobody," said Luciano. "Sure, here and there we would squeeze some guys, but on the other hand, look at all the money we was puttin' in circulation just from other good businessmen buyin' our protection."

Luciano was clearly trying to embellish history with such statements. As will be shown later on in this chapter, Luciano would remain a major focus of international drug dealing investigations for nearly two decades. His base in Italy was a major point for narcotics trafficking from the Mideast, and many major cases of the FBN had ties to Luciano.

Luciano's claims that he advised caution on Genovese and the other mobsters supposedly were ignored. Even Genovese and Costello sensed the way things were going and told Luciano as much. Luciano relented.

"For Chrissake keep me out of it," he told the conclave, reportedly jesting, by his account, by saying "or I'm gonna have to take out an ad in the *New York Mirror* and declare myself."

Again, Luciano's account was self-serving. Narcotics trafficking would be a foundation for his operation in Italy. There was no evidence in this period that Genovese started to dabble in drug trafficking, but later on that would all change in a major way. Costello, despite claims by some that he did deal in drugs, would vehemently deny that allegation.

The Havana meeting broke up right after Christmas 1946. Everybody went back to their hometowns. Genovese had the new home in Atlantic Highlands to enjoy, and Costello had the luxury of an apartment in Manhattan and a lovely country manse in Sands Point, Long Island. But Luciano stayed on. Life was good for him in Cuba. He left the Nacional and moved to a house in the exclusive Miramar section, not far from the home of Cuban President Grau.

Wealthy Americans would invite Luciano for dinner, and he had the run of the country, talking with the Cuban president and enjoying freedom without the constraint of Italian or American police and their ubiquitous surveillance.

"During those days, Luciano was almost completely happy," reported Cirules. "Havana was becoming the ideal place for him."

But not for long, as it turned out. Newspapermen from the U.S. spotted Luciano in Havana. Stories started to appear back in the States. By February 1947, Luciano's presence in Cuba was simply too much for American officials to ignore. At first, Cuban officials tried to underplay Luciano's presence. However, Harry J. Anslinger, the head of the FBN, suspected that with Luciano in Cuba his mob friends were making trips to and from the island to move narcotics and drugs that the U.S. had exported there. To pressure the Cubans, the U.S. restricted the export of legitimate narcotics to the country. This was something the Cubans couldn't ignore. Hospitals and doctors began to run out of needed drug supplies.

Under such pressure, the Cuban government finally arrested Luciano and his two bodyguards, whom he had been living with at the Miramar villa. It was all done very politely, yet Luciano's lawyers in Cuba said that he was the subject of a "political persecution." Despite such protests, Luciano had to go, and President Grau ordered Luciano deported as an undesirable alien. On March 18, 1947, Luciano boarded a Turkish ship, the *Bakir*, bound for Italy. He paid his own first-class passage of $300 and spent his travel time playing cards with some of the tourist-class passengers. When the *Bakir* docked in Italy, Luciano was promptly jailed, although that didn't last very long. While Luciano had lost his potential base in Cuba, he would eventually regroup in Italy and become what American officials had always feared he would be: a major international narcotics trafficker.

The drug pressure on the Cubans has been the accepted story of how Luciano was frustrated from using Havana as his convenient home away from home—the U.S. mainland. One alternative explanation offered by Cirules is his barebones theory that Genovese and other mob bosses, including Lansky, couldn't tolerate Luciano so close to New York and through some unspecified alliances with some American intelligence officials made Luciano's position in Cuba untenable. While the theory is a novel one, there is no proof or documentation presented that Genovese or the others wielded such influence against Luciano. Frankly, Genovese had more than Charlie Lucky to worry about. Costello was his chief rival for the acting control of the family during Luciano's exile, an exile that would never end in his lifetime.

Chapter Thirteen

BACK IN NEW YORK AFTER THE HAVANA CONFERENCE, things seemed to have quieted down for Genovese. A check of the newspaper headlines after the Boccia case ended in 1946 revealed virtually no mention of Genovese through the end of the decade. Now and again, the Boccia case would garner a mention but always in a historical context and with the perfunctory mention of Genovese's name as the big fish who beat the case.

The absence of Genovese from the newspapers didn't mean that he wasn't busy. It was just that there was nothing for law enforcement to hang its hat on for an arrest. True to his word when he talked about having legitimate businesses, Genovese tended to his Lower West Side Colonial Trading Company on Hudson Street, which dealt with waste paper and rags. There was a second such company on the same street. Then there was Erb Strapping on Thompson Street, a business that he would take an interest in during the next decade.

Genovese also maintained a foothold close to home in New Jersey. He had an interest in a poultry farm in Middletown, New Jersey, from which he sold chickens. Genovese sold the farm in 1948 for about $38,000. Records also show that in July 1948 he and some partners established the Atlantic Highlands Wharf Company. The company handled freight and passenger transportation at the yacht harbor in the coastal town, which happened to be were Genovese had a home. It wasn't a lucky venture. Genovese would later remember that the steamship company had to be liquidated after two years because of a lack of business, particularly after he and his two partners couldn't get approval to have gambling on the vessel.

The businesses—while they lasted—enabled Genovese to show legitimate income. But he didn't become the man Judge Leibowitz once called the "overlord of crime in New York" by recycling scrap paper and rags. Cops were aware that Genovese and others in the New York mob had their hands in gambling operations, notably the Italian lottery, which was a staple for years in the immigrant community. In essence, the lottery worked as a numbers operation in which customers bet on which combination of numbers, usually three digits, would come up randomly.

As explained in a congressional memo found in old government files, the lottery in the U.S. was composed of a number of companies, each of which has a "bank," an entity that had no fixed location but moved around each week. For years, the New York lottery was keyed to a legal lottery in Italy, where each Saturday in each of the Italian provinces five numbers were drawn randomly. The resulting numbers, a total of fifty, were then transmitted to the U.S., where the various banks contributed to a "take" in each business, the memo stated. Genovese's role in all of this was to settle territorial disputes among the various banks as they vied for customers.

But with the advent of World War Two, the numbers from the lottery based in Italy weren't obtainable. So a different system was devised in New York City in which the numbers picked as winning in the lottery were selected from the "handle," or the last three digits of the amount of bets placed at a racetrack on a particular day. Bets were placed by customers all over the city, usually in bars, barbershops, and social clubs, and the cash was taken by runners to the central bank for the operation. The system, according to investigators, was run on the level.

At one point, Genovese was said by Anna to be making for himself $20,000 a week from the policy operation in New Jersey alone. His take could have amounted to $1 million a year throughout the metropolitan area in just the Italian neighborhoods alone. The lottery operation survived the way it did because there was plenty of police corruption to help the mob. This was repeatedly underscored in a series of investigations, among the most notable being one in 1950 that centered on Harry Gross, a man who controlled four hundred betting establishments and who provided the key as a government witness to the extent of corruption in the NYPD plainclothes division. So many cops were implicated in wrongdoing that the entire division was replaced with rookie officers. Genovese had the Italian lottery to line his pockets, and it was never clear that he was involved in police corruption, even though his associates in the crime family were involved in gambling operations that needed police protection.

After the war, Genovese kept a relatively low profile, unlike Costello, whose political activity made him a continuing target for reformers. One headline Genovese garnered was in August 1949, during the Manhattan trial involving bizarre allegations of wiretapping that implicated two men, John G. Broady and Edward Jones, a former U.S. government treasury agent. Both men were involved with a Brooklyn car dealership known as Kings County Buick Corp., the sole distributor of the car model in the borough.

Genovese wasn't involved in the allegations of illegal bugging. Rather, Genovese, Costello, and Joe Adonis were mentioned by prosecutors as being among those, including politicians and policemen, who had received cars ahead of customers who had placed their orders before them. The secret list of preferred customers was titillating for the tabloids and got headlines about an auto black market in the city. Broady testified and matter-of-factly claimed that the late police commissioner Lewis Valentine told him that Costello and Adonis had a standing offer of over $2,000 to anyone who could tip them off about wiretaps on their telephones.

But in the end, the evidence against Broady and Jones on the wiretapping turned out to be small beer, and both were acquitted of the private bugging, which they had claimed had been authorized by company directors. A charge of grand larceny was dismissed after the jurors disagreed by a vote of 11 to 1 to acquit, the lone holdout being the jury foreman.

But down at police headquarters on Centre Street, the department's investigators were picking up intelligence about Genovese's rackets in lower Manhattan, particularly along the waterfront and in the gay bar scene in Greenwich Village. His suspected involvement in narcotics was also on the radar of federal law enforcement, while his involvement in gambling was well-known. Yet the problem for the NYPD in particular was that Genovese and the rest of the members of what cops called the "syndicate" or "combination" were pretty brazen about being seen in public, not necessarily committing crimes but consorting openly.

Genovese and his chief lieutenants made a habit of congregating in their old haunts off Mulberry Street in Little Italy. There were a couple of choice locations, one being a club known as the Alto Knights, which years earlier had been the Café Royale. The origin of the name for the place was uncertain, with some thinking it had some connection to opera singing. During Prohibition, it had been a location for bootlegging deals, and then it was the place that out-of-town gangsters would visit first on a trip to New York.

For the NYPD, the frustrating thing about a place like the Alto Knights was its location. The premises were about two or three blocks from the ornate police headquarters building. It was almost like Genovese and his partners were snubbing the cops as they congregated out in plain view on Kenmare and Mulberry Streets, doing nothing more visible to the naked eye than talking, smoking, and posturing. The group was observant and always on the lookout for police surveillance, as were the people in the neighborhood.

"Actually, they don't do anything but meet, plan and scheme, to keep their own enterprises and to plan new ones, legitimate and illegitimate," was what a frustrated Chief Sherman Willse of the NYPD would remember later about the activity. "However, they are very watchful. The location is their own."

Folks living and working in the area of Kenmare Street couldn't be counted on to cooperate with cops because of the reputation of

Genovese and those who met with him on the street, said Willse. The watchfulness also had a way of armoring Genovese and the others from assassination attempts.

To be sure, bosses like Genovese, Costello, and others weren't unknown to the public. Each had legal issues that made it into the newspapers and kept them at times in the limelight. But by 1950, the sea was changing politically, and the gangster life, while thrilling and exciting to many, was starting to collect liabilities for those involved. Costello in particular was a known power in the New York City Democratic bastion of Tammany Hall. His influence came mainly through the hold he had over district leaders, not to mention the money he had access to and the value of his bad reputation. Genovese had his own set of connections, mainly through the Lower West Side of Manhattan. While there was a time when it was valuable for politicians to count them both as allies, the atmosphere in New York and Washington was going through some profound changes, an indication of how some public sentiment was drifting away from seeing gangsters as okay people.

Mayor William O'Dwyer may have very well sensed in 1950 that the political matrix was shifting when he decided in May to resign, ostensibly because of concerns about the health of his wife. O'Dwyer's decision stunned the political establishment, particularly because a year earlier he had won reelection. But out in Brooklyn, District Attorney Miles F. McDonald, the one who tossed in the towel finally on the Boccia murder case, had geared up another grand jury to look at the extensive network of police protection rackets that worked hand in hand with gambler Harry Gross and his fellow bookmakers. The investigation would ultimately come close to James Moran, O'Dwyer's top aide and confidante, who over the years was suspected of running his own moneymaking rackets.

O'Dwyer would never be directly implicated in Moran's ceaseless moneymaking hustle, for which he would ultimately be convicted and sent to prison. But O'Dwyer could sense the trouble it could all mean, and after resigning, he took a job as the U.S. ambassador to Mexico, essentially moving away from the prosecutorial fury that was developing but, as would be shown later, not far enough away to prevent having his image tarnished.

Taking over as acting mayor was Vincent Impellitteri, who had been Democratic leader of the city council. A new election was scheduled for November 1950, and Impellitteri decided to stand for election on the Experience Party ticket, having lost the Democratic primary to Ferdinand Pecora, an Italian immigrant running on the Democratic-Liberal line who after becoming the first chairman of the Securities and Exchange Commission became a state supreme court judge. A third candidate would be Edward Corsi, a Republican.

Starting with a large disadvantage because of the large number of Democratic registered voters, Corsi immediately started mudslinging, raising the specter of organized crime in connection with both his Italian-American opponents. In what was a last-ditch effort to swing the electorate, Corsi took to the airwaves to say that both Impellitteri and Pecora had the backing of the mob: Impellitteri was supported by Thomas Lucchese, while Pecora was backed by none other than Genovese, Costello, and Adonis, three of the mainstays of the Luciano crime family.

Corsi argued that Impellitteri's surviving as a candidate after his loss in the Democratic primary was evidence "of a split in the underworld" and not problems within Tammany Hall. In one sense, Corsi was right, in that Costello and Genovese were rivals for power in the crime family. There was a split looming in the mob, but it wasn't what Corsi made it out to be. Genovese and Costello had come to an understanding that allowed both to survive as co-acting bosses of the crime family, something that was still years away from being settled.

Corsi asserted that Costello and Genovese had always been powers in Tammany Hall, but added that when O'Dwyer, whom they had supported in 1949, had resigned, their plans to continue their influence had been upset. Thus, Corsi reasoned, Genovese and Costello threw their support to Pecora. Corsi's evidence was slim: he claimed that newspaper publisher Generoso Pope had said he had to consult with Costello and that Costello had decided to back Pecora. Despite Pecora's rebuttal that he had only met Costello three times in the past, Corsi said that "frightened men from the underworld" had told him of other meetings between the two men.

As far as Impellitteri was concerned, Lucchese's crime family didn't want to go along with Genovese and Costello and so supported the acting mayor. Lucchese's aspiration was to "take over New York City and be king of the underworld," said Corsi.

In reply, Impellitteri's spokesman compared Corsi's tactics to that of Nazi minister of propaganda Joseph Goebbels. Impellitteri's support came from the people of the city, said his spokesman, Herman Hoffman.

Meanwhile, Impellitteri was not above using mob smear tactics and did his best to drive Costello's name into the mix in his own way. Since Pope had said that Costello was backing Pecora, Impellitteri said that was an indication that the mobster would be the de facto head of the city, much like Corsi accused Impellitteri of fronting for Lucchese.

"I am not questioning Judge Pecora's character . . . but I say he is no more than a respectable front for the lowest, vilest elements this town ever saw," Impellitteri said in a radio address.

Impellitteri did win the election but not by much, beating Pecora by fewer than 230,000 votes. Corsi ran a very distant third. In retrospect, the mob baiting in the election seemed infantile. But on the other hand, it showed how toxic such an association could be for a politician who was close to any Italian gangster. A new derogatory term, "Costelloism," had crept in to the political lexicon. Only a few short years earlier, that had not been the case.

New York City's electoral antics in 1950 weren't the only way Genovese, Costello, and the rest of the mob got dragged into the public eye. In April 1950, the Kansas City underworld boss Charles Binaggio and his driver, Charles Gargotta, were gunned down in a gambling den. The killings were part of a spate of two dozen gangland style slayings in the past three years. Newspaper editorial boards like that at the *Kansas City Star* lashed out against the "national threat of organized crime," and such cries reverberated in Washington, DC, where a mild-mannered, bespectacled unknown, Senator C. Estes Kefauver of Tennessee, took the initiative and created a special committee to investigate. With a working budget of about $150,000, the Special Committee to Investigate Organized Crime in Interstate Commerce got to work. Frank Costello would have something to worry about. But Vito Genovese wouldn't. No, Vito's problem would come from somebody closer to home who would wind up doing more to hurt him than any congressman: his wife, Anna.

Chapter Fourteen

THE ASSOCIATED PRESS STORY THAT RAN in some of the newspapers hardly rated a mention beyond a few lines. Datelined from Freehold, New Jersey, the October 17, 1950, dispatch reported that Anna Genovese, wife of "underworld figure" Vito Genovese, had filed for divorce. She claimed, the story reported in the last sentence, that the mobster had deserted her in 1948.

The story got little play in the press, relegated to a brief mention in the *New York Daily News*. But in the world of the Mafia, the news was a big deal. Any civil court case involving a major mobster like Genovese had the potential to air secrets he would rather keep confidential. A divorce action could also expose his financial dealings. If there were any personal scandals in the relationship, well, they would also be fair game for the media if the case ever went to trial or legal documents were filed. Somebody like Vito Genovese had a great deal he would want to keep under wraps. But in New Jersey, the laws of disclosure were fairly liberal for the time, and there would be a point where it could all come out, with little Genovese could do to shield himself from prying eyes.

There would also be another looming problem for Genovese in a divorce case. The Mafia was not a world where old-timers looked kindly on men who mistreated their wives. If there was any scandal of abuse in the marriage, Genovese would lose face not only with the public but also among the other Mafiosi. Then of course there was the possibility that crime family secrets would somehow be exposed by a vindictive spouse. That could also be very damaging. If Don Vitone couldn't control his wife, how would that look to the others in his world? He had been thrown a dangerous curveball by Anna, and it was not something he could ignore in the courts.

Those who remember Anna Genovese said she was a woman of fine-boned features, coiffed hair that was often in a beehive style, and a light complexion. She also wasn't the warmest of people, sometimes aloof and distant. The latter may have come from the fact that the men in her life had been problematic. Her first husband, Gerardo Vernotico, was a bit of ne'er-do-well, getting in and out of trouble as a street criminal before he was garroted by a person or persons unknown. He reportedly cheated on Anna, something that was at the root of their divorce. Genovese, the man who wed Anna next, had his own notoriety, and when he fled to Italy, it was Anna who was left holding the bag. She not only had to take care of his business dealings but also the three children who were part of the household.

The four-page complaint for divorce filed by Anna in Monmouth County Superior Court alleged that Genovese had "abandoned" his wife on January 5, 1948. The significance of that date wasn't made clear, but according to Anna, for the next two years she was on her own. Anna claimed she was destitute of means of support, "except through her own exertions, by which she is unable to earn sufficient money for her support." Meanwhile, Genovese, said Anna in her complaint "was possessed of property of substantial value and is in receipt of an income amply sufficient from which to maintain and support" her in a manner "suitable to her station in life."

Anna did acknowledge to the court that Genovese had contributed $120 a week for her support but indicated that clearly wasn't enough. The bottom line was that Anna wanted the marriage dissolved and Genovese to support her. Anna also wanted to resume using her maiden name: Petillo.

Records show that Genovese was served with a copy of the complaint at his large home at 130 Ocean Boulevard in Atlantic Highlands, where he was living with his daughter, Nancy, and Anna's son, Philip. Actually, the papers were served on Genovese's son-in-law Patsy Simonetti, who was married to the gangster's daughter.

It was in late October 1950 that Anna, noticing that Genovese had not responded to her complaint for divorce, asked the court to grant her a default judgment, essentially giving her everything she had asked for. But six months later, Anna's attorney filed a motion to abandon the divorce action. Obliging her, New Jersey Superior Court Judge Donald H. McLean signed an order dismissing the complaint on April 6, 1951.

With his problems with Anna behind him, at least for a while, Genovese had official proceedings of another sort to deal with—the Kefauver hearings in the U.S. Senate. Kefauver launched what would turn out to be a fifteen-month series of hearings in 1950 that tried to pry the lid off of organized crime's main source of income—gambling. By 1951, Kefauver revved up for another series of hearings in which he and his committee would call numerous gangsters—Frank Costello, Joe Adonis, Joseph Profaci, and Thomas Lucchese—to testify. A marque witness would turn out to be Costello, who decided, on the basis of what some of his gangster friends thought was a good move, to testify. Costello had been dogged earlier by rumors that he was into narcotics, and he believed testifying before the committee would be a perfect way to defend himself and show how legitimate he had become.

Costello may have impressed many as a suave businessman, but his appearance before the committee was a public relations disaster. Since his attorney, George Wolf, didn't want Costello's face to be televised, the cameras just focused on his hands. The image was telling. As Costello spoke, often evasively, his hands betrayed his turmoil. He fidgeted, alternately clasping his fingers or a handkerchief, toying with a glass of water, or drumming on the table. It was a performance one newspaper columnist called "the ballet of the hands."

Costello was combative with the committee and at one point walked out of the room. His performance would later earn him a contempt of Congress indictment, for which he would serve twelve months in prison. Costello's belief that he could help himself by testifying was the wrong move. He just looked and sounded guilty of something.

If Vito Genovese was watching Costello's performance on television, he knew that if he took the stand he would be similarly in trouble. In March 1951, Kefauver's staff tried to serve Genovese with a subpoena, but he did a good job of making himself scarce. For weeks, Genovese became an expert at not being seen by investigators. The postmaster for the local town of Atlantic Highlands told investigators that Genovese was seen one morning leaving the house at about 5:30 A.M., a very unusual time for him to be out. Genovese got in his Buick and drove away. Neighbors reported isolated sightings of Genovese, but even a review of his telephone call records gave investigators no clue. Reporters, scratching around for a story about Genovese's absence, visited his old haunts near his home in Atlantic Heights and learned that people there thought he was a fine citizen, a good customer for local merchants, and generous, too.

"He always talked sensible to me," said barber Anthony Gardner, who gave Genovese shaves and haircuts. "Vito is a smart man. There is no doubt about it."

Another barber, Lawrence Maroni, told a reporter that Genovese was "to me, just a good customer . . . very particular." He often left a dollar tip. At a nearby firehouse in Atlantic Highlands, some firefighters said that Genovese contributed to their department by buying about $25 worth of raffle chances for a car.

By May, Rudolph Halley, chief counsel to Kefauver's committee, had to admit that the slippery Genovese had totally frustrated efforts to subpoena him. The committee wanted to question Genovese, "a known Brooklyn racketeer," about the Mafia and the city's policy operation, said Halley. Anna Genovese, already in the midst of her matrimonial case against Genovese, gave a statement to investigators in private but provided no help in locating her estranged spouse or any information about his business dealings or criminal associates.

With no witness, the committee was left with little to say in its proceedings about Genovese in 1951, aside from the fact that some witnesses made cursory references to knowing him. There was a brief mention of Genovese's criminal record, and failed New York City mayoral candidate Edward Corsi reiterated the old allegations he had made about Genovese, Costello, and others having influence over his political rivals in the 1950 campaign.

While Genovese didn't want to testify, there were plenty of other mobsters who decided to appear before Kefauver's committee and talk, even if they didn't have much to say. Costello was combative. Joe Profaci and Joe Adonis gave monosyllabic responses. Some took the Fifth Amendment and declined to say anything.

But one who had no problem telling the committee things was Willie Moretti. An old-line gangster from the Prohibition days, Moretti lived in northern New Jersey and had a reputation for being an old gunman and killer. Moretti, known as "Willie Moore," was a relative of Costello, to whom Costello delegated some of the administration of the crime family.

"Willie had lots of men," recalled Valachi. "He was like independent. He had his own little army. That was the way we expressed it among ourselves. That was the way we thought."

But later in his life, Moretti was said to be suffering from advanced syphilis, and there were concerns within the mob that he might not have control over the things he did and said. Costello was said to have assigned medical care for Moretti when he was going through his less lucid phases. Eventually, it was deemed okay for Moretti to testify.

When Moretti testified on December 14, 1950, he seemed to provide some comic relief for the committee, and his appearance prompted the *New York Times* to subhead its story as "Moretti Praised By Committee for Rags-To-Riches of Dice and Horse-Playing." Moretti talked openly about his gambling and the horses. He recalled starting out as a young street kid in Philadelphia shooting craps and then working his way up to horse racing and a shot at featherweight boxing.

Kefauver and the others on the committee seemed amused by

Moretti's banter. At one point, the chairman asked him how money was made at the racetrack, and the old gangster said, "Bet 'em to place and show. . . . You've got three ways of winning. Come out to the track sometime and I will show you."

Moretti was asked what gangsters he knew, and he didn't hold back, citing Capone, Luciano, Costello, and Genovese. He told the committee that "everything's a racket, everybody has a racket of his own."

As amusing as Moretti may have seemed to the Kefauver committee, his performance did not please Genovese, who saw it as a sign that the old man was losing his marbles and becoming more unpredictable as his illness advanced. As Valachi remembered, Genovese used Moretti's situation as a way of justifying his murder and getting rid of a Costello ally at the same time. Genovese would say to people that while what was happening to Moretti was sad, if he had lost his mind he would want someone to kill him so as not to do something that would harm others in the crime family, explained Valachi.

The contract to kill Moretti was an "open contract," one that didn't have to be rushed. Whoever had the opportunity first could put Moretti out of his misery.

It was October 4, 1951, around 11:30 A.M. that Moretti's cream-colored Packard convertible pulled up and parked outside of Joe's Restaurant on Palisade Avenue, just opposite Palisades Amusement Park. Moretti met four men who were already waiting for him at the eatery, and they all went inside, where they were heard laughing and joking, sometimes in Italian. A waitress left the room.

Then, as described in the *Daily News* account, shots rang out and terrified restaurant workers peered into the room to see the 57-year-old Moretti on his back, his shoes pointed towards the door, his maroon tie dangling over his shoulder, and blood covering his face and chest. "Willie was dead and his assassins had fled," the paper said.

An autopsy revealed that Moretti was felled by two shots—both to the head. Cops recovered a total of four slugs from the scene, including one embedded in a wall. Investigators quickly ruled out robbery as a motive since Moretti had $2,000 cash in his pockets.

Outside in the Packard was found a newspaper opened on a seat to the racing section. The *Daily News* reported that the paper had Moretti's last bet checked off; it was for $500 on the horse Auditing in the third race at the Belmont Park racetrack on Long Island. Auditing came in fourth in a six-horse race.

Investigators from many agencies jumped on the Moretti case, and theories circulated that he was slain in connection with a brewing police scandal. But Valachi would later claim to have the exact insight. He told Peter Maas that a key man in the restaurant when Moretti arrived was one John Robilotto, a sometime loan shark who was part of Albert Anastasia's operation. Robilotto would be indicted in 1952 for the murder, but the case would ultimately be dismissed for lack of evidence.

Moretti's funeral was one of those Mafia spectaculars, drawing ten thousand onlookers to the Corpus Christi Church in Hasbrouck Heights, New Jersey. Moretti's old friends Costello, Genovese, Adonis, and Anastasia all sent floral displays to the funeral home— at least, that is what some of the cards indicated. However, none of them were reported as having shown up.

Although Genovese had laid low during the Kefauver hearings and had stayed away from spectacles like Morelli's funeral, he remained very much on federal law enforcement radar. He was considered one of the leaders of the American Mafia and had a reputation that put him in a direct line of fire from Washington, DC. If nothing else, the Kefauver hearings had made it clear to the American public that Genovese and his mobster pals ran many of the rackets, notably gambling, which was "the life blood of organized crime," and they seemed immune from the cops.

But in 1952, U.S. Attorney General James Patrick McGraney vowed to go after as many of the Italian-American racketeers as he could by finding a way to strip them of their American citizenship and send them back to Italy. Federal immigration agents began looking at the records of over one hundred gangsters with a fine-tooth comb, trying to come up with something to haul them into court over. Once officials focused on the naturalization applications of some of the big crime bosses, it became apparent that some of them had failed to disclose earlier arrests on their forms. If the omissions were considered willful, then McGraney had something to use against the mob. Thomas Lucchese, Joseph Adonis, Frank Costello, and Vito Genovese himself all seemed to have misstated their criminal records, and McGraney took advantage of the opening. In November and December 1952, in various court actions filed against gangsters in New York City and Detroit, the U.S. government accused them all of lying and began denaturalization proceedings.

Each of the lawsuits to take away the citizenship of the mob bosses was set in a different venue. In the case of Genovese, the government filed a civil action in Newark federal district court, alleging that when he filed to become a citizen in 1935, he lied in his interview about his criminal record, claiming he had not been arrested or convicted of any crimes when in fact the opposite was true. Genovese had a skein of at least eight arrests and had twice been convicted of crimes. None of those events, the government charged, had been disclosed when Genovese applied to become a citizen.

It would take about two years for Genovese's fight with the immigration authorities to work its way to a court hearing and another year for there to be a final decision. But in the meantime, Genovese had to again do battle with Anna, the tempestuous wife who had a year earlier pulled back on her lawsuit for divorce. The immigration issue was serious enough and could have serious repercussions for Genovese. But the crime boss's problem with his disgruntled and scorned spouse was something more pressing and something that he would never live down.

Chapter Fifteen

FOR REASONS KNOWN ONLY TO HERSELF, Anna Genovese, despite all of the problems she claimed her spouse dumped on her, decided in early 1951 to give a more conciliatory approach a try. After dropping her divorce action in April 1951, she settled for a weekly sum of $200 in maintenance payments from a man considered one of New York's most powerful mobsters.

It Anna expected things to be better with that kind of money, they weren't. In early December 1952, she filed another matrimonial case, asking for more money from a man she claimed was pulling in $20,000 a week from the Italian lottery business.

"That was barely enough to maintain the state of life to which she was accustomed," papers filed in Freehold state court claimed. Instead of $200, Anna wanted $350 a week, plus $5,000 to pay her lawyers.

Although Anna had said in the earlier divorce action that Genovese had abandoned her in 1948, it seems as though they may have been living together, at least until March 1950, when she found living with him intolerable. She said he beat her, blackened her eye, and once set her hair on fire. Genovese was an ogre, Anna said, and his cruelty "endangered her health and made her life extremely wretched." Well, things must have turned pretty bad because the couple had been sharing a twelve-room house that Anna said had been refurbished with $250,000 in renovations, including the addition of imported carpets, marble staircases, and a twenty-four-carat gold dinner service. She left it all, she said, to live in a walk-up apartment at 134 West Houston Street in Manhattan.

Aside from the lottery cash, Anna said that her spouse owned nightclubs, horse racetracks, and dog tracks and that during a trip to Europe just after the war she carried $100,000 cash for both of them. Vito was flush with cash from all his rackets, she said.

Not so fast, Vito replied in the face of Anna's claims. He had nothing to do with the lottery, nightclubs, racetracks, or dog tracks. He was just the general manager at Colonial Trading Company in Manhattan, a waste paper company, where he gave and took orders. For that, said Genovese, he took home $107 a week, and that was after taxes Now that Anna was taking more shots at him in court, Genovese countersued for divorce.

The case didn't get into meaningful court sessions until March 1953, when both Anna and Vito Genovese made appearances. As often happens in civil cases, there were some last-minute attempts at reconciliation, said to have been prompted by Anna's daughter, Marie, from her first ill-fated marriage. Genovese rebuffed that effort, and then Anna took another shot, going to see Frank Costello in Manhattan to ask him to intercede. "I begged him to get Vito to take me back," Anna recalled.

Costello, a soft touch who at this point of his life was the one mob boss sitting above Genovese on the crime family totem pole, obliged Anna and talked to Vito. But it did no good. Vito never called his wife, she recalled. Slighted by Genovese, Anna proceeded to take the stand in the case. If the cops wanted a road map to the mob boss's rackets, Anna gave it to them.

In two days of testimony, Anna laid out Genovese's gangster life: the lottery, the secret ownership of nightclubs, his hidden interest in legitimate businesses, kickbacks from the waterfront in Kearney, New Jersey, and narcotics. The money was stashed, she said, in bank vaults not only in New Jersey but also in New York City,

Switzerland, and Naples, Italy. She told of his brutality, including a broken nose and assorted injuries that Anna said she was so ashamed of that she never visited a doctor. At the same time, Anna admitted that the couple was rolling in money, saying, "Money was no object, I never knew the value of it."

Anna admitted playing the role of dutiful wife of a mob boss. Every Tuesday and Thursday, there would be meetings at her house, she recalled, of the boys from New York City. Her lavish entertainment was set for the likes of Frank Costello, Albert Anastasia, and Longie Zwillman. Anna also said the parties were wild and weird, especially with her husband.

"They were wild parties," Anna said. "You should see the kissing parties. The games. Oh, the drunken parties."

She didn't spell out who was kissing whom, but it was a fair bet it wasn't among the boys. Don Vitone had a roving eye for the girls, and the only reason he wanted a divorce was that he wanted to make a move for the wife of Tommy Calandriello, who worked with Genovese on the New Jersey docks, she said.

Although Anna expressed shock at the "kissing" ways of her spouse and his friends, there were plenty of stories to emerge about her. When he took the stand, Genovese said that the real reason Anna left his house was because she liked New York City. There was an "element" he didn't want her to associate with in Manhattan, and although he didn't go into detail, it revolved around the nightclubs in the West Village that she ran, like the Caravan Club and some others. Anna gained a reputation over the years for catering in her places to the lesbian crowd, which was a significant part of the city's social and sexual history. Anna herself had a reputation for being bisexual, although Genovese didn't go into that kind of detail. More to the point of their deteriorating relationship, Genovese claimed that Anna was simply interested in another man, someone he identified as a "doctor," although he didn't elaborate.

As it turned out, cops over the years had heard allegations that

Anna had an interest in women, and at one point, according to an old prosecution memo unearthed recently by the muckraking website The Smoking Gun, detectives investigating the old Boccia murder had quizzed a 23-year-old woman with the first name Gwen. The cops had asked Gwen about her relationship with Anna, whom she said she had met over the years at the Caravan Club. Gwen was asked pointed questions about whether she was a lesbian, and she denied it, according to the document.

As Gwen explained things, Anna had befriended her and even got her a job as a cashier at the Caravan Club, "stating that she likes Mrs. Genovese who befriended her," cops said. Gwen and Anna had a relationship based on fondness for each other, enough so that Anna had confided that she had been celibate for six years since she last saw her spouse, the memo stated. The document appears to be from September 1954, which would put Anna's period of sexual inactivity with Vito beginning at about 1948, around the time of their separation. While intriguing, the memo never explained why the cops wanted to know if Gwen had information that would lead to Genovese's incarceration since he was no longer a fugitive in 1948, something that raises questions about its veracity.

The police also believed Gwen had lived for a time with Anna in Manhattan. At the time she was questioned by cops, Gwen said that she had her own apartment on the Upper West Side but that for a time she had stayed with Anna, who would wait up for her until 5:00 A.M. In her testimony, Anna denied living with Gwen something that retired New York detective Clifford Geiger disputed as a witness in the matrimonial trial.

As terrible as her husband allegedly treated her, Anna admitted that there was a time when he lavished her with money and material goods. Genovese gave his wife jewelry, she said, adding that she never was short of money. A year earlier, in talking to congressional investigators, Anna said that she never had to pay any household bill.

"If I needed anything, I called up the grocer or the butcher and Vito paid all the bills," she told one investigator.

But Anna's testimony in court contradicted what she told congressional investigators and raises questions about whether she was being truthful or instead just being a vindictive wife. While she told the divorce court about having lavishly entertained for her spouse and his friends, Anna told the congressional people that she wasn't around for Genovese's meetings at the house with his friends. Anna also claimed that she personally handled $20,000 a week due her husband from the Italian lottery, but she gave a different story to congressional investigators, claiming she had never heard of the lottery.

There were more contradictions. When asked pointedly by a congressional investigator if she knew the source of Genovese's income, Anna replied that the only income she knew of was from the Colonial Trading Company in Manhattan. But a year later, Anna claimed Genovese had all sorts of illicit sources of cash. It was a remarkable change in her story and her knowledge at a time when she had been separated from Genovese for at least two years. Anna's claimed lack of awareness about her husband's finances astonished the congressional staffer, committee counsel Joseph Nellis.

"You keep telling me you live in moderate circumstances, don't know about his financial background, don't know anything about how he earned his income. I keep throwing these facts at you, which are matters of public record, and you don't know anything about them," said a skeptical Nellis.

"I am trying to the best of my knowledge," Anna replied. "These things were never discussed with me."

It is unlikely that Genovese or his attorneys were aware of Anna's earlier interview with Nellis. Had they been, they probably would have used Anna's words to contradict her court testimony. But in any case, when it came to Genovese's turn to testify, he tried to show that she was being unreasonable. He admitted that Anna and he had many squabbles over the years and that she would leave for short periods and then return. When he tried to talk with her about the problems, Anna would reply, "Don't bother me, I am nervous." The way Genovese recounted things, after the couple separated in March 1950, he approached his mother-in-law, Concetta Petillo, and bemoaned what was happening. English was his second language, and at times his heavily accented diction showed it.

"Why she do this to me for?" Genovese asked Petillo. "Why she want to step on my heart for? I am a good husband, a good provider. Mom, why don't she come back?"

Reporters in the courtroom seemed a bit incredulous with Genovese's sob story about his beseeching his mother-in-law. This was one of New York's most ruthless gangsters, a man believed to have been behind a number of murders as he clawed his way up the rackets. As the *Daily News* noted, "The performance didn't bring out a single handkerchief."

Genovese's lawyer, Joseph Mattice, called over twenty witnesses to refute Anna's testimony. One of them was Elizabeth Boccia, a New Jersey woman who served as a cook for the Genovese household for a salary of $50 a month, plus board. Boccia denied that Genovese ever beat Anna, cursed her, or threw lavish parties for gangsters. Anna even complained that life in the house was like living in a morgue, Boccia recalled, adding that the couple fought a lot, usually over money. She never saw Genovese engaged in brutality.

"He was always a perfect gentleman," according to Boccia.

Another witness was builder Dominic Caruso, who strongly denied Anna's claim that he took cash payments from Genovese from the Atlantic Highlands home. Caruso said he recorded the money he made on the books, and he detailed that the Genovese home had been originally purchased for $38,000 in 1946, well below the value of $250,000 Anna had placed on the property with furnishing and renovations. Caruso put a value on the property of about $53,000. But that valuation seemed a bit low, considering the renovation that had gone on. A visitor said that the inside was "very elaborate," with a marble staircase and ironwork that led to a large living room and dining area with an immense fireplace. Both the living room and the dining room faced Raritan Bay, with a beautiful view. Outside was an outdoor barbecue with a food preparation area, all of which also faced the bay. One mural depicted an angel and a horn of plenty hovering in the air over an image of the house on the bay, symbolic of Genovese's life in America.

During her testimony, Anna made the titillating claim that Genovese had at one time had an affair with Mary Radice, the wife of her husband's friend Frank Radice from Thompson Street in Manhattan. Mary Radice was labeled by Anna as Genovese's "ex-mistress and procurer," even claiming that Radice had offered her own 15-year-old daughter to Genovese for sex.

"You should know why I am angry at Mrs. Genovese, my own daughter was mentioned in this," Mary Radice testified. Radice would later go on to sue Anna Genovese for defamation.

Other witnesses were brought in to chip away at Anna's credibility, one even saying she was known as "Flo Dingbat," slang for a scatterbrained person. Queens bartender Edward Talerico said that the owners of the Caravan Club were Anna's brothers Ferdinand and Nick and not the "syndicate" as she claimed. Talerico said the broken nose Anna blamed on Genovese was actually given to her when she got into a brawl with some sailors at the club one night in 1944. Anna also had a hand in loansharking, said Talerico, adding that he should know because he was in the usurious moneylending business with her. A local doctor from Atlantic Highlands said that when he once treated Anna for a headache and stomach pains, he saw no bruises on her that indicated she had suffered a beating.

After the testimony ended, it was Judge McLean's job to sort things out and decide if Anna was due money or if Vito had made the case for divorce. But before that was to happen, the full impact of the case was being felt with law enforcement. When she showed up at the courthouse to testify, Anna was served with a subpoena from a Hudson County grand jury in New Jersey that was probing crime and corruption on the New Jersey waterfront. Days later, investigators with the New York State Liquor Authority sought Anna to learn more about the claims she had made about crime syndicate interests in four night clubs that had come up in her testimony: Club Savannah, reputed to be owned by Anthony "Tony Bender" Strollo; the 82 Club, a gay and lesbian venue; the Moroccan Village, a hangout of Don Vitone, and Anna's Caravan Club, which had been stripped of its liquor license years earlier for being a disorderly place. Joining in on the rush to get Anna's testimony was the New Jersey Law Enforcement Council, a public body that had the job of looking into anything it wanted.

After her court appearance and her sensational allegations about her husband, Anna Genovese would testify all over the state. The divorce case still had many months to go and would grab its share of newspaper headlines, but among Genovese's associates in the Mafia, things weren't sitting well. For a devout Roman Catholic like Joseph Profaci, a mob boss in Brooklyn, the tales of sex—lesbian sex at that—and wife beating grated against his religious sensibilities. Old time mobsters weren't above having mistresses and girlfriends, but that kind of thing was to be done discreetly. Anna and Don Vitone's public airing of their dirty laundry exposed too much.

Anna's lifestyle may also have contributed to the death of Steven Franse, a Lower West Side mob associate who ran the Club 181 at the time when it ran into trouble for openly gay activity and selling liquor after hours. Franse was a nightlife staple in other clubs, such as Club 82, and reportedly helped Anna run her operation. In his biography, Valachi related that Genovese blamed Franse for Anna's strange fixation on the club scene while he was overseas and through Tony Bender arranged for Franse's murder by strangulation in June 1953.

The larger problem was that Anna's allegations came on top of the Kefauver committee disclosures and seemed in part to confirm the evidence that the mob was able to infiltrate businesses and run criminal combinations in a whole host of areas. How did Genovese allow Anna to get away with it? As Peter Maas would later say, the mob was "google-eyed" that Genovese didn't stop her. Valachi later said that the underworld was abuzz with speculation that Genovese should have Anna killed for what she did. But he faced a dilemma.

If she was harmed in any way, suspicion would immediately fall on Genovese. The other fact was that Genovese seemed to have a genuine love and affection for Anna, announcing that he would take her back into his fold if she wanted to drop the whole matter.

But the matter wasn't settled, and it would fall to Judge McLean to figure out what to do with the very messy case of Genovese v. Genovese. Genovese had fallen $8,000 behind in the support payments he had agreed to, and the court threatened him with jail. Genovese's lawyers got a reprieve from an appeals court and came up with the idea of selling the Atlantic Highlands home since Genovese said he was broke, having to sell his 1949 Buick to pay for the appeal.

The case dragged on through the summer of 1953, and finally the court allowed the Genovese home to be sold in part to pay a $32,000 lien of Caruso's construction company. Earlier, Genovese began what must have been a very humbling and degrading experience of selling off the furnishings and artwork in the house to pay legal obligations. An auction at O'Reilly's Plaza Art Galleries in Manhattan drew a standing room only crowd of several hundred. Items did sell, but not for anything near what Genovese had paid. A bed with a mirror, glass, and satin headboards sold for $160 to two women: Genovese reportedly had spent $5,000 on it. A Mosler safe that Anna once said held tens of thousands of dollars in cash was sold for $45. The combination was included; any contents had been long ago removed. A pink-and-white alabaster lamp, carved into the shape of a dancing girl, fetched $75. The sale was expected to fetch about $10,000.

It was finally in September that Judge McLean decided to dismiss Anna's lawsuit for maintenance. He stated that Anna should go back to live with Genovese, but he needed more time to figure out how much back alimony and lawyers fees were owed. McLean ruled that Anna had not proved the allegations against Genovese and, likewise, that her spouse had not proved the claims in his suit for divorce. The results were a standoff. All that courtroom drama and all those allegations didn't prove anything as far as McLean was concerned. In early 1954, an appeals court sustained both dismissals and the tawdry saga was over, for a while anyway. Anna went on living in Manhattan, and Genovese downsized to a smaller rented ranch house in Atlantic Highlands. He still had a view of the harbor and the distant Manhattan skyline, that is, if he walked a few blocks closer to the shoreline.

Chapter Sixteen

THE VERY PUBLIC FIGHT WITH ANNA had ultimately cost Genovese his nice, spacious New Jersey home. The next battle Genovese endured would threaten his status as an American citizen. The federal government had chosen Genovese as one of a number of Top Hoodlums to go after in an effort to revoke their citizenship, the first step to deporting them. It wasn't a fast process. Papers had been filed by the U.S. government against Genovese in the fall of 1952. It was after the matrimonial case was over in mid-1954 that Genovese and his lawyers found themselves trooping into court again, this time into federal court in Newark, where the denaturalization case was to be decided.

As a prelude to the actual trial, Genovese was asked to appear in November 1954 for a special deposition before a government attorney and give detailed answers about what had happened when he applied for citizenship in 1935. At that time, Genovese had not only filled out a citizenship application but also was questioned by a federal examiner, who took down his answers. The crux of the government's complaint against Genovese was that he concealed his criminal record in making the application, claiming he had not been arrested when in fact he had been at least eight times.

Genovese's deposition, a copy of which surfaced during research for this book, took place in the Newark federal building on September 8, 1954. The government was represented by Assistant U.S. Attorney Albert G. Besser and a lawyer from the old Immigration and Naturalization Service. Handling the case for Genovese was New Jersey attorney Ascenzio R. Albarelli and an attorney out of Washington, DC. From the beginning, Genovese related the story noted in chapter two about how he thought that going into the U.S. Army at the age of 19 during World War One somehow carved out a path to citizenship. He was relatively young at the time, but based on what he said in the deposition, Genovese seemed to have had a lackadaisical attitude about the documents he signed back in 1917.

"I thought I was a citizen," said Genovese.

He learned in the 1930s, after returning from a pleasure trip to Italy with Anna, that in fact he wasn't a citizen, and he then filed what he called "first papers in order to become a citizen." The real crux of the government's case was that Genovese had lied about his criminal record when filing for citizenship, and when asked in the deposition if prior to 1935 he had been convicted of a crime, Genovese got evasive.

"I don't know what you call a crime. I never committed a crime in my life outside of carrying [a] concealed weapon to protect myself," answered Genovese. "That is all, I never shot anybody, nor stolen, never harmed anybody."

Genovese admitted getting arrested and convicted twice for carrying a gun, once in 1917 and then in 1927. So Genovese essentially admitted that the application for citizenship contained falsehoods. He had done some of the government's work towards proving its case. But Genovese's defense was that he was never asked about the convictions and that the immigration examiner didn't seem to want to know about some of his misdemeanor crimes.

"Did they ever ask you whether you were convicted of a crime?" Genovese was asked by the government lawyer.

"They asked me if I was convicted of a felony," replied Genovese.

"You felt these were not felonies, is that correct?"

"That is the way I felt, and I told them."

As Genovese explained it, the immigration service examiner said they were not interested in misdemeanors. He also quibbled about whether he was actually arrested on some occasions, as opposed to self-surrendering to cops. Genovese also had trouble remembering things and got angry when he was asked if he ever killed anyone with a car, a reference to the Prospect Park incident of 1924.

"I never killed anyone with a car," Genovese insisted.

Genovese also took umbrage over the fact that cops took him into custody over the Prospect Park case, which led to the death of one man

"It is not common sense. I am in the car. I am thrown out of the car, somebody else was driving the car. I almost got killed. Do you call that an arrest?" said a combative Genovese. "If the police want to take me in for an arrest, I won't resist. I won't resist an arrest. I have more respect for law and order."

At one point, Genovese was getting so angry that he threatened to clam up and assert his constitutional right against incriminating himself. But he didn't. He continued to testify, and the government attorneys brought out more arrest records, fingerprint files, and photographs.

The questioning turned to Genovese's old New Jersey estate in Middletown, which had burned down, and the crime boss got sarcastic when the government attorney said he was trying to help him remember.

"You are trying to help me!" exclaimed Genovese. It was the kind of help he didn't need, aimed as it was to strip him of his American citizenship.

Ultimately, Genovese said the immigration examiner put his responses on the citizenship questionnaire without reading it back to him and without giving him a chance to examine it. The rest of the deposition dealt with Genovese's family and his children. In the end, he tried to create the impression that he gave the immigration officials what they wanted on the questionnaire and that any errors were from a misunderstanding on their part.

Genovese's denaturalization case finally went to a court hearing in November 1954 before Federal Judge Phillip Forman. The central issue in the case had not changed: Had Genovese willfully lied in failing to disclose his numerous arrests in the years before he filed his citizenship application? To prove its point, the government brought in the same documents it had introduced two months earlier in the deposition that showed Genovese's arrests from 1917 through 1930. Also testifying was a New York City precinct officer who verified some of the documents as showing when Genovese was arrested and what he was arrested for.

On the witness stand, Genovese acknowledged most of the arrests and the circumstances, particularly the Prospect Park auto accident homicide charge. One case, a contempt of court charge filed against him in Hoboken, New Jersey, in 1925, he didn't have a recollection about. Under questioning by the government, Genovese talked about his three children and in particular noted that Marie, known also as Rose Marie, was Anna's child from her first marriage and that he had adopted her. As was not unusual of parents back in that time, Genovese said he never disclosed to Marie that she was adopted and also didn't tell anyone so as to assure the child never found out. "I didn't want the neighborhood to know she was my adopted child, I wanted her to think I was her father," said Genovese, explaining that he kept the secret from Marie until she got married in 1947.

The crux of Genovese's testimony came when the government lawyer asked him about the questions he was asked about his arrest record by the immigration examiner, whose name was never mentioned in the testimony.

"Now, Mr. Genovese when you told this unidentified person about your arrests and convictions for misdemeanors, what did he say, what did he tell you?" the government lawyer, Albert G. Besser, asked.

"What he told me, that he asked me about felony, city prison or federal penitentiary," Genovese answered. "I told him I had the arrest and had two misdemeanors against me. He just put his head down and wrote something and said 'Go ahead, sign.'"

"Did he say that doesn't matter?" Besser asked.

"No, I don't remember him saying that," replied Genovese. "I think he said 'We are not interested,' something like that. 'We are not interested in misdemeanors.'"

When Genovese was asked if the examiner had wanted him to enumerate each arrest separately, he said, "There was no specification of that because he said, 'Go ahead, sign,' and I signed."

Listening to Genovese, Judge Forman found his recollections of events concerning the making of the citizenship application to be "very vague," with a lack of memory about who filled out the various forms. Forman wasn't impressed.

"Have you ever been arrested or charged with violation of any law of the United States or State or any city ordinance or traffic regulation? If so give full particulars." That was the key question on the application. That was question number 31 on the citizenship application, and it was a major problem for Genovese. It was quite clear from all of the records that he had been charged or arrested ten times dating from 1917 through 1934.

Genovese insisted that in the course of the naturalization proceedings, he had been asked whether he had ever been convicted of a felony and that he had responded that he didn't know what that meant. Genovese also said that when he was given an explanation, he was told words to the effect that a felony meant that he had served time in a state prison or been convicted of a federal offense that led to a sentence of over a year in jail. When Genovese mentioned he had a couple of misdemeanor arrests, he was told by immigration officials they weren't interested in that.

But weighing the evidence, Forman found that the government had proved that Genovese had replied falsely to the question about his criminal record, giving the answer "no." As far as Forman was concerned, Genovese had willfully given false information and his citizenship should be revoked, a drastic remedy, the court acknowledged. The date of the court's ruling was August 16, 1955.

Genovese would appeal Forman's decision, but to no avail. Today, anyone looking at Genovese's original petition for naturalization will see the large letters "CANCELLED" stamped on the pages.

Chapter Seventeen

ALTHOUGH VITO GENOVESE WAS STRIPPED of his citizenship, he didn't lose his ability to run the rackets and gain power in the Mafia. He may have been patriotic in his own perverse way, but Genovese was a gangster and had a crooked image to uphold as a matter of principle. Luciano wasn't going to be coming back, and Frank Costello, having already spent fifteen months in prison for contempt of Congress, was in a battle for his life, facing multiple federal counts of income tax evasion. Not to be outdone by Genovese, Costello was also fighting his own denaturalization proceedings, adding to his legal distractions. Genovese, at least, was free to walk the streets and consolidate his power.

Among the big industries impacted by the Mafia was the garment industry, one of New York City's largest manufacturing bases for decades, particularly among the Jewish and Italian immigrant communities. Garment firms eventually consolidated their manufacturing operations in an area just below Times Square on Seventh and Eighth Avenues, in an area stretching from about Thirty-first Street to Thirty-ninth Street, if you count the fur district. Allied businesses such as fabric companies, notions, and trucking firms also shared the business district. It was all such a consolidated, narrow-profit-margin industry in the years just before and just after World War Two that it was easy for organized crime to focus its efforts at control.

Trucking was a critical choke point for the manufacturers because they had to ship their product in several stages of the manufacturing process. For that reason, truckers had the manufacturers over a barrel and could set up cartels to fix prices and divide up territories. Garment firms had little leverage against the truckers since speed of delivery in the business was paramount. If a manufacturer missed store deadlines, he or she might as well send the stuff straight to a liquidator. The competition was that brutal. Manufacturers also needed cash, sometimes on a quick basis, and when banks failed them, they could always turn to Mafia loan sharks. The unions were another critical player, and if a manufacturer could avoid unionization or get sweetheart deals to avoid the formal labor contracts, that also allowed money to be saved.

Since Jewish and Italian workers were employed in large numbers in the garment business, it was Jewish and Italian mobsters who used the industry as their racket. The Italians had the trucking part of the business sewn up, while the Jews were notable labor racketeers and moneymen, along with some of the Italian loan sharks who worked Seventh Avenue. Among the most notorious of the early Jewish gangsters in the garment industry was Louis "Lepke" Buchalter, once a bootlegger who graduated to be a leader and killer in the Murder Inc. combination, a mix of Jews and Italians who carried out murders in the 1930s and 1940s. In the garment area, Buchalter became a major labor racketeer, using violence and threats of strikes to get his way, that is, until he was captured in 1939 and then executed in 1944, the last major gangster to get the death penalty in New York State.

With the older Jewish mobsters like Buchalter gone, by 1956, according to FBI intelligence files, Vito Genovese was believed to have control over the Italian Mafiosi in the garment industry. An informant told the bureau that Genovese had so many rackets that he had only a "loose" control over the garment area of Manhattan. It was rather the Jewish mobsters, led by Meyer Lansky, who seemed to exert more authority through businessman like Benjamin "Boom Boom" Levine, a wealthy garment manufacturer said to have nonunion shops manufacturing clothing. Lansky also was said to have control over officials at the International Ladies' Garment Workers' Union, according to the FBI files.

Genovese's control over the garment area was decentralized in that a number of his crime family associates controlled various segments of the business, more or less as his surrogates in shakedowns of companies. Among them were Joseph "Joe Stretch" Stracci, Michael "Trigger Mike" Coppola, James Plumeri, and Anthony "Fat Tony" Salerno, one of the garment industry's major loan sharks. John "Big John" Ormento was said by federal officials to have been on the payroll of at least one garment-trucking firm owned by Max J. Posner. Thomas "Three Finger Brown" Lucchese, who headed his own faction and owned a legitimate garment-manufacturing firm, also exercised control over some of the cutting rooms in the industry. Cutting rooms were essential parts of the garment production process at the time because that was where the fabric was cut into the desired shapes for sewing, which was often done at sewing rooms located elsewhere.

Another ally of Genovese with sway in the garment industry was John Dioguardi. Known in the press as "Johnny Dio," Dioguardi started out as a low-level gangster making illicit alcoholic beverages during Prohibition and then moved into garment industry racketeering with Plumeri when Buchalter died. Although aligned on the record with Lucchese's crime family, Dioguardi was one of the principal racketeers in the fashion industry, where crime families had the territory divided up and sometimes worked together to protect their mutual interests. A tough character who was not above taking swings at news photographers, Dioguardi was a suspect in the acid blinding of newspaper columnist Victor Riesel.

Sitting above the fray in the garment area was Genovese, considered in 1956 among the preeminent Mafia bosses in the nation. He also had another area of influence: the waterfront, specifically the New Jersey side. Or so investigators believed. When Anna Genovese testified to a Hudson County grand jury in New Jersey in March 1953, she was asked about allegations she had made in her matrimonial case about her husband's sway over the waterfront. Specifically, she had alleged that Genovese got payroll kickbacks from longshoremen at a number of piers, involving Tommy Calandriello, the man whose wife Anna believed her husband had lusted after.

It was never learned precisely what Anna told the grand jury in her two hours of questioning. But the resulting indictments named eleven people—but not her estranged husband—on charges they made usurious loans to longshoremen. Two years later, the Waterfront Commission, a bistate agency of New York and New Jersey, filed administrative charges against six dock workers on charges stemming from a different kickback scheme in which longshoremen had been forced to pay in order to get good jobs at a naval ammunition terminal. Again, Genovese was not charged.

A more intriguing possible tie of Genovese to the New York waterfront emerged back in the 1940s during an investigation into the murders of shipyard foreman Charles Edward Butler in 1943 and union official John Flaherty a year later. Investigators ascribed both killings to an entity known as the Black Hawk gang, an obscure name later linked to Genovese when he was finally arrested in the Boccia case in 1945. The gang was said to be part of Genovese's link to the underworld. Two reputed members of the Black Hawk group turned informant and said the killing of Butler was sparked by fears that he was going to tell the FBI about a payroll-padding scheme at a Brooklyn shipyard. But a police investigator later debunked that claim when he found no evidence of payroll shenanigans. In any case, apart from his reputed tie to the Black Hawk crew, Genovese was never implicated in the case.

But if investigators weren't able to tie Genovese into any waterfront rackets, at least not enough to charge him, he still had a substantial connection to the docks and piers through his involvement in a company known as Erb Strapping, located at 180 Thompson Street in Manhattan on the Lower West Side. The story of how Genovese became involved in the company, which specialized in securing cargo for shipping, showed the value of his reputation—good or bad—in lining his own pockets through a waterfront legitimate company.

In an interview with the FBI given in 1958, Eleanor Erb Pica, whose brother formed Erb Strapping, said she had met Genovese about ten years earlier at the Piano Bar in his hometown of Atlantic Highlands. The bar was owned by Genovese's daughter and son-in-law, and the mobster could be found there regularly. Pica said Genovese was always someone who gave her good advice, and she sought him out for help in the strapping business. As a result, Pica told the FBI, Genovese became a shareholder in the company.

According to the FBI memo, Genovese would show up for about half of a normal workweek at Erb Strapping and supervised the warehouse, gave advice, and secured some customers. Questioned by the FBI, Pica said she never talked with Genovese about his personal business and didn't know about any of his other business dealings. Any payments the company made to Genovese were reflected on the company books.

Federal authorities were looking at just about every business relationship Genovese was said to have, including real estate in lower Manhattan and Seacoast Liquor Distributors, Inc., in New Jersey, a firm allegedly run by his son, Philip, and his daughter, Rose Marie. But as in the case of Erb Strapping, nothing came of the probe.

Given his stature, Genovese was sought out by businesses well beyond Manhattan and New Jersey. Such was the case of Joseph Cosso, an executive with the Long Island–based company of County Line Steel Corporation of Amityville. In an interview with *Newsday* in 1958, Cosso recalled how he turned to Genovese when he needed capital to expand the company, getting a $30,000 investment from him in return for a one-quarter share of the ownership.

"Vito is a natural-born salesman," Cosso told reporter Bob Greene, "and a smart businessman. He figured we were on the upgrade and it would be a good investment."

Cosso knew Genovese from the old neighborhood of Greenwich Village and said that Genovese would try to salvage local youths, including himself, from a life of crime. Said Cosso, "It was Vito who took us in hand and straightened us out. He's been helping me ever since."

The experience of Cosso with Genovese seemed to fall in line with what other legitimate businesses did in courting the mob boss.

In exchange for Genovese's largesse, the companies got someone with contacts who, if the stories are to be believed, actually put in some work hours. Nothing wrong with that, provided it was all legitimate. Genovese could then show regular, legitimate sources of income. Government records showed that federal prosecutors and the FBI looked into Genovese's interests and never found anything amiss, including any extortion schemes. It also seemed that Genovese paid his taxes, although at one point earlier in his life, Genovese settled a $160,000 back tax bill with Uncle Sam. Rival mobster Costello famously claimed he paid his taxes but in reality failed to do so fully.

Chapter Eighteen

Vito Genovese never thought he was as smart as Frank Costello, at least in some ways. But as things turned out, Genovese knew enough to keep his finances straight, and while Costello did have a hand in a number of big business ventures, Genovese wasn't doing badly, either. Despite the sensational disclosures and allegations that Anna had made in the matrimonial trial, Genovese didn't get touched by prosecutors because of the things she said. However, Costello, as smart as he was, made some terrible mistakes at a time when the Mafia was approaching a state of turmoil—and violence.

Costello had problems on a number of fronts. Some of his allies were getting bumped off, notably Willie Moretti, or in the case of Joe Adonis, were deported as undesirables. Legal issues like his denaturalization case, the contempt of Congress conviction, and seemingly endless probes by the IRS were proving to be distractions. Prison over the contempt case pulled Costello out of circulation and made it difficult for him to stay on top of mob business, although reports circulated among federal officials that his wife, Loretta, took an apartment in Milan, Michigan, and that he was able to sneak out of prison to visit her.

On the street in New York, Genovese was building his power base. The publicity that prosecutors have given him about his being the biggest gangster in America only added to his stature. In reality, the mob viewed him as a key boss, even though Costello was at least as important. But the problem for Costello was that he was in the crosshairs of the IRS and the taxmen were not going away. Methodically, agents had compiled a list of Costello and his wife's expenses, everything from the purchase of flowers for a cemetery to the building of a family mausoleum and plenty of other expenditures like those Costello made for his girlfriend Thelma Martin. The result was that the Costellos were spending in some years more money than they made. Based on what was called a net-worth analysis by the government, Costello was indicted in March 1953 for evading $73,000 in taxes after spending $200,000 more than he made over a four-year period.

On May 13, 1954, a federal jury in Manhattan convicted Costello of income tax evasion. Costello wasn't sent to prison immediately because he took numerous appeals, all the way up to the U.S. Supreme Court. But in May 1956, while certain appeals were pending, Costello agreed to start his five-year prison sentence and surrendered. With Costello now in jail, the Mafia needed to figure out what to do and who was to take his place.

The Mafia doesn't like a power vacuum, and recently released FBI records show that when Costello went away, a number of high-ranked mobsters called meetings to figure out what to do now that Uncle Frank was gone. One gathering of thirty-five men at the St. Moritz Hotel in Manhattan took place just five days after Costello surrendered. Among those said to be present were Vincent Alo, Mike Coppola, Joseph Rao, and Meyer Lansky.

An informant stated that those present at the St. Moritz meeting decided that Costello's usefulness to the Eastern Syndicate was at an end and his replacement should be picked. Vincent Alo, a force in the garment-trucking industry, was supposedly picked to replace Costello, with gangster Charles "the Blade" Tourine picked as an enforcer. But that information about Alo's selection was suspect. Another FBI informant plugged into the mob world said that he had heard nothing about Alo ascending to power and he didn't think Alo had enough standing to rise to that position. The story also had Genovese out of the process, something that he would not have stood for.

As happens when leaders of the Mafia are killed or in prison, lots of names are thrown around as successors to the once powerful, and that is what happened in the case of Costello. Several names were tossed around, some without any real basis. But all of the speculation and ruminations were thrown into doubt when on March 11, 1957, the U.S. Supreme Court handed Costello a reprieve when it agreed to hear his appeal on the tax conviction and set him free on bail after he had served about eleven months. Costello went home to Loretta. But now Genovese no longer had a clear shot at the title of boss of the family. Something had to give.

The May 2, 1957, assassination attempt of Frank Costello is one of those choice moments in the history of the New York Mafia. It has been told many times, most recently in my *Top Hoodlum: Frank Costello, Prime Minister of the Mafia*. Suffice it to say, Costello survived and only received a glancing wound to his head in a bungled shooting by Vincent Gigante. But the message to Costello was clear: his days were numbered if he attempted to remain as boss.

As Valachi remembered events, Genovese didn't fear a reaction from Costello but rather his main ally, Albert Anastasia, the murderous gangster from Brooklyn known as the Mad Hatter and Lord High Executioner. To consolidate his forces, various members of the crew of Tony Bender, the key captain in Genovese's combination, were called to a meeting at a hotel on Manhattan's West Side and given areas of the city to cover in case there was a retaliation for the Costello attempted hit.

"We were told," Valachi told Maas, "we got to get ready, there could be war over this."

Valachi said he covered East Harlem and had five shooters under him. Meanwhile, Genovese retreated to his home in Atlantic Highlands with dozens of men. He wanted a show of loyalty and strength and had everyone come in to pay him respect. To explain what had happened to Costello, Genovese related how he was forced to take a preemptive strike because Costello was actually gunning for *him*. As Valachi remembered, Genovese anointed himself head of the family and appointed Gerardo "Jerry" Catena, another New Jersey–

based mobster, as his chief advisor or underboss, a role the murdered Willie Moretti had once played for Costello.

About two weeks after the shooting of Costello, Gigante was arrested and later brought to trial for attempted murder. Ever the stand-
up guy, Costello took the witness stand and said he couldn't identify
who had shot at him. Gigante was acquitted, and his mother,
Yolanda, shouted out, "It was the beads! It was the beads!" referring
to the rosary beads she had in her hands throughout the trial.

Ironically, Gigante and Costello became friends of sorts after the
trial, with Costello having the big-chinned prizefighter to his home
once as a guest of honor over dinner. But such things didn't happen
between Genovese and Costello. They were now enemies to the
core. Costello would go quietly, relinquishing power and spending
his days between his homes on Central Park West and Sands Point,
Long Island, where he grew orchids. He also bore with him the message Anastasia once gave him: be wary of Vito Genovese and any
attempt he might make to smooth over problems.

Anastasia was one of those Mafiosi whom people either admired,
hated, or feared. Sometimes it was a combination of all three senti-
ments. Decades earlier, Anastasia had learned the ropes as a killer
doing contract murders for Murder Inc., and he eventually became a
power in the Brooklyn waterfront rackets. Over the years, he gained
a reputation as an erratic, volatile man whom many in the mob were
wary of. He had become underboss to Vincent Mangano, leader of
one of the Mafia families in the city, but had other ambitions.
Costello considered Anastasia an ally, and for that reason Genovese
viewed "Don Umberto," as Anastasia was called, with suspicion
and as a potential stumbling block in his path to take control of the
old Luciano family.

"Everybody knew that Albert is a mad hatter," said Valachi.
"With him it was always kill, kill, kill. If somebody came and told
Albert something bad about somebody else, he would say 'hit him,
hit him.' At the table there was no telling how he would be."

One thing was clear. Anastasia wanted Mangano out of his way,
and in 1951, the boss of the family disappeared. His body was never
found. An emboldened Anastasia told the ruling Commission that

Mangano had to be killed because the old boss had been plotting to kill him and he needed to act in self-defense. The Commission bought the argument and allowed him to be the boss of the old Mangano family.

Anastasia's newfound status as boss did make him careful about his security. He had bodyguards and lived in a palatial home in Fort Lee, New Jersey, surrounded by a wall as well as menacing guard dogs. He knew he had to be careful in what was now a very unstable Mafia world with Genovese on the prowl for preeminence.

It would take six years after the disappearance of Mangano before Anastasia got his own just desserts. As recalled by Valachi, Genovese contacted an Anastasia underling named Carlo Gambino and convinced him to go along with a plot to depose Anastasia. "Without Vito backing him . . . Carlo never would have went for it."

But helping to convince Gambino to back Genovese, according to Valachi, was the Scalise affair. Frank Scalise was for all purposes considered the second-in-command of the Anastasia family. But he apparently developed a bribery scheme in which he sold Mafia memberships for as much as $50,000. When Anastasia learned of the membership racket, he ordered Scalise to be killed over what Valachi said was the crass commercialization of the process of becoming a made man in the Mafia. In a grisly postscript to Scalise's demise, his brother Joseph, after loudly proclaiming that he would seek vengeance for his sibling's demise, went missing in September 1957. Valachi would later report that Joseph was lured to the home of another Anastasia lieutenant and killed, then his body was dismembered and disposed of, likely in some private garbage-carting trucks.

Gambino was well aware of what had happened to the Scalise brothers, and that gave him an extra reason to realize that Anastasia could turn into an enemy in the blink of an eye, even for some of his own people. Anastasia was also reportedly losing big at the racetrack and abusing his underlings because of that. With Gambino in with Genovese, the plot for Anastasia's assassination went into high gear.

The murder of Albert Anastasia the morning of October 25, 1957, as he sat in a barber's chair at the old Park Sheraton Hotel in Manhattan was another one of those singular events in Mafia history that has been retold many times. It is tale that doesn't need to be forked over again here in much detail. As hits go, it was masterfully carried out by two gunmen who had wrapped the lower part of their faces with scarves. Anastasia never had a chance and was hit five times and died in a pool of blood on the floor. His bodyguards had conveniently left the barbershop just before the shooting started.

Cops found two handguns near the scene of the slaying. Those might have offered some clues, but this was 1957 and not modern times with DNA evidence, ballistic technology, and surveillance cameras. Like the 1931 killing of old boss Joseph Masseria, the murder of Albert Anastasia would remain unsolved to this day. In recent years, there have been reports that the slaying was carried out by a three-hitman team working at the behest of Carlo Gambino, who took over the crime family. But none of those men were ever charged.

The killing of Anastasia devastated Costello. The loss of his main ally against Genovese meant that Costello was vulnerable. It was Costello alone who had to face Genovese, and he believed his days were numbered. Costello's attorney, George Wolf, remembered visiting his client at his Central Park West apartment and finding Anastasia's brother Tony already there and both men clutching each other and sobbing. "This means I am next," Costello said quietly to Wolf, a prediction that mercifully proved inaccurate.

Anastasia's funeral—such as it was—proved to be a good indication of his stature among his Mafia associates. Hardly anyone showed up. There was no funeral mass. Instead, there was a burial at Green-Wood Cemetery in Brooklyn, just blocks away from the dockland that Anastasia had once ruled. The ground was not consecrated because Green-Wood is a nonsectarian burial place, open to all faiths. Anastasia's family showed up, as did a handful of officials from the International Longshoremen's Association, and the graveside rites, spoken by a priest over the metal casket, lasted only about seven minutes. A few hundred spectators did peer through the fence at the cemetery's perimeter, but there wasn't much to see. The whole service was unspectacular and nothing like the funerals mob bosses of the past were given.

Eventually, a flat bronze plaque level with the ground would be placed on the spot where Don Umberto rests. It is a simple marker, embossed with his birth name, Umberto Anastasio, as well as the dates of his birth and death. A visitor to the cemetery has to look carefully for the grave, as it is obscured now by shrubs. About the time Anastasia was put in the ground, another mostly obscured event occurred in Paris. An attorney there argued on behalf of his convicted client in a drug case that the defendant had Anastasia as a client. The event rated a tiny mention in the American newspapers. Soon, the story of the Mafia and drugs, as well as the involvement of Vito Genovese, the man who conquered Anastasia, would become much bigger news

Chapter Nineteen

THE RESIDENTS OF BEAUFORT AVENUE in the town of Livingston, New Jersey, were used to limousines and big cars turning into the driveway at number 288. The house at the end of the road was one of those ornately constructed stone dwellings capped by some Gothic statuary, all of which made it look like some garish Transylvanian castle. There was a swimming pool and the peacocks had their own enclosure. Ruggiero Boiardo, known to his friends and most of the world as "Ritchie," was a man of years who was shown a great deal of respect. He had earned it all from his days as a bootlegger, street gangster in Newark, head of the local Italian lottery, and survivor of an assassination attempt and for his ascension to the ranks of the Mafia.

There were stories that Boiardo gained his nickname "the Boot" from the way he would stomp those he beat. But according to one newspaper columnist who would write an obituary of sorts about Boiardo when he died in 1984, he gained the sobriquet from his role as a milkman and numbers operator in Newark's First Ward, which was then populated by poor immigrants who shared a corner telephone booth. The story goes that Boiardo spent so much time answering telephone calls there that whenever his customers asked where he was, they were told he was "in the booth," which in the diction of the First Ward was pronounced "boot."

But at least to his immediate neighbors, Boiardo liked to say he was just a talented stonemason who did well enough to afford the palatial thirty-acre estate with the swimming pool and a unique collection of statuary, in which he was depicted riding a horse and surrounded by likenesses of his children and grandchildren. The property had enough space that Boiardo's children were able to have their own homes on the estate. Visitors would stop by and pose for photographs by the statutes or, if they didn't dare trespass too far into the property, by the two stone guardhouses by the front gate. There were also stories that a certain area of the property was used as a gangster crematorium to dispose of bodies.

Sometime before noon on November 10, 1957—at least as far as investigators could determine the accuracy of the date—the caravan of limousines driving into the Boiardo estate was more impressive then usual because of the human cargo they carried. Some of the big bosses of the New York Mafia had earlier driven to a restaurant parking lot in New Jersey and were then escorted to the waiting limousines, which took them the rest of the way to Boiardo's estate. Those men in the cars were some of the preeminent bosses of La Cosa Nostra: Joseph Bonanno, Sam Giancana, Carlo Gambino, Stefano Maggadino, Joseph Ida, Joseph Zicarelli, and of course Vito Genovese. The group, which composed the key members of the ruling mob Commission, arrived just before noon and would stay into the next morning, fed no doubt from Boiardo's restaurant, Sorrentino. The men would want for nothing.

When big things happen in the Mafia—and Anastasia's murder was big—the top mobsters do what other executives do—they hold a meeting. Crime historians have detailed the famous conclave of gangsters that took place in November 1957 at the Apalachin home of Joseph Barbara in which, among other things, the Anastasia assassination was discussed. But the Boiardo meeting was more intimate, a kind of pre-summit in advance of Apalachin. There was one main item on the agenda: the Anastasia hit. According to an FBI informant, the meeting was called so that the Commission members could be "feeling the pulse" of those in attendance about what had happened just weeks earlier in the Park Sheraton barbershop. It was then decided that the meeting at the home of Barbara in upstate New

York was needed to tell other members of the Mafia around the country why it was necessary to kill Anastasia.

It was Vito Genovese who is credited with pushing for the big meeting for the national leaders. He had much on his agenda, including trying to justify the bloodshed involving Costello and Anastasia. The big questions centered on where should it be held. Sam "Mo Mo" Giancana of Chicago figured his home turf would be good. Nationally, the Mafia was spread out across the country in about a dozen areas. But the main focus had always been New York City and its environs like Philadelphia, Pittsburgh, and Buffalo. Some of the main leaders of the Commission were New York–based, so it made sense that a big meeting should take place in the Northeast, close to New York City and major airports so that the out-of-town members could have relatively easy access.

The venue finally selected was the estate of old-time mobster Joseph Barbara on a hilltop road at a dead end southeast of the town of Apalachin, near Vestal, New York. The big event was set for November 14, just a few days after the earlier meeting at the New Jersey home of Boiardi. Travel arrangements for the dozens of men who were to attend involved some secrecy. Barbara made some local motel reservations and told some of the visitors that they didn't have to sign the registration form, that "Joe" would take care of things the next morning. Some of the men who flew in from out of town over a two-day period did so with reservations made under false names. Room bills were to be paid for by Barbara's company, the Canada Dry Bottling Company of nearby Endicott. It was planned for them to all eat well: Barbara had ordered nearly 250 pounds of meat, steaks included.

The story of how law enforcement, almost by chance, learned of the Apalachin meeting is one that has been part of mob lore ever since it became part of American consciousness. It happened to be that on November 13, a day before the men were to enjoy steaks and other parts of a large repast at Barbara's home, two New York State Police officers, Sergeant Edgar D. Crosswell and Trooper Vincent Vasik, received information about a bad check someone had used at the Parkway Motel on Route 17 in Vestal. In conversation with Mrs.

Helen Schroeder, wife of the motel proprietor, the two state cops learned that Barbara's son had reserved three double rooms to be paid on the account of his father's bottling company. The younger Barbara told the motel proprietor that his father didn't yet have the names of the guests who would be attending but that the event was a convention of some Canada Dry men.

It turned out that the Parkway Motel was only one place used by the Apalachin mobsters for overnight accommodations. Some used the Arlington Hotel in Binghamton. They came from as far away as California and as nearby as Scranton, Pennsylvania, and upstate Utica. A great many arrived from New York City. Some flew in to a nearby airfield, but many more drove. In one car came Vito Genovese, his cousin Michael from Pittsburgh, and Gabriel Mannarino, a reputed gangster and bookmaker from Pennsylvania who served as the driver.

Carlo Gambino, the newly minted boss of the late Anastasia's family, took a train to Binghamton with his cousin Paul Castellano, at which point both rode in a borrowed car with Genovese's old friend Mike Miranda. New York City dock boss Carmine Lombardozzi of Brooklyn drove up to Apalachin with garment trucker Natale Evola, as did Joseph Riccobono from Staten Island. Those flying in were California attorney Frank DeSimone, considered a boss of the Los Angeles wing of the Mafia, who then made the final leg of the trip by car with Pennsylvania mobster Russell Bufalino. All totaled, there were at least sixty-two men—some key members of the Mafia, some associates.

By about noon on November 14, Crosswell and Vasik returned to the Parkway Motel with an agent of the federal Alcohol Tobacco and Tax Unit of the Treasury Department. There, they observed the auto of James Lac Duca and saw that six guests who had occupied some of the rooms earlier reserved by Barbara had left the motel. After checking out the Canada Dry bottling plant and noticing no activity, the three law enforcement people drove to Barbara's home on the hilly cul-de-sac.

It was at the Barbara house that the three law enforcement officials noticed that there were up to eight cars parked in the driveway, and they began to record the license plate numbers. It was then that up to a dozen men came out from the rear of the garage, followed by others. At that point, Crosswell and his two colleagues sensed there was something going on and called to a nearby state police head-quarters for more uniformed officers. A roadblock was set up at the only exit leading from the Barbara estate.

As the extra cops arrived and the mobsters learned of the road-block, they started to panic and attempted to leave Barbara's home in haste, grabbing whatever rides they could or tramping through the fields. They were largely but not entirely unsuccessful and were rounded up. Vito Genovese got into a car with Bufalino, and both were among those stopped at the roadblock. Michael Genovese was found in the same car as three other Pennsylvania mobsters: James Osticco, Gabriel Mannarino, and Angelo Sciandra. Garment trucker Evola was another traveler who was stopped at the roadblock as he tried to drive away in a Cadillac sedan with Frank Cucchiara of Boston.

One of those trying to leave Barbara's home on foot was Mafia boss Joseph Bonnano, who was found in a cornfield near the house. When questioned by the cops, Bonanno admitted being at the meet-ing. Another one trying to escape through the woods was Santo Trafficante, late of Havana and Florida, who was corralled by a state trooper.

All the vehicles were searched, but nothing incriminating was found, not even weapons. A number of the men present, including Carlo Gambino and Joseph Montana, had valid pistol permits. None of the men were wanted in New York State or their home states. Many of the guests, when asked by the cops, said the purpose of the meeting was to visit Barbara, who was ill. Wisely, Genovese only told the cops who he was and then said he didn't have to answer any more questions.

Not everyone stopped and questioned at the Barbara estate was a big-name Mafia boss. A number of them were relatively obscure men from upstate New York. But geographically, the participants came from all over the country. Officials determined that about half of the men were native-born Americans, while thirty-three were born in Italy, mostly in Sicily. While none of the participants had active arrest warrants or were wanted, ten had gambling records, and four had narcotics arrests in their past. Genovese, Bonanno, Miranda, and Vincent Rao were viewed by investigators as major narcotics violators, although they didn't have any drug arrests at the time of the conclave.

Crosswell and his colleagues, while suspicious of the gathering, agreed that there was insufficient evidence to charge anybody with anything. It turned out to be a number of Italian-American men, all with gangland connections, coming together in one place for what was ostensibly a social gathering, a barbecue. But at a time when the Mafia was well a subject of public discussion, debate, and folklore, the meeting of the large group of men at the Barbara home triggered months and years of investigations and tons of newspaper headlines.

While the state cops couldn't find anything legally wrong with the gathering, other officials tried hard to pin something on the crowd. Genovese was called before the State Commission of Investigation, and when asked why he had attended, he said he had heard it was a social event and thought he could sell some steel, even though he had never before met Barbara. At that point, Genovese had an interest in a Long Island steel fabricating company. Genovese explained more detail about his travel to Apalachin, recalling that he had flown to Binghamton with four others, including Michael Miranda and Jerry Catena. During the drive from the airport, Genovese said the group had talked about the countryside and the weather. Once at Barbara's estate, Genovese said he had a steak sandwich.

Genovese was one of scores of witnesses called by the commission in its effort to find out what the meeting in Apalachin was all about. While investigators recognized that at least eight of the participants, including Genovese, were said to be ranking leaders of the Mafia, there wasn't enough evidence to show that the group had committed a crime in gathering at Barbara's estate.

The commission was mindful of the speculation in the press and

by the public that the true purpose of the meeting was to be an organized crime "summit" of sorts. But the investigative body, appointed to the job by Governor Averell Harriman, admitted it didn't
want to throw its weight behind any theory or speculation and essentially said it didn't know what the Barbara conclave was all
about.

But if the state commission couldn't figure out what Apalachin
was all about, federal prosecutors in New York thought they could.
They hauled Genovese and many of the other Mafiosi before a
grand jury and then, when they weren't forthcoming or were evasive about the reason why they all gathered at Apalachin, indicted
twenty-seven of them for conspiracy and perjury. They were all
convicted at the trial level, not surprising given the furor in the
media over the Mafia.

Government prosecutors reasoned that it was quite clear that the
meeting in Apalachin was planned well in advance and that the defendants had agreed to hide that fact in their answers to the grand
jury. That was the essence of the conspiracy charge. The trial judge,
Irving Kaufman, said in charging the jury that the defendants could
be convicted of conspiracy if it was shown they agreed to cover up
that a meeting took place and its purpose.

But on appeal, the U.S. Court of Appeals for the Second Circuit
saw through the government's case and determined that there simply was no proof about what the true purpose was for the meeting
and hence there could be no proven perjury or conspiracy case.

"The fact that none of those present admitted that he was asked to
attend a meeting for other than social purposes and that at least
some of those present must have lied, does not warrant a jury's con-
clusion that any or all lies were told pursuant to an agreement made
on November 14," the appeals court said. "There is nothing in the
record or in common experience to suggest that it is not just as
likely that each one present decided for himself that it would be
wiser not to discuss all that he knew."

Given the outcry nationwide about the Mafia and the Apalachin
meeting being a sinister conclave of gangsters, it made sense for the

individual defendants to decide for themselves to give as little information to the grand jury as possible without there being a big conspiracy, the appeals court ruled.

"In the face of such a hue and cry, it is just as reasonable to suppose that each one present would of his own volition decide that the less he said about Apalachin, and the more innocent his statements made the occasion to be, the better for him," the judges concluded.

The three-judge appellate panel unanimously threw out the convictions, with one member of the court, Judge Charles Edward Clark, noting that in all the years of investigation not a shred of legal evidence emerged to show that the Apalachin meeting was for an illegal purpose. Clark also took a shot at Trooper Crosswell, noting that he was like the fictional Inspector Javert as he had tried without success for thirteen years prior to the barbecue to make a case against Barbara. Crosswell may have gotten wind that a meeting was happening, but aside from innuendo, the only thing certain was the bizarre nature of the gathering, said Clark.

"But that gets us nowhere; common experience does not suggest that plotting to commit crime is done in convention assembled," Clark noted.

The law, once again, came down in favor of Genovese and his other Mafia cohorts. They were freed from the yoke of a federal conviction. It was a stunning blow to the federal government and its nascent efforts to go after the Mafia.

Although Genovese was again able to dodge a legal bullet by not being charged in the federal case, his stature had taken a hit over the Apalachin debacle. Some of the nation's major crime bosses had been humiliated in the crazy frenzy to get away from the police roadblock. Their names, criminal records, and their associates' names would be bandied about in the newspapers, books, and television programs for years. Besides the loss of face and anger, the Mafiosi were now on the radar of the FBI, even if its director, J. Edgar Hoover resisted believing in the Mafia's existence. If Genovese had called for the meeting to push himself as a big boss, justify the Anastasia hit, or set Mafia policy in areas like drugs, he was the easy scapegoat for all of the problems the summit caused.

An indication of how deep the resentment was over the failure of Apalachin surfaced a few years later when Chicago crime boss Sam Giancana was overheard on a wiretap berating Buffalo Mafioso Stefano Maggadino for helping organize the meeting at Barbara's estate.

"Well, I hope you are satisfied," Giancana pointedly said to Maggadino. "Sixty-three of our top guys made by the cops."

"I gotta admit you were right," replied Maggadino. "It would have never happened in your place."

"You're fucking right it wouldn't," Giancana said angrily. "This is the safest territory in the world for a big meet. We would have scattered you guys in my motels. We would have given you guys different cars from my auto agencies, and then we would have had the meet in one of my big restaurants. The cops don't bother us here."

Giancana had a point. The Apalachin venue, in a small-town setting, was too susceptible to attracting attention. The earlier pre-summit at the Boiardo estate in New Jersey had worked perfectly. In the end, Genovese had proved too trusting of the judgment of others. He only had to look back a few weeks to recall how smoothly the Boiardo conclave went. As Valachi would later recall, Genovese had thought about holding things in Giancana's territory but was persuaded to have it at the home of Barbara, an old friend of Maggadino, in an effort to avoid big-city police investigators. Well, that certainly didn't work out well.

Chapter Twenty

WHAT THE WORLD CAME TO KNOW about the agenda for the meeting at Apalachin has been the product of a collection of conjectures and drips and drabs from people like Valachi, who was not present but had become an acolyte of Vito Genovese. Nothing is very certain, but the meeting agenda was assumed by many in law enforcement to have been set by Genovese, and apart from his making his pitch to be the preeminent boss of the Mafia, he probably also included a warning that the bosses get out of the drug business.

"All the rackets, particularly narcotics, were to be regulated from the top," said Renee Buse in the book *The Deadly Silence*, the story of the FBN's offensive against the heroin racket of the mob. "All illegal activity must bear the approval of 'The Right Man.' Any hood who might decide to swing a deal on his own would have his head blown off. No man could operate outside the syndicate and the syndicate could operate only under the dictatorial direction of its overlord."

The overlord according to the FBN, was "the Right Man," Genovese. While the popular myth was that the Mafiosi didn't want to deal in narcotics, that was largely fiction. For decades, the mob had been dealing in drugs, and the situation had deep roots in the Mafia's international connections, which the FBN in the 1950s was trying to target. It would prove to be a major undertaking.

After World War Two ended, heroin smuggling began to grow in

Europe, mainly with the Italian Mafia organizations, which teamed up with the laboratories in Marseille, France, that were run by Corsican criminals and were well equipped to process the opium from places like Turkey. Italian Mafiosi were then able to smuggle the heroin product abroad. After his deportation to Italy, Luciano was able to get involved in the heroin operations and was considered by both Italian and U.S. officials to have become a major drug trafficker, despite his pleas to the contrary. The developments became a major focus of the FBN, particularly for legendary investigators like Charles "Charlie Cigars" Siragusa, Tom Tripodi, and the agency's iconoclastic leader, Harry J. Anslinger.

At least in the early phase, the FBN was focusing on Albert Anastasia as a major trafficker. As far back as 1951, when Anastasia was a feared killer but not yet boss of his own family, federal agents were focusing on him as a possible conduit for heroin from Italy. Luciano still remained the big prize, but according to FBN records, Anastasia was suspected of smuggling wholesale lots of heroin from Italy to the U.S. through a suspect known as Joseph Pici. This information had been developed as part of a probe into Luciano and other members of his Italian-based crime group.

Siragusa, who earned his nickname for the ubiquitous cigars he always had with him, learned of Anastasia's possible connection during a coffee shop meeting in Genoa with an informant who had his own criminal record as a notorious black marketeer dealing in smuggled cigarettes. According to a letter Siragusa sent to an investigator for the U.S. Senate, the informant told Siragusa that a seaman named Gino on a vessel in the port was carrying a thirty-pound load of heroin from Pici for delivery to Anastasia in New York. But Anastasia got spooked at the last minute, saying things were dangerous in the States, and he told Pici not to make the shipment.

"It is probable that Anastasia probably was referring to the recent commotion caused by the Senator Kefauver Senate Crime Investigation Committee; that Gino the Italian seaman has been a narcotics smuggling courier for Joseph Pici during the past year," Siragusa stated. A short time later, Siragusa returned from his overseas posting in Italy and the drug investigation into Anastasia didn't develop enough information to indict him, although when he was killed in 1957, there was a news report out of Paris that implicated him in a drug deal there.

While Anastasia did raise suspicions about heroin trafficking, federal and Italian investigators had other targets that proved to be just as high-value and important. Top of the list was Luciano, who was well positioned to exploit the trafficking situation in Italy, where for years heroin was not considered an illegal substance. According to a report by a committee of the Italian Parliament, the years between 1953 and 1958 saw a great expansion in drug smuggling activity to a point of a dangerous "mania." One French-Corsican group had at least twenty-two boats plying the coast from Savona to Palermo in order to connect with major Sicilian Mafia groups. The period proved to be a dangerous one, with numerous killings and shootings marking the activity.

Luciano avoided being involved in this fractious period of smuggling but kept ties to the native Italian group and built financial ties with them, according to the parliamentary report. But by October 1957, just days before the assassination of Anastasia and a few weeks before the Apalachin summit, a group of American and Italian Mafiosi met in Palermo in what would turn out to be another critical meeting, this one to decide the future of the heroin trade.

The Hotel della Palma, also known as the Hotel des Palma, has remained one of Palermo's more opulent destinations. With its private conference rooms and splendor, the hotel was the appropriate setting for what investigators said turned out to be a five-day Mafia parlay. Among those spotted by police at the hotel were Luciano, Joseph Bonanno, his uncle Joseph Bonventre, Carmine Galante, Frank Garofalo, and John di Bella. Rounding out the list were Giuseppe Genco Russo and Gaspare Magaddino, two top Sicilian Mafiosi, as well as Vito Vitale, said by investigators to be a liaison between the Americans and the combination of Corsican and Sicilian drug traffickers. Vito Genovese, fresh from engineering the Anastasia murder and preparing for his own summit in Apalachin, was not in attendance.

Also present, according to police, was a shadowy Italian businessman named Santo Sorge, who spent his time between New York and Italy running a number of businesses. Sorge, while not necessarily a Mafioso, was deemed important enough that the conference didn't get underway until he arrived in Palermo on October 12, 1957, an Italian court would later find.

The main objective of the Palermo summit was to create a drug smuggling organization involving the Americans and Sicilians, define their various roles, assure channels for processing payments, and make sure there was a mechanism to settle disputes, parliamentary investigators would later reveal. Heroin smuggling was to take on a more international operation by including the Americans.

After Palermo, things didn't happen quickly. But in the United States, the FBN was primed for making cases, and under the direction of Anslinger, Siragusa, and others started watching the trafficking and gathering evidence. A number of smuggling routes into the Western Hemisphere had emerged, and they included Canada and the Caribbean. In the U.S., local Mafia families in New York became involved, and it was then that the FBN decided to focus on major players like Genovese, who had long been suspected of being involved but had kept himself apart from such legal trouble.

By the time of the Apalachin conclave, the FBN had put together information on major narcotics traffickers in what became known as *The Mafia Book*, a lengthy compendium of United States–based Mafiosi that included biographical details, summaries of their criminal records and business interests, and where they ranked in terms of importance in terms of narcotics and their dangerousness. The book was later published for the public by HarperCollins Publishers in 2007.

Vito Genovese was among those listed in *The Mafia Book*. Don Vitone was noted as being a "financial backer for international narcotics smuggling" and the "reputed head of the N.Y.C. rackets." There were plenty of other Apalachin gangsters listed, including Russell Bufalino, Joseph Bonanno, and Carlo Gambino. But among the FBN leaders, Genovese had emerged as a major target and a key to destroying the Mafia's drug connection.

"Genovese is the most important man in the mob and our prime target," George Gaffney, the FBN's district supervisor in New York stated. "Every government agency's been after him, but for forty years he's been thumbing his nose at all of us. Our intelligence on him is very extensive and goes back for years, but to build a case against him is a different matter."

Part of the problem was the fact that Genovese had never been concretely tied to any narcotics trafficking. Allegations are quickly and easily made in law enforcement, but proving them in court is another matter. Anna Genovese had raised numerous claims about her spouse in the matrimonial case years earlier, but nothing had ever come of them. Genovese claimed to be just a poor wage slob, living in a rented house in Atlantic Highlands.

The Mafia myth of no involvement in narcotics was about to be exposed for the sham it was as Gaffney's unit began to focus not only on Genovese but also on a number of his top Mafioso cohorts. There was garment trucker Natale Evola, who along with others was finally cleared of federal conspiracy charges stemming from Apalachin when a federal appeals court threw out the convictions. Other big names were John Ormento, the portly Long Island gangster, and the very unstable and vicious Carmine Galante. Another garment industry name being watched was Benjamin Levine, who had become extremely wealthy from the clothing business, as did Lucchese crime family member Andimo Pappadio. From the depths of Little Italy was Joseph "Joe Beck" DiPalermo, one of the three DiPalermo brothers who seemed not to have legitimate jobs but were constantly being tied to the narcotics business. The list of characters was extensive, and for that reason the work to build a case against them—even some of them—would be daunting.

Chapter Twenty-one

THE LIFE THAT LAY AHEAD for Nelson Silva Cantellops seemed from the outset to be one destined for ordinary obscurity. Born in San Juan, Puerto Rico, in June 1924, Cantellops, whose name has been likened to that of a musk melon, started school at the age of 6, later entered a vocational school where he learned a bit about carpentry and farming, and finally was placed in high school, which gave him a grounding in business skills. A year of college followed, and then Cantellops went into the U.S. Army from 1945 to 1946, and by the time he was discharged, he went back to business school for a while.

In short, Cantellops seemed destined for nothing special as a young man, and it showed. At least, nothing special in Puerto Rico aside from managing the Old Colony Canteen, which he did for about nine months and then tried running a gambling concession before he decided to travel to the United States with a few thousand dollars in his pocket. After a short stay in Chicago, where he quit a restaurant job after a few days, Cantellops traveled to New York City, the Bronx specifically, where he took up with a woman named Elena, one of several relationships he would cultivate over the years—including a marriage—in which he would father seven children and adopt one.

Cantellops was one of those rolling stones who would travel from place to place and woman to woman. His existence didn't amount to much. Criminal cases were certain to follow, and they did. In New Jersey in the early 1950s, Cantellops was convicted in a swindle in which immigrant job seekers were defrauded of money paid for what they believed would be job referrals. After he came out of prison for that scam, Cantellops got hit in New York City with a one-to-three-year sentence for attempted forgery, although he only served about six months. He also got hit with an eight-month sentence for marijuana possession. All in all, Cantellops didn't get released from a cell until about January 1955.

Once freed, Cantellops scratched around, making a living by selling stolen clothing and merchandise and working in a numbers operation in Manhattan. It was then that Cantellops's life took an auspicious turn, one that would eventually lead to the unraveling of some of the Mafia's largest heroin operations in the city and would in the process ensnare Vito Genovese in the case that would destroy his dream to be the top boss of the mob.

But Genovese wouldn't enter the picture for a while. Instead, the meeting of Cantellops and the drug dealer known as "Guayamina" occurred on a winter morning at the corner of Fifty-third Street and Ninth Avenue, the location from which they distributed heroin to various pushers. In turn, the pushers would get the product out to customers. It was an arrangement that started to make Cantellops some money and whetted his appetite for more.

Working the street business, Cantellops was really at a very low rung in the heroin trade. Guayamina wasn't much higher. They likely didn't have a sense at this point that they were at the tail end of a heroin trail that began in Turkey, moved to Marseille, then Sicily, and thence to Cuba, where porous borders and pliant customs agents let the product move on easily to Florida and other places for distribution in the United States. But it was around this time that things became unstable in Cuba with the advent of a revolutionary movement led by Fidel Castro. Although Castro wouldn't succeed in taking over Cuba for a good three years, the rebel activities were causing smugglers problems because of the need for the Havana government to be vigilant about all kinds of smuggling. For that reason, Mexico and Puerto Rico became choice transshipping places for Mafia heroin when Cuba became too problematic. The mob didn't completely abandon Cuba but needed to resort to the other venues to assure continuity.

The mob also constantly needed people willing to play a role in smuggling the dope, and the timing couldn't have been better for Cantellops, a low-level player looking to become bigger. By the summer of 1956, Cantellops had met the Mafia-connected players who would help him play a bigger role in the heroin distribution racket: Joseph DiPalermo, John Ormento, and the brothers Carmine and Ralph Polizzano. Ormento, an alumnus of Apalachin, and the Polizzano brothers were all big players in the heroin racket and had the connections to make things work. There would be others, but those men proved to be pivotal in getting Cantellops to join the racket as a courier.

Cantellops knew full well the kind of people he was getting involved with and what would happen if he ever talked to the police or screwed up. "You just disappear," he later said. Cantellops also had heard of a fellow named Genovese who was bigger than everyone else and whose job was to enforce "the rule, the law."

But Cantellops never did disappear or do anything to earn the wrath of his smuggling overseers, at least not in the early goings. By March 1955, Cantellops began making trips as a drug courier, with his first being to Las Vegas, where he met another courier at the famed Golden Nugget Casino, picked up a shipment of heroin, and then traveled to Los Angeles for the trip back to New York. The trip netted Cantellops $1,000, pretty good money for those days.

Another trip he made with a fellow known only as "the Mexican" showed how the network had been set up to exploit the Caribbean connection. The trip, for which Cantellops would earn $1,500, was initially to Miami. He traveled with the Mexican, who, about a day after they arrived, traveled to Havana on an overnight trip. After the Mexican returned, both he and Cantellops drove to Pompano Beach, where at a motel they picked up two pieces of cheap luggage and then drove back to Miami. Once back in Miami, Cantellops took the luggage and boarded a bus for New York with at least twenty pounds of heroin in tow. After arriving back in Manhattan, Cantellops took the luggage to a room he had rented in East Harlem. Then others in the drug operation showed up to take care of the product.

Cantellops made a number of trips to Miami, and each time was told it was always possible that he might have to go to Cuba to pick up the heroin. In most of the cases, Cantellops drove from Miami with Carmine Polizzano to Key West, where the drug connections were made, after which Cantellops went back to New York. By the fall of 1956, because of the fomenting Cuban Revolution, it became difficult to supply the drugs from Cuba using Key West as a transit point. Joseph DiPalermo and a woman named Jean Capece even went to Cuba during the period, but they apparently were unable to work things out and raised suspicion upon their return to the United States when Capece was found by customs agents to be attempting to bring in $9,000 in consecutively numbered $100 bills in her bra. The network began to then consider Mexico as a route.

But Cantellops was fearful of using Mexico as a smuggling route because he thought the authorities there would arrest him, and he came up with the idea of using the Island of Vieques, or Isla de Vieques, some thirteen miles off Puerto Rico's east coast, as an alternative route. In November 1956, when Cuba was becoming more untenable for importing heroin, Ormento and Carmine Galante, a member of Joseph Bonanno's crime family, took Cantellops up on his suggestion of Vieques. The resulting plan involved a series of clandestine meetings and sailboat trips around the Caribbean that were worthy of a cheap spy novel plot. After arriving in San Juan, Cantellops met in the city of Rio Piedras with an intermediary who gave him some money for the drugs. After being paid, Cantellops went to a town on Puerto Rico's coast, hired a small launch, and crossed the channel to Vieques.

Tourist bureaus say Vieques, some fifty-two square miles in size, is one of those quiet, lush, uncrowded spots of natural beauty. Even

as of this writing, the island, which was once a U.S. Navy ammunition depot and training area, is touted as being filled with undevel-
oped beaches, where one can experience "tropical bliss," so much
so that visitors risked being "spoiled for life." But, Cantellops didn't
have time to play tourist or enjoy the scenery. He spent the night
after his arrival in a boarding house on the island and the next morning went to the harbor on the eastern end of Vieques and looked for
a particular boat and its skipper. A problem developed when the description of Cantellops the boat pilot had didn't match the person he
was looking at. Actually, it was only the height that was off, but the
mariner, who went by the name "Perez," still demurred and remained suspicious.

"You have to come with me to San Juan and see the boss because
I didn't come here just for nothing," said an exasperated Cantellops.

Somehow the fact that Cantellops was willing to take the mariner
back to San Juan impressed him enough that he relented.

"Well, I could be wrong, so, anyhow, I am going to trust you," the
skipper said and handed Cantellops the package of nine pounds of
heroin, which was wrapped in sturdy, waterproof marine canvas.
Catching the next launch back to San Juan, Cantellops rented three
rooms, the better to avoid being noticed by staying too long in one
place. Next, Cantellops went to a hardware store and bought some
waterproof wrapping paper and gift-wrapping paper and Scotch
tape. Back at his room, Cantellops opened the canvas luggage he
had received from the boat captain on Vieques and repackaged the
heroin into three packages, which he mailed over the course of two
days back to the General Post Office in Manhattan on Thirty-fourth
Street.

Sending drugs through the mail can be suicidal for a smuggler.
But in the case of the Vieques load, everything went according to
plan. Back in New York, Carmine Polizzano told Cantellops that the
mailed shipments had arrived, and he took him to see Ormento, who
paid him several hundred dollars. For a tip after a smuggling trip,
Cantellops would also be given an ounce of heroin, which if he
wanted to he could sell on the street.

Through 1956 and even into 1957, Cantellops was also involved in various other shipments that he picked up in Chicago, Philadelphia, and elsewhere. In one trip to Cleveland, Vincent Gigante, Genovese's driver and the man he would later hire to do the abortive hit on Costello, drove Cantellops, and along the way he dropped an interesting tidbit on the lowly courier: Ormento would try to introduce him to somebody very important, somebody known as "the Right Man," Vito Genovese.

Cantellops had only a passing familiarity with Genovese, although he knew from his reputation that he was a very big and powerful man in the syndicate. But over at FBN headquarters in New York, Genovese was the big fish, the biggest of targets all the investigators were angling for. But a man of Genovese's stature would not be an easy target. Undercover agents were able to penetrate a drug operation only so far, and often police needed to get someone to cooperate—a snitch, a rat. It was FBN agent Anthony Consoli who got the break.

According to the account in the book *The Deadly Silence* by Renee Buse, Consoli picked up an addict one day who admitted that he got his heroin from Cantellops, someone Consoli wasn't familiar with but whose name became a crucial lead. But in the early going, the addict couldn't identify Cantellops from any mug shots and didn't know anything about his family or his address. The deals the addict had with Cantellops were always furtive purchases where drugs were quickly passed in exchange for money.

Consoli's plan was to try and find this man named Cantellops and perhaps convince him to cooperate regarding others who were higher up the chain of command in the drug network. It was classic tradecraft for a narcotics agent, and sometimes it worked. Other times it failed. But within a couple of weeks of Consoli finding the addict, the druggie reported that Cantellops had indeed been arrested by the NYPD on a narcotics possession charge. This would have been sometime after September 1956.

Consoli visited Cantellops in the city jail known as the Tombs down on Centre Street. But the meetings, at least in these early goings, were fruitless. Consoli remembered that Cantellops kind of rambled but when asked a direct question clammed up and stayed silent, according to Buse. The lowly Puerto Rican drug dealer thought he had good reason to stay silent. Ormento, DiPalermo, and others in the drug network had promised him that if he ever got arrested, things would be taken care of: lawyers secured, money for bail raised, and his family's needs seen to. But as time went on, none of those promises were kept.

"You know as well as I do, Nelson," said Consoli, "that the mob's letting you go down the drain. No lawyers, no bail, nobody cares what happens to you. You can go to jail for the rest of your life and they won't raise a finger to help you."

To underscore the trouble he was in, when Cantellops went to trial on the state case, no defense attorneys showed up. The court appointed counsel, but he pleaded guilty anyway and got a four-year prison sentence, to be served in Sing Sing. It was then that Consoli and the others at the FBN made their move and got Cantellops transferred to an upstate county jail with a special legal writ for the purposes of getting him to testify to the agents back in Manhattan.

The interrogation of Cantellops took time and patience. Consoli and the other agents walked him through numerous transactions and trips, piecing together scenarios and constructing a schematic of the network from the middle-level managers to the big operatives like DiPalermo, Ormento, Galente, and others. Cantellops illuminated how the drug operation in June 1956 planned to supply him with narcotics to expand into the Spanish-speaking market. It was during one of those planning meetings, said Cantellops, that he first caught a glimpse of Genovese talking to Carmine Polizzano on East Fourth Street in Manhattan. Thinking nothing of it, Cantellops said he approached the two men, but he was told in no uncertain terms by Polizzano never to disturb him when he was talking to "the Right Man," a reference to Genovese. By itself, the chance spotting of Genovese with the drug-dealing Polizzano proved nothing. But it was a tiny piece of the puzzle the federal agents were trying to finish in order to get Genovese.

The plan to expand the operation was discussed a number of times, including once in October 1955 when Cantellops said he was asked to explore the Spanish policy banks on the Lower East Side of Manhattan for use as possible fronts for narcotics distribution points. Taking over the locations, which were based mainly around Eldridge Street, would take an investment of between $100,000 to $150,000, said Cantellops. Such an outlay would be a substantial investment, and for that, said Ormento, the group needed to get the approval of the Right Man. It was actually during that meeting that Cantellops told his bosses that because of the turmoil in Cuba, the Island of Vieques might be a good distribution point.

Cantellops proved to be a goldmine of information for the agents and prosecutors, including Assistant U.S. Attorney William Tendy, who headed the narcotics unit for the Manhattan U.S. attorney's office. When he was a high school dropout growing up in East Harlem and the Bronx, Tendy had seen a great deal of drug dealing and knew what heroin could do to the addicts ensnared in its grip. But unlike others in his environment, Tendy finally straightened out and flew right. He graduated college, attended Fordham Law School, where he earned his Juris Doctor degree, and in 1954, began life as an attorney in private practice. In 1956, Tendy became an assistant U.S. attorney in Manhattan and took on the job of coordinating the office's narcotics squad, the so-called junk squad because of its heavy concentration on heroin cases.

By 1957, with Cantellops on board as a cooperating witness, Tendy's unit began to sculpt a criminal case. But relying on one witness is sometimes dangerous for prosecutors. Corroboration was needed, and in the case of Cantellops, there were many things he had claimed to have done for the syndicate that needed to be verified as best they could be. He had also made claims about meeting Genovese, whom he placed in important meetings with other conspirators. So, at the very basic level, it was important to show that

Genovese knew Cantellops, otherwise the case would be difficult to prosecute.

It fell to FBN agents James Hunt and Francis E. Waters to surveil Cantellops when he was brought before Genovese by another gangster in an East Side German restaurant. During his time in Europe, Genovese had developed a fondness for German food, which he acquired, according to his wife, from visits to Germany in the period around World War Two. Cantellops was able to attend the meeting because he had not yet been arrested in 1957 for drugs. Hunt and Waters, while seated at the bar, overheard Genovese say that Cantellops was "all right." It was a single remark, and years later, critics of the government would say it was a very slim reed on which to build a criminal case. But, according to Hunt's son, also named James, who went on in later years to lead the Drug Enforcement Administration office in New York, his father recounted the story to him and also would later testify about it in court.

While some criticized the FBN and federal prosecutors for using Cantellops as the only substantial witness, a number of federal judges would agree that there were a number of other men, all involved with someone in the drug ring, who directly or circumstantially corroborated what Cantellops himself had told investigators. The time was right for the federal government to bring the case against Vito Genovese, "the Right Man," and the others to an indictment.

Throughout 1958, Genovese became aware that the FBN was closing in and had a major case brewing against him and some of the big names in the Mafia for heroin trafficking. Genovese had a big bull's-eye on his back, and he knew it, particularly since he had already been called before a federal grand jury. So, in early July 1958, he clammed up when he was called before the U.S. Senate to testify before a select committee probing illegal and improper activities in labor relations and certain industries, notably the garment industry, where Genovese had a presence and power. The hearings were chaired by Senator John L. McClellan, a Democrat from Arkansas, and had among its members Senator John F. Kennedy of

Massachusetts and as its counsel Kennedy's brother, Robert F. Kennedy.

In announcing the hearings, McClellan said that Genovese was "probably the most important witness to be called" and portrayed him as the king of crime, reciting his history of arrests, his time in Italy working with the U.S. Army, and his various associates such as Costello, Luciano, and the late Anastasia. Other Mafioso witnesses subpoenaed included Mike Miranda, James Plumeri, and Thomas Lucchese, as well as garment-trucking boss Abe Chait. To make the hearings more of a draw for the news media, McClellan noted that some of those subpoenaed had attended the Apalachin get-together a year earlier.

Genovese appeared in the Washington, DC, hearing room on July 2, 1958, along with attorney Wilfred Davis, and if McClellan expected him to give them details of any sort—aside from his name—he was very much mistaken. In answer to over 150 questions put to him, Genovese invoked the Fifth Amendment privilege against self-incrimination, even when asked to confirm his birth date or whether he was a citizen—which at that point he was not because he had been denaturalized a few years earlier by a federal judge.

When asked about the Boccia murder, his business interests, whether he owned safe-deposit boxes, and various claims made by his wife Anna about his wealth, Genovese gave the same monotonous answer: "I respectfully decline to answer on the ground the answer may tend to incriminate me."

The committee had also called Natale Laurendi, an NYPD detective who was assigned to the Manhattan district attorney's office, who testified that the office believed Genovese was worth about $30 million. Laurendi also raised the 1943 murder of Carlo Tresca, noting that investigators had received information from a source close to Genovese that the anti-Fascist editor had been critical of Genovese, but he stopped short of saying the mobster had ordered the murder.

Getting nothing from either Genovese's or Miranda's testimony, a frustrated McClellan said that both men were despicable and that their refusal to cooperate had dishonored those who had sacrificed their lives for the freedom of American society. But that was grandstanding by McClellan. Genovese knew very well that he had more to worry about than being called unpatriotic.

Chapter Twenty-two

IT WAS ON JULY 5, 1958, AT ABOUT 8:00 P.M., five days after he appeared and didn't answer questions on Capitol Hill, that Vito Genovese was arrested by agents of the FBN at his rented home at 68 West Highlands Avenue in Atlantic Highlands. The arrest, as they say in cop parlance, was without incident, and Genovese had time to dress in a conservative gray suit with matching accessories. He was taken into Manhattan by agents and awaited arraignment.

By the time he got to court on July 8, Genovese learned the full extent of the case and how many others were charged with him after Judge William B. Herlands unsealed the indictment. It was a large narcotics case, with a total of thirty-nine defendants named, including the DiPalermo and Polizzano brothers and the garment district business powers Natale Evola, Benjamin Levine, and Andimo Pappadio, as well as mobsters John Ormento and Carmine Galante. A host of lesser names were also in the indictment. But one more important additional defendant turned out to be Vincent Gigante, the loyal driver of Genovese and suspected shooter of Frank Costello.

In court, Manhattan U.S. Attorney Paul W. Williams said that Genovese was the controlling force behind the drug conspiracy and that his associates called him "the Right Man," as an indication of his stature and importance to the group. Gigante, who unlike Genovese appeared in court in rumpled clothing that fit poorly on his bulky figure, was described by Williams as being Genovese's "protégé . . . a rising star in the underworld and the number-one boy of this man Genovese."

Genovese and Gigante made different impressions to court spectators. The well-dressed Genovese seemed placid as he sat behind horn-rimmed glasses. Gigante, looking as if he had slept in his clothes, which he likely had, seemed like a hulky dimwit, with his mouth drooping half-opened as he listened to the proceedings. This being the 1950s, bail conditions had to be set, and Williams asked for high amounts for the time: some $50,000 for Genovese and $35,000 for Gigante.

Genovese's attorney, Wilfred Davis, said that Williams's portrayal of Genovese was "grossly inaccurate" and that his 60-year-old client was a family man and a small businessman who paid his taxes and lived a quiet family life in New Jersey. Genovese's business was with Erb Strapping, the dockland consolidator and repacking operation, said Davis. But Judge Herlands wasn't moved and kept Genovese's bail at $50,000. Gigante didn't have a prayer he would getting his bail lowered, so his attorney didn't try. But both men were able to post the required bonds and walked out of the courthouse shortly after noon on July 8. Genovese ran into a few reporters as he left the building. Of the indictment, Genovese said, "It is ridiculous, it is not even funny."

From the looks of it, the indictment certainly wasn't anything amusing. It charged that Genovese and the others had conspired over a three-year period beginning in February 1955 to import heroin into the United States through Cuba, Puerto Rico, Mexico, and other countries. A federal official later estimated the amount of drugs moved by the syndicate to be around 100 kilos, or 220 pounds. The plot, according to the indictment, ran right up until the date of the indictment and involved numerous actions by various defendants. But while Genovese was named as a conspirator—and the main one according to prosecutors—he wasn't listed in any of the so-called overt acts involved in the conspiracy. Genovese had been smart enough to keep himself away from handling drugs. But, if Cantellops was to be believed, Genovese was the person who had given approval, not only for his involvement but also for the overall plans to expand the operation into the Spanish-speaking neighborhoods.

The indictment not only signaled legal trouble for Genovese but also created problems for him in the mob. He now had to focus on the criminal case, and in the world of organized crime, when a boss has to spend time thinking about pressing legal matters, his attention to and control over the crime family becomes challenged. In the back of Genovese's mind and those of his street captains, soldiers, and associates was the thought about what would happen to his status as a boss should the worse happen and he be convicted. But, at that point, such things were in the future, and because Genovese was out on bail, he had the ability to meet with his lawyers and plan his legal strategy.

However, it soon became apparent that things were unstable in the mob right after the indictments hit. This became clear on the evening of July 18, 1958, a little over a week after the Genovese indictment, when Cristoforo Rubino, a 38-year-old heroin trafficker who was well connected in the international smuggling business, met his untimely end as he talked with an associate outside a Democratic Party political club in the Bushwick section of Brooklyn. A car stopped outside the club, and while the driver stayed in the vehicle, a second man got out and fired five shots. Rubino fell into the gutter with a bullet in his head and one in his shoulder. Rubino's associate suffered a graze wound on his chin.

As it turned out, Rubino had been on the radar of law enforcement for a long time and was considered a major link to Luciano in Italy. But after a two-year exile in Europe, where he had fled after being indicted in the United States, Rubino had decided to return, and after getting bail, he was preparing to talk about all his contacts in the U.S., including Genovese.

"Rubino was Luciano's courier and high up in the dope racket," Assistant U.S. Attorney Joseph F. Soverio Jr. announced after the killing. "We expected him to give us all the necessary information on the New York narcotics activity."

Soverio went on to explain that Rubino was scheduled to testify to a federal grand jury the week he died. His testimony was expected to help build the government's case against the newly indicted Genovese, the prosecutor added.

It remained unclear just what information Rubino had to tell the government. Luciano had long been considered a major smuggler of heroin from Europe to the U.S., and it would have fit into the prosecution's theory about the international ties charged in the Genovese indictment. After all, the European heroin had been funneled for years from Europe to Cuba in the days of the Batista regime, and Rubino might have been able to provide information about any such links to the New York conspiracy. But Rubino took anything he knew to the grave.

The killing of Rubino played into the reputation Genovese had of seeing witnesses against him disappear or die, such as happened in the Boccia murder prosecution. But, while it was never shown that Genovese had any connection to the Rubino hit, it really didn't matter because Cantellops, the key witness in the Genovese case, was under the government's protection.

As the conspiracy trial got closer, some of Genovese's codefendants were fugitives. The most important was Ormento, who fled the scene about a month before the big roundup when a smaller drug case against him was announced. Ormento didn't go very far, leaving his Lido Beach home on Long Island for an apartment in the Bronx with his pal Nick Tolentino, another drug suspect. Another gangster who fled was Galante, who traveled clandestinely to a ranch house on Pelican Island, off the coast of New Jersey near Toms River.

Genovese, out on a hefty bail package he didn't want to forfeit, stayed at his home in Atlantic Highlands, playing the role of the quiet neighbor and father. It was at the house on the evening of Saturday, December 6, 1958, at about 8:00 P.M. that Genovese answered a telephone call that would prove to be one of the most bizarre events in the case, and one that only added fuel to the notion that Genovese was being set up by the government to be the fall guy on a weak case. The caller, Genovese would remember, identified himself as "Begendorf," a man who said he had once worked for the FBN and had met the mobster at his office on Thompson Street about two years earlier. The caller, whose full name would turn out to be Benjamin Robert Begendorf, told Genovese that he wanted to meet him at his Atlantic Highlands home to discuss "certain matters."

Facing a large criminal case and being a major crime boss, Genovese was not about to agree to meet a stranger in his house. But Begendorf was insistent about seeing Genovese and told him he was stopping by in an hour. Fearful now and unable to reach his attorney on such short notice, Genovese called his daughter Nancy, who lived next door and asked her to come over. He also called a woman neighbor as an extra witness for whatever happened.

Begendorf rang Genovese's doorbell at about 9:00 P.M., and when the door opened, Genovese recognized the caller as a man who had visited the Thompson Street office earlier. Seeing Nancy and the neighbor, Begendorf said he wanted to talk with Genovese alone, something the mobster insisted he wouldn't do.

"There is nothing that you can talk to me about that you cannot say in the presence of my daughter and my neighbor," said Genovese.

Begendorf, while reluctant to speak in front of witnesses, finally asked Genovese a question.

"How are you doing with your case?" said Begendorf.

"I don't know," answered Genovese.

"Well, there is nothing to do, you will never hear anyone mention your name in that trial," Begendorf explained.

"Well, what do you mean?" asked Genovese.

"Well, you know what I mean," said Begendorf. "There is a lot of publicity attached to your name. You have had a lot of publicity and the U.S. Attorney wanted to get some publicity, he wanted to get the nomination and become Governor."

Begendorf was referring to the fact that Williams had resigned from his post as a Manhattan U.S. attorney the day after he announced Genovese's indictment to run for the governorship of New York State. An old associate of famed prosecutor Thomas Dewey, the 55-year-old Williams had garnered some support from Republican Party members but didn't get enough, and by August had released his delegates so they could support the candidacy of Nelson Rockefeller. In the November election, Rockefeller defeated the incumbent Averill Harriman.

Genovese said he didn't know what Begendorf was talking about. Begendorf inquired of Genovese if he was going to waive a jury trial and asked about his bail package, finally pressing him to see if he could call again next week to talk privately.

Genovese, who recalled the details of the strange meeting in an affidavit later filed with the court, seemed puzzled and troubled by what Begendorf was doing by showing up at his home. Genovese was also angry that Begendorf had gotten his private telephone number and said he was going to file a complaint with the telephone company. With that, Begendorf said that he currently worked for the U.S. Customs Service and that he had found Genovese's number through his office.

The next morning, Genovese and his attorney, Wilfred Davis, went to the federal courthouse. There Davis met with the trial judge, Alexander Bicks, and the new U.S. attorney, Arthur Christy, to brief the judge. Christy agreed to investigate what had happened and to find out who Begendorf was. The following day, Christy told the court and Genovese that Begendorf did in fact work for the Customs Service and that he had been interrogated about his visit to Genovese's home. Begendorf did admit to making the visit but denied that he had initiated any conversation as Genovese had alleged.

After the matter came to the attention of Judge Bicks, Begendorf submitted his own affidavit and indeed admitted that he had telephoned Genovese and visited him at his home. The visit and call, said Begendorf, was something he did on his own initiative and not as part of any government investigation. But he denied telling Genovese his case was a frame-up, a word not actually used in Genovese's account of the strange meeting.

"I did not say that he was framed, nor that the indictment against him was obtained for purposes of publicity or discuss with him the waiver of a jury trial," said Begendorf in his affidavit. "There are also further inaccuracies in the affidavit of Vito Genovese concerning our conversation."

Begendorf never did specify why he had decided to make the visit to Genovese and what his purpose was. The situation became more confused when one of the defense attorneys representing one of the other defendants in the narcotics case received a copy of a government memorandum that stated that Begendorf had for a time been assigned to the investigative squad involved in the narcotics investigation, contrary to an earlier claim by the government.

Genovese had always claimed that he had been framed. After the strange visit by Begendorf and the information that he had worked in the narcotics unit, Genovese's defense team believed that there should at least be a hearing with the taking of testimony to sort out where the truth lay. They apparently never did get the full-blown hearing. But evidence later surfaced, in the form of a Civil Service Commission proceeding that stated that Begendorf did say during the visit to Genovese's home the things the mob boss alleged were said. This led to Begendorf being fired.

The Civil Service Commission found that Begendorf's dismissal was justified because, in part, he discussed with Genovese "the progress of his narcotics trial, criticizing the methods of the officers who arrested Genovese and stated that the prosecution had nothing on Genovese, and that his arrest was for publicity and political effect only." Essentially, the commission believed that Begendorf did make damaging statements to Genovese and did so after he had been told by his superiors to refrain from any participation in the case against Genovese. All of that was later summarized in a federal Court of Claims decision upholding Begendorf's termination. But that was all some years in the future. Begendorf's actions were at the very least unprecedented in law enforcement and raised questions about the way the case evolved against Genovese, fueling for some the idea that he was set up. However, it did nothing to derail the imminent trial of Genovese and over a dozen of his codefendants.

Chapter Twenty-three

THE TRIAL OF VITO GENOVESE and fourteen others of his codefendants in the giant drug conspiracy case began with jury selection in early January 1959. With the trial coming so soon after the Apalachin meeting and all of the firestorm of publicity about the Mafia, defense attorneys tried to get the initial jury pool of over two hundred potential jurors tossed and to begin the selection anew. But Judge Bicks shot that request down. By January 9, a panel of seven women and five men was picked, along with four alternates, to hear the evidence in a case that was expected to go into the spring.

It was on January 12 that U.S. Attorney Arthur Christy gave the government's opening statement to the jury, the overall summary of the case and what the prosecution hoped to prove. Opening statements are not evidence, but they do give both sides a chance to sketch out the evidence and indicate how the opponent's proof might fail. The big drawing card to the case was Genovese, and that is where Christy started, at the top of the conspiracy pyramid.

"Among the executives in the conspiracy, and by that we mean those who had a hand in the policy and strategy, were men like Vito Genovese and Benjamin Levine," said Christy, the latter being one of the defendants whose case was severed from the trial but who was alleged to be a major financier of the operation.

"These men moved out of the shadows at those moments when their presence was necessary for some decision or other, and, as in any organization or business, the men at the higher echelons, of course, seldom have much direct contact, much contact with the people who perform the actual work," explained Christy.

The next level of conspirators included those who participated in the planning and ordered deliveries of narcotics to be made, and Christy named them: Natale Evola, Rocco Mazzie, Joseph Di-Palermo, and Carmine Polizzano. Two other names were mentioned, John Ormento and Carmine Galante, but they weren't on trial because they had fled around the time the indictment was unsealed. Joseph's brother Charles DiPalermo was named as one of the men who would watch the couriers to make sure none of them went astray, a job Carmine Polizzano also performed.

Christy threw all of the other defendants into the mix as well, naming Vincent Gigante as an overall gofer and Jean Capece, the woman who got caught bringing greenbacks into the United States in her bra, as someone who assisted Joseph DiPalermo.

The jury got a taste of the scope of the drug operation when Christy described how they made their pickups of heroin in Florida, Las Vegas, Cleveland, and Puerto Rico. The prosecutor alluded to only one specific allegation about Genovese: that he was present during a key strategy meeting of the group in the Bronx back in September 1956. This would be crucial evidence that Cantellops would relate when it came to his turn to testify. But Christy never mentioned Cantellops's name to the jury in his opening; the panel would learn about him soon enough.

As opening statements went, Christy's was fairly straightforward and staid. Christy was prep school educated and attended Yale before joining the navy in World War Two to become a commander. He stayed away from the fire and brimstone and self-righteous posturing common with government attorneys. He had a pastime as a carver of scrimshander, a patient pastime involving the whittling of whale teeth and wood, which he engraved and gave to friends as gifts. Christy and the other trial attorneys for the government were up against some veterans of the criminal defense bar who thrived on being tough with government cooperating witnesses and weren't easily intimidated.

But the Genovese case wasn't Christy's first big rodeo. He had prosecuted Frank Costello in 1953 in the gangster's contempt of Congress case, winning a conviction. Christy rose steadily through the ranks, leading the office's criminal division, becoming chief assistant, and in 1958, after Williams left to run for governor, being appointed as a United States attorney.

For such an important case, the trial in its early going didn't generate a great deal of newspaper and media attention. Part of that may be because much of the initial testimony revolved around information from cops and drug agents, as well as cooperating witnesses, about drug purchases and search warrant executions. It was pretty dry stuff for the most part, dealing with smaller pieces of the mosaic that prosecutors were trying to assemble to implicate Genovese and the others.

Cantellops finally took the witness stand on January 22 for his direct examination. Initially, Cantellops went through a short series of questions to see if he was a mentally competent witness to testify, something Judge Bicks found that he was. Christy and the other prosecutors then took turns walking him through the details of his troubled and unremarkable life, from his birth in Puerto Rico to his various run-ins with the law. Prosecutors often would bring out the worst in their cooperating witnesses as a way of preempting the defense attorneys or to at least try to blunt the unsavory aspects of the witnesses' lives. Cantellops readily admitted that he got into trouble with the labor scam in New Jersey and the forgery case in New York. He then described his first links to narcotics smuggling with Guayamina, and from there prosecutors tried to inch the case closer to Genovese and some of the other defendants.

One critical episode recounted by Cantellops involved the German restaurant meeting where he said Ormento presented him to Genovese, who was overheard by FBN agents saying that Cantellops was "all right" for working with the heroin ring. It was a rather slim reed in the government's proof since it relied almost completely on Cantellops's version of what was said by Ormento as a preface to the meeting and the testimony from the two agents about what they overheard Genovese say in the busy restaurant.

But the next time Cantellops testified about Genovese, he claimed to have more details that showed the mob boss actually taking part in a meeting that had more substance to the conspiracy. As Cantellops recalled, it was at the end of August or early September 1956 that he attended a meeting at the Bronx home of Rocco Mazzie, one of the others in the drug gang. It was early evening when Cantellops said he drove to the same German restaurant with Ormento, Evola, Galante, and Pappadio. In terms of the company Cantellops was keeping at that moment, the lowly Puerto Rican was with some heavy hitters. Ormento was one of the Mafia's major drug dealers for years, as was Galante. Evola and Pappadio were powers in the garment industry and controlled trucking and manufacturing combinations. Evola in particular was a close friend of crime boss Joseph Bonanno and had earned the moniker "Joe Diamond" when serving as an usher at Bonanno's wedding; the groom had lost the diamond ring he was to give his wife, only to find it in the cuff of Evola's pants.

Ormento then made a telephone call, and the group of four drove to the West Side Highway, where they met another car. Cantellops said he and Ormento entered the car, which was driven by Gigante. In the backseat, said Cantellops, was Genovese. "This man is doing a good job for us, he is helping us and doing a good job for us," Ormento told Genovese, testified Cantellops. Ormento then told Cantellops that Genovese was in fact "the Right Man."

According to Cantellops's testimony, it was then that Genovese told him that they were all going to a meeting to discuss territorial issues in the drug business and that he, Cantellops, could make some money by helping the syndicate. That someone of Genovese's stature in the mob would talk to a lowly operative like Cantellops would strike some at the time and even years later as very improbable. But that was the testimony, and it remained a crucial part of the record.

Next, according to Cantellops, the two automobiles were driven to Mazzie's home and everyone entered except Genovese and Gigante, who remained in their car. In the meeting, Cantellops said, he, Evola, Massie, Ormento, and Pappadio talked about the distribution of narcotics in the Spanish-speaking market of the East Bronx, to be achieved by using policy banks and eliminating competition from existing drug peddlers and other policy operators. Evola and Pappadio thought the plan could work in as quickly as a month and a half.

After about twenty minutes, Genovese entered the house and asked what had been decided, and when he was told the details, he said that he had to know when to send his men—presumably for the policy operations—into the Bronx zone, testified Cantellops. Others in the group later told Cantellops that he would be the main contact man for the distribution ring, and he recalled that he did make drug deliveries in the area.

The testimony about Genovese was very incriminating, but was it plausible? Would he so openly put himself in such jeopardy by conversing with Cantellops in the presence of others? Some in law enforcement were skeptical. After all, Genovese was supposed to be the Mafia's major player in New York City, if not the nation. Why would he want to get his hands so dirty? Defense attorneys tried to cast doubt on Cantellops's testimony, but they had little to really go on. He had a criminal record, that was true, and Cantellops didn't deny it.

Other witnesses called by the government seemed to corroborate part of Cantellops's testimony about various drug deliveries. That was important circumstantial evidence for the case. But as it turned out, there was no evidence to directly or even circumstantially corroborate Cantellops's testimony about the Bronx meeting that was so incriminating for Genovese. The one bit of corroboration for the Genovese link was that of the two FBN agents, James Hunt and Francis E. Waters, about what they overheard in the German restaurant meeting.

Cantellops was on the witness stand for a total thirteen days, three on direct examination and the remainder under cross-examination. Genovese's lawyers didn't call any witnesses, although lawyers for five of his codefendants called a total of a handful of people to the stand. So, after a thirteen-week trial and a trial transcript that ran for over 6,700 pages, the case was ready for the jury. Judge Bicks read a twenty-thousand-word charge, which took about eight and a half hours, and on April 2, he ordered the panel of what finally wound up as six men and six women to begin deliberations.

Despite the length of the trial and the mountain of testimony, the jury was convinced quickly. After a day of deliberations, on Friday night, April 3, the jury convicted Genovese and fourteen others of being part of the international heroin conspiracy. The verdict was announced shortly after 10:00 P.M. in a packed courtroom. Genovese was observed giving a slight grin as the verdict was announced. Evola, Gigante, and the DiPalermo and Polizzano brothers were among those convicted. The only defendant acquitted was Louis Fiano, a 48-year-old man already serving a twenty-year sentence for an earlier drug conviction in California.

Despite protests by government attorneys, Judge Bicks allowed Genovese and four others to remain free on previously posted bail. But since he had now been convicted, Genovese had to post $100,000 on top of his previous bail amount of $50,000. Bicks gave Genovese until the following Monday to raise the amount, which he did. Unlike current practice in federal court, when there are often weeks or months between a conviction and sentencing, Genovese and the other defendants were ordered to return to court on April 17 to learn their fates.

The day of sentencing, Genovese arrived at court smartly dressed in a grey overcoat, suit, and tie. He also sported a fedora and sunglasses as well as a smile for the news photographers waiting outside the Foley Square courthouse. Inside, with a total of fifteen defendants to deal with, Judge Bicks had to spend the whole day listening to arguments about why he should be harsh or lenient. The prosecutors painted the defendants, particularly Genovese, as the worst type of criminals and called for tough sentences. The defendants, through their attorneys, asked for leniency. The betting by armchair legal experts was that Genovese faced as many as five years, possibly ten.

But when it came time to sentence Genovese, Judge Bicks hit the mob boss with fifteen years and a $20,000 fine. Asked if he had anything to say, Genovese replied, "All I can say, your honor, is that

I am innocent." Joseph DiPalermo also got the same sentence, and, like Genovese, had his bail revoked. The other defendants got sentences ranging from five to ten years.

The one thing that impressed Bicks was the amount of letters he got from the public on Gigante's behalf, something the jurist had never seen before. Gigante also had a large rooting section in the court and one the same size outside the building. Members of the clergy and even people from the Children's Aid Society wrote to the court to laud Gigante and his work against juvenile delinquency in Greenwich Village. Gigante got hit with seven years but was allowed to remain free on $50,000 bail pending an appeal, which was certain to come.

Attorneys for Genovese rushed to the appeals court and got his $150,000 bail reinstated, so he was free pending his appeal. But he faced other legal problems as the federal government moved to seize his property. Meanwhile in May, the twenty-seven men who had attended the ill-fated Apalachin meeting two years earlier were indicted on the conspiracy charge that they had agreed to lie to conceal the true nature of the conclave, a prosecution that drew a great deal of attention and later led to convictions, which were finally overturned in 1960.

Since he was a free man pending his appeal, Genovese was called in June before the State Investigation Commission, which had been tasked with looking into the Apalachin barbecue at Joseph Barbara's estate in November 1957. Although he had been convicted in the drug case, Genovese was given immunity from prosecution by the commission, and on June 16, the now 61-year-old Mafia boss told the panel that he had flown and driven to the upstate event with two of his friends, Joe Ida and Dominick Oliveto of New Jersey, because he had hoped to maybe sell Barbara some steel, as previously noted. Genovese had an interest in a Long Island steel company and thought the visit would be a good opportunity.

But as it turned out, an ailing Barbara had a heart attack. Outside the house, Genovese said he congregated around the barbecue pit for about an hour, where he had a steak sandwich and a soft drink.

The only other people he knew at the Barbara house were Michael Miranda and Jerry Catena, said Genovese. The event was his curse.

"I should have broken both my legs before I accepted that invitation," said Genovese ruefully. As a result of all the publicity and furor, Genovese said he was a target for being "framed" in the narcotics case.

"Everybody knows Vito Genovese, thanks to the press," said Genovese. "They introduced me to the world."

"He [Ida] told me we were going to a barbecue party as I took it for granted that it was a barbecue party," Genovese testified.

One of the commissioners, Goodman A. Sarachan, quizzed Genovese on why a man like Barbara, who owned a soft drink bottling plant, would be in the market for steel. Sarachan was skeptical of Genovese and told his attorney, "I certainly don't believe a lot of what he says, I tell you that very frankly."

In a strange coda to the whole Apalachin saga, just days after Genovese had testified to the commission, Joseph Barbara Sr., the supposed host of the conclave, died of a subsequent heart attack in upstate New York. He really, truly did have a chronic heart condition, something that may have been the only true thing in terms of everything that was said about that infamous summit of the mob.

Genovese had actually been named as an unindicted coconspirator in the big Apalachin case but didn't have to worry about legal troubles from it. But two of his old cronies in the drug case, John Ormento and Carmine Galante, thought they could duck their legal troubles altogether by going into hiding. They needed to run because the evidence in the Genovese case has implicated them heavily in the conspiracy. That tactic worked for a while in that their case was severed from that of Genovese for the trial, but the federal investigators just never quit.

Both Ormento and Galante were hiding in plain sight. But where? That was the question. Ormento, after leaving his Lido Beach home, settled into an apartment in the Bronx, while Galante stayed away from his Manhattan and Brooklyn haunts to hideout in the South Shore area of New Jersey. Both men assumed they could beat the cops in hide-and-seek, but chance and good detective work proved them wrong.

In the case of Ormento, rumors began to fly that he had been murdered and that Galante had fled the U.S. There was a murder that would be connected to Ormento's case, although it had actually nothing to do with him. Federal Bureau of Narcotics agents James Hunt and Martin Pera had gone to the Forty-Eighth Precinct in the Bronx to probe the murder of a 70-year-old man who had been bashed in the head with a lead pipe. The victim also happened to be an associate of Genovese, reportedly as a chemist who helped the drug operation.

Hunt and Pera showed some photographs of some reputed strong-arm men to a detective in the precinct. The supposition was that a mob goon had been hired to finish off the poor old chemist. The agents hit pay dirt. The detective recognized one of the photographs as that of Nick Tolentino, whom he had run into not long ago in a Bronx apartment building. Tolentino, it turned out, had gone into hiding after he was indicted in a different heroin ring.

On March 30, 1959, just as the Genovese trial was in its last days, the two agents went to the building at 1466 Gun Hill Road in the Bronx just before 10:00 P.M. The agents had the good fortune to run into Ormento as he happened to be coming down the stairs. It turned out Ormento had been living in a $110-a-month apartment upstairs and was heading down to see Tolentino, whose rent on the lower floor was $125 a month. Both were busted. Ormento admitted that he had occupied the third-floor apartment in the building and that it was Tolentino who had cooked all their meals. The apartment had been a prison of sorts because Ormento and Tolentino had not left the walk-up in nine months. Sometimes at night they would go up on the roof to get some fresh air and walk for an hour as exercise.

"What were you two hiding from?" Hunt asked.

"Who's hiding?" was the reply.

While Ormento and Tolentino were hiding out in cramped apartments in the Bronx, Galante had sheltered himself in the relative luxury of a private home on Pelican Island, just off a spit of land accessible by causeways from the New Jersey shoreline. Federal agents had racked their brains trying to figure out where Galante was. There were reports he was in Canada and Latin America. Telephone and mail records were checked, and his relatives were watched in the hopes that Galante might show up. Intelligence reports indicated Galante had made some trips at night to New York City proper, so it seemed logical that he was close by.

It was the evening of June 2, 1959, and two FBN agents, after tracing a telephone call to a house on Pelican Island, were in the middle of a surveillance operation when at about 10:00 P.M. they saw three men enter a white Chevrolet convertible at the house being watched. One of the men looked like Galante, so the agents followed the car in the middle of a downpour. The convertible eventually headed north on the Garden State Parkway. While the agents were able to get closer to the car, they couldn't tell for sure if it was Galante they saw in the front passenger seat. The agents called the New Jersey State Police, which sent a unit to intercept the Chevrolet at the next toll stop. As related in *The Deadly Silence* by Renee Buse, the federal agents then rolled up, took one look at Galante, and knew they had their man. The 49-year-old Galante, one of the nastiest and most dangerous of the Mafiosi in the drug business, was held on $100,000 bail and pleaded not guilty to the narcotics indictment. The two men driving in the car with him were charged with harboring a fugitive.

Why any judge would give suspects and Mafiosi like Ormento and Galante bail after they had proved so elusive is a mystery. But this was in the 1950s, and it seemed like the presumption was that even dangerous criminals should be bailed. In the case of Ormento, he apparently went back to his home on Long Island. But that didn't mean he would stop causing trouble. The next thing he got involved in was one of the most unusual twists in the entire Genovese conspiracy case: Nelson Cantellops's supposed recantation of his testimony.

After he was sentenced in April 1959, Genovese filed various appeals, and on June 20, 1960, the U.S. Supreme Court shot down his request for the high court to hear his case. Things were looking rather bleak for Don Vitone. But before the Supreme Court took that action, Genovese's defense attorney, Wilfred Davis, attended a rather bizarre meeting at Our Lady of Mount Carmel Catholic church in the Bronx on January 26, 1960. Present were another attorney known as Herbert S. Seigal, who had ties to Ormento, a priest from the church, a notary public, and lastly, Cantellops himself.

As Davis would later describe it in his own affidavit filed in Manhattan federal court, Cantellops, in the presence of the others, swore that all of the testimony he gave about Ormento and Galante in Genovese's trial was false and untruthful. During the church interview, Cantellops didn't want to discuss his trial testimony about Genovese, but he insisted that he lied about Ormento and Galante, particularly about an alleged meeting he had with them in a restaurant in Manhattan, which had been brought up in his testimony at trial. It turned out the Cantellops interview was recorded, and a transcript filed with the court by Davis showed the relevant portions.

Davis asked Cantellops if Ormento and Galante sent him on a trip to Puerto Rico in either 1956 or 1957, as he had testified. To all questions about that subject, Cantellops answered "No."

"They never sent you on such a trip?" asked Davis.

"No," replied Cantellops.

The transcript showed that Cantellops also claimed that FBN agents had "suggested" certain elements of his testimony.

While Davis was reluctant for reasons that remain unclear to mention Genovese's name, the lawyer did ask Cantellops if he ever traveled to the Bronx with Ormento in a car, and again the witness answered "No."

If Cantellops's recantation was true, then he never went to the Bronx meeting as he testified he did, riding in a car with Genovese to the Mazzie house. Thus, he could not have heard Genovese ask at that time if final arrangements had been made about the territory concerning the Spanish-speaking market. It could be the kind of evidence Davis needed to overturn the verdict and get a new trial.

Davis used the transcript in requesting that the court grant Genovese's request for a new trial, based on a sworn, notarized statement by Cantellops, which he said he was making to "clarify my past errors." Davis also said in his court papers that in August 1960 he had learned that Cantellops did indeed claim everything he testified to about Genovese was false.

But the old adage that if something is too good to be true it likely isn't was apt in the case of Cantellops's recantation, or let us say "alleged recantation." It turned out that the whole song and dance involving Cantellops, the priest, the church, and the lawyers was basically the result of bribery and a hoax. For while John Ormento was out on bail in his drug case, he was up to no good in an effort to try and corrupt the criminal justice system.

In the end, it turned out that Cantellops was paid off to recant his testimony, and when he was caught by FBN, he withdrew his recantation. The entire scam was uncovered during a hearing before Judge Bicks and was spelled out in a lengthy ruling he made in which he shot down Genovese's efforts to have his conviction thrown out. It is the kind of thing that makes judges view any time a witness recants testimony with suspicion.

Here is what happened as related by Judge Bicks. It was early January 1960 that Cantellops got some telephone calls from someone who was never identified that in substance said he would be paid if he recanted certain parts of his testimony. At some point, it was Ormento who turned up the heat and called Cantellops, telling him that unless he went along with the plan to change the testimony "all would not go well for him," as Judge Bicks delicately put it.

For going along with Ormento's plan, Cantellops was to be paid an initial $3,000, with the promise of up to $30,000 more if he followed a script that was going to be dictated by the Long Island mobster. On January 24, Siegel was contacted by Ormento, who wanted the attorney to verify that the fellow he had talked with was in fact Cantellops. Eventually, in a kind of Keystone Cops routine, Siegel and another attorney, Amadeo L. Lauritano, shadowed Cantellops as he met with Ormento at a restaurant in the Bronx. The lawyers slinked around outside and then decided to go into the eatery and buy sandwiches in an effort to appear inconspicuous.

The two attorneys said they couldn't be sure that the man was Cantellops. At one point, Siegel and Ormento met Cantellops in the attorney's office. Even Ormento had suspicions that he was being conned and blurted out "You are not Cantellops!" Finally, Cantellops related some incidents from the Genovese trial, and Ormento was satisfied that he was in fact the witness who needed to be corrupted.

After the January 27 church meeting where he signed a notarized document—which Ormento wrote—recanting his trial testimony, Cantellops went to Siegel's law office and got money in cash totaling $3,000 from Ormento. That cash was the down payment for the recantation.

But the scheme fell apart. Within days of the payoff, Cantellops gave statements to federal prosecutors and FBN agents about the bribe from Ormento. However, according to court records, even with a grand jury probing the bribe, Ormento continued to try and get Cantellops to go along with the scheme. But even with some poorly made audiotapes that Ormento tried to use to bolster the recantation, Judge Bicks saw through the scam. The recordings, said Bicks, "were forced and cajoled, not made under oath and the product of bribery."

While the effort to overturn the verdict by bribing Cantellops turned out to be a disaster, Genovese's attorneys nevertheless pressed their appeals. But Bicks shot them down, as did the Court of Appeals. The eminent lawyer Edward Bennett Williams even took on Genovese's case, raising the argument that the government had not turned over the notes of some of the FBN agents and a federal prosecutor who had debriefed Cantellops. But at least at the appeals court level, those arguments didn't work. Finally, in February 1960, Vito Genovese lost his bid to stay out of prison while Williams took his case to the U.S. Supreme Court. He had run out of options and had to surrender to begin his fifteen-year sentence.

Chapter Twenty-four

VITO GENOVESE'S LAST MOMENTS as a free citizen of these United States occurred on February 11, 1960, when he walked into the U.S. Courthouse on Foley Square to give himself up in the chambers of Judge Sidney Sugarman. Dressed in a dark wide-brimmed hat, shirt and tie, and a dark overcoat, Genovese looked like he was going to a funeral. He seemed grim. When reporters asked him if he had anything to say, Genovese, as the *Daily News* reported, "gritted his teeth and fought to hold back tears, but said nothing."

After surrendering, Genovese was held in a holding pen for about two hours and then led out of the courthouse and past a horde of television, newsreel, and newspaper reporters, who barraged him with questions like "Are you the head of the Mafia?" Genovese managed a grin but said nothing. He was taken to a nearby detention center to wait for the Bureau of Prisons to decide where to send him.

A bus took Genovese with some other newly minted prisoners to the prison in Lewisburg, Pennsylvania, and then he was bussed to his new home: the federal prison in Atlanta, Georgia. The packet of documents that accompanied him claimed that he was "a menace to society and a habitual criminal." His criminal record was extensive, the records added, noting that Genovese "is considered by some to be the chieftain of the Italian underworld in this country." For good measure, his attendance at the Apalachin "gangland convention" was also noted.

As menacing as Genovese was made to sound in those Bureau of Prison records, the 62-year-old man who was examined by prison doctors seemed anything but forbidding. At 167 pounds and just over five feet, seven inches tall, Genovese was slightly overweight by modern standards. His blood pressure was high, 182 over 110, he had pains in his right side, and his feet ached. He was also missing a few teeth and bore the scars from the infamous Prospect Park accident in 1924 and spinal surgery in 1946. Genovese also complained about the effects of past bouts of bronchitis, a harbinger of the emphysema that was to come thanks to his habitual heavy smoking. He also seemed to be bothered by high places, an indication that he suffered from a form of vertigo. Simply put, Genovese was an old man and not aging well.

As part of the process of figuring out what to do with Genovese, prison officials assessed his intelligence, recording his IQ at 84, which was considered low average, although that kind of arbitrary classification apparently had no impact on his ability to thrive in the world of crime. Later, that IQ score was upped to 95. Genovese himself said he only finished the third grade in school in Italy. But he had worked for years as a businessman, something prison officials noted in recommending that he be given work in the prison greenhouse or a job as an orderly.

Given his age, officials didn't recommend that Genovese take any schooling, although it wouldn't be precluded if he wanted it. But one thing Genovese did want to partake in was the practice of his old Roman Catholic faith. Prison officials thought that was a good idea and encouraged Genovese to attend prison services and take the sacraments.

When it opened in 1902, the Atlanta federal penitentiary was the largest facility in the federal system, with room for three thousand inmates. It had some large sports facilities, such as a baseball diamond, handball courts, and basketball courts, as well as boccie courts, a popular item with Italian inmates. When Genovese arrived in 1960, he found himself in some good company. Numerous mob figures had been sent to Atlanta, among them Joseph DiPalermo, the infamous "Joe Beck" who was convicted along with Genovese in the heroin case. There were some lesser luminaries, but one who stood out was Joseph Valachi, one of Genovese's old acolytes from the Bronx. As it turned out, Genovese shared a cell with eight inmates in Atlanta, and for a time one of them was Valachi.

As Valachi remembered, Genovese might have been considered an ailing old man who wanted to appear to be a practicing Catholic, but he ruled his domain among the prisoners. As related by Maas in *The Valachi Papers*, Genovese held sessions with inmates two nights a week to arbitrate disputes and dispense favors. During a visit Maas made to Atlanta in researching the book, he was told that one prison guard said that Genovese was such a poor boccie player that the other prisoners who went up against him in the game had to eat crow and lose on purpose.

Valachi initially said that Genovese was cool to him in Atlanta. The main problem was that Genovese believed Valachi had remained allied with Tony Bender, something the mob boss viewed with suspicion. But over time, Valachi convinced Genovese that he also had problems with Bender, whom he accused of foolishly leading him to believe that if he surrendered in a narcotics case he would only get a five-year sentence. In that case, Valachi got a fifteen-year sentence and wound up in Atlanta.

During his initial stay in Atlanta, Valachi was charged in another heroin case back in New York and brought there for trial in a case he believed was a frame-up. Valachi said he had no doubt about the guilt of some of his codefendants—including Vincent Mauro, Frank Caruso, and Albert and Vito Agueci—but insisted he had nothing to do with their heroin dealings. Mauro and Caruso turned into fugitives, and Albert Agueci, after making bail, was found dead in an upstate field after being strangled and then set on fire with gasoline. It was also reported that Agueci's body had been carved up and about thirty pounds of flesh taken from his body while he was still alive.

Valachi went to trial in December 1962 with eleven others and was found guilty. He received a twenty-year sentence to run concurrently with the fifteen years he was doing in Atlanta. But federal agents believed that Valachi had information that could be useful and had him go through some questioning before he was returned to Atlanta.

Back in Atlanta, Genovese at first accepted Valachi back into the fold of prison life. But at the same time, Vito Agueci had been convicted of the narcotics charge and was now incarcerated in Atlanta, where it seemed to Valachi that he had Genovese's ear. Valachi, ever paranoid in the prison culture, believed Agueci was telling Genovese that Valachi was an informant. Agueci appears to have wanted to divert attention away from himself since, as Maas would later report, he would turn into an informant for the FBN. (Genovese would later deny to prison officials ever knowing anyone named Agueci.)

Valachi's paranoia was further stoked when Genovese remarked about the disappearance of his once-trusted underboss, Tony Bender. It was April 1962 when Bender disappeared after he left his home in the company of two other men, telling his wife that he wouldn't be gone for long. Bender, who was under suspicion for drug trafficking, was never seen again. Genovese commented to Valachi that whatever happened, "It was the best thing that could have happened to Tony. He wouldn't be able to take it like you or I." It was a sign that Genovese knew or suspected that Bender was dead, and it didn't make Valachi feel any better.

The one episode that really made Valachi dread prison life close to Genovese occurred when the crime boss started telling him how "bad apples" had to be removed before they spoiled the whole barrel, a simple metaphor, Valachi thought, for the need to get rid of informants. With that, Genovese gave Valachi a kiss, "the kiss of death." Fearful, Valachi requested that the prison put him into solitary confinement, but after a brief stay in the "hole" and a fruitless attempt to talk with George Gaffney of the FBN, he was ordered back into the general prison popular.

Valachi saw threats all around him. On the morning of June 22, 1962, Valachi was walking in the prison yard when he noticed three men loitering behind the baseball grandstand. To Valachi's paranoid mind, the men appeared to be waiting to ambush him, and in fact, they started to approach him. He had to act. Picking up a two-foot-long piece of iron pipe that was nearby on the ground, he went into a rage and struck a man he thought was DiPalermo who happened to be walking by. But Valachi had struck the wrong man. His victim whose head was split open and body beaten to a pulp wasn't old Joe Beck but rather John Joseph Saupp, who was in Atlanta for a bank robbery conviction. Valachi didn't even know him.

Saupp died after about two days in a coma. Valachi now faced a murder charge on top of all his other legal troubles. He had only one way out: cooperation. As the public later came to know, the death of Saupp compelled a guilt-ridden Valachi to become one of the most significant cooperating witnesses for the federal government in the history of law enforcement. There would be other cooperators after Valachi, particularly those like Sammy "the Bull" Gravano, who helped the FBI nab John Gotti. But it was Valachi who was the man who gave the American public, as well as the FBI and Congress, its first vivid picture from the inside of the Mafia—or La Cosa Nostra—and in the process showed how a boss like Genovese wielded his criminal power.

Peter Maas in *The Valachi Papers* put the whole Atlanta episode in perspective best: "This seemingly senseless killing by apparently so unremarkable a hand would end with Valachi becoming the first person to unmask the Cosa Nostra, whose very existence had been the subject of fierce debate, even in law enforcement circles. Almost overnight, as a result, Valachi's name became as familiar as that of Capone, Luciano, Costello, or Genovese."

Of course, at that time, with Capone dead, Luciano in exile, and Costello "retired," it would only be Don Vito Genovese who really had anything to fear from what Valachi would reveal. If Genovese hated the publicity he got after Apalachin, he had yet to see the worst of it.

Chapter Twenty-five

BY THE TIME JOSEPH VALACHI WAS TESTIFYING before the U.S. Congress, Vito Genovese had been transferred from the Atlanta penitentiary to the U.S Penitentiary in Leavenworth, Kansas. Genovese had been supposedly ruling the roost in Atlanta among the inmates in terms of his reputation and power. He was also believed to have been the recipient of food stolen from the Atlanta commissary, so he was sent farther way from the old inmates he had been familiar with in the Mafia.

But in Leavenworth, Genovese became very aware, from the newspapers and magazines he read, about the things Valachi was saying about him to the FBI. While he may have secretly enjoyed what the turncoat was saying about him, Genovese told officials in Leavenworth that Valachi was either crazy or telling "involved" stories in a bid to win his freedom. Yes, Valachi had been his cellmate in Atlanta, but he had nothing to do with his getting that assignment and never signed any inmate's request, including that of Valachi, to bunk in the cell. Genovese also disputed Valachi's description of the mob boss's power behind bars and said he never was asked by Valachi to talk with any inmates. As far as the murder Valachi committed, Genovese said that he had nothing to do with it, stating that he was in the visiting room the morning the killing occurred and that when he was informed that one of his cellmates had committed the crime, Genovese had asked, "Which one?"

Valachi began his public testimony before the U.S. Senate committee on September 27, 1963, and as far as Washington, DC, was concerned, it was the only show worth anything in town. Adding spice to the event was the claim that Valachi had a $100,000 contract on his head, something that warranted a protective cordon of capitol and local police, FBI agents, and U.S. marshalls. As the *Daily News* described on the opening day of the Valachi hearings, "The seven senators sat google-eyed as, for the first time in memory, a witness in the Senate Caucus room blandly related how he had committed a murder—and volunteered that he had carried out other killings under Cosa Nostra orders."

Valachi also gave a primer on life in the mob, describing the blood-letting ceremony in which an inductee to the Mafia had his finger pricked and held the burning picture of a saint as he swore loyalty to the life of crime. But Valachi also described numerous historical murders that served as the underpinning of the modern mob, beginning with the killing of Joseph Masseria in a Coney Island restaurant in April 1931. Genovese was part of the group of gangsters who coaxed Masseria to go to the lunch and were present when he was shot dead, said Valachi.

After Masseria was killed, Salvatore Maranzano pulled together the mob in New York City, anointing himself as the big boss, said Valachi. But that didn't last too long because Maranzano became greedy and plotted against the likes of Genovese and Lucky Luciano, the very men who helped catapult him to power. Valachi said that he got wind of Maranzano's plan to execute Genovese, Luciano, and others and that it was Genovese who approached a group of Jewish gunmen under the control of Meyer Lansky to take out Maranzano. It was on September 10, 1931, that Maranzano was ambushed in his Park Avenue office by a group of shooters led by Red Levine, explained Valachi.

The stories told by Valachi to the senators became the spine around which a good portion of the history of La Cosa Nostra, or the Mafia, has been set. Much of the old history has been retold numerous times and in various formats—books, movies, television series—and has become ingrained in the American culture. Critics have argued that Valachi wasn't that significant a figure in the mob, although he was connected to major players like Genovese. But little has emerged to challenge his basic story line, although his wife, Madeline, disavowed him after he testified, saying he was a womanizing lout whom she gave up on years ago.

Back in Leavenworth, prison officials noted that Genovese didn't seem the least bit disturbed about the things Valachi was saying. "He has created little difficulty here, and the recent publicity has caused very little comment," according to a note from the Leavenworth warden to his superiors in Washington in August 1963. Other prisoners sometimes approached Genovese, but he said he gave them a polite "good morning" but then brushed them off, said the warden. For the most part, Genovese didn't appear to have any close friends in Leavenworth, and when he was confined to the hospital unit, the staff watched closely, knowing his links to the mob, for anything suspicious but found none. The only person Genovese said he ever was close with behind bars was a cellmate he had in Atlanta known as Angelo Paccione, a man with a "crippled leg" whom Genovese felt sorry for.

Still, when he testified publicly in September 1963, Valachi labeled Genovese as the "the boss of all bosses" who was running three branches of La Cosa Nostra from his cell in Leavenworth. Valachi said he didn't fear Genovese now and was giving him a kiss of death right back by testifying.

Moving to more contemporary crimes, Valachi said it was Genovese and Frank Costello who ordered the 1952 murder of suspected federal informant Eugene Gianni, who was gunned down in Harlem. The contract, according to Valachi, was farmed out to Tony Bender. Gianni turned out to be an informant but was also trying to work an angle with the mob when he was killed, stated Valachi.

One way Genovese could have run things from Leavenworth was by personal prison visits from friends and relatives or by letter. But prison records showed that Genovese by August 1963 wrote only to his attorney, his daughters, Nancy and Marie, his son, Philip, and, surprisingly, to his wife Anna. Visits were again limited mostly to his children—Marie Esposito, Nancy Simonetti, and Philip Genovese.

His attorney, Wilfred Davis, paid him visits to discuss legal strategy. His brother Michael, long considered an associate of the crime family, visited Genovese almost every month from August 1962 through August 1963. The one problem with Michael's visits was that he and his brother would sometimes lapse into Italian, which drew a warning from prison guards to stop or the visit would be terminated. After a while, prison officials told Michael Genovese that if he wanted to visit Leavenworth again he needed to make a request in writing before he showed up.

Michael Genovese complied with the prison request and made additional visits to see his brother, as did attorney Davis. Curiously, an unidentified representative from the NYPD visited Genovese between August 1963 and August 1965, as did a representative from a New York prosecutor, also not identified. There was no indication what was said in those law enforcement meetings. But thought was given by federal officials that if Genovese was transferred to a facility like the McNeil Island Corrections Center, a federal facility in Puget Sound in the state of Washington, the move "possibly [could] induce him to cooperate further with the government." That phrase was also curious because it suggested the Genovese, the boss of the Mafia, had provided some cooperation.

Having lost his final attempt to get his case overturned, Genovese became resigned to prison life and settled into a sedentary routine. The one legal hope was that he would challenge the legality of his sentence. Genovese's health kept him in periodic stays in the hospital unit at Leavenworth since July 1962, and by all indications he was a model patient, described as "a most cooperative patient, with an excellent attitude." The doctors must have loved him. So did the prison's Catholic chaplain. It seems that Genovese attended Mass regularly, and he had "shown a keen interest in the Catholic program and takes an active part in all Catholic devotions," said prison officials in a 1965 memo. What's more, Genovese made his Easter duty and regularly took the sacraments, which means he must have gone to confession.

For a man of advancing years, suffering from emphysema, heart problems, and the effects of bladder cancer, there wasn't much physical work Genovese could do in prison, although he did visit the Leavenworth recreation yard. To pass the time, Genovese read magazines and books from the prison library. Those at least kept him up-to-date on what was going on back among his old Mafia associates.

Don Vitone had a fearsome reputation in the underworld. Everyone knew that. Yet in his interaction with the prison staff, he seemed like a genial grandfather. If he had animosity because of his situation, Genovese didn't show it, not against the prison staff, the U.S. government, or the court that had consigned him to a life behind bars. "He related that he was well satisfied with his treatment here and had considerable praise for the medical and institutional staff," was how one of Genovese's annual prison reviews described him.

Chapter Twenty-six

HIS SLEEP CAME IN FITS AND STARTS.

Vito Genovese may have praised the way his jailors treated him and his infirmities. But at night, his anxiety about dying behind bars and never seeing his family again took its toll. Sleep became difficult. He stayed awake thinking about what life had been and what it had become. Genovese had a hard time falling asleep, and when he did there were the nightmares. What exactly terrorized him during sleep was unclear. Maybe he was dreaming about those he had killed or brutalized. He had done and seen enough in life to stoke all kinds of terror.

The inability to rest put Genovese into a vicious cycle of erratic heartbeats known as "premature ventricular contractions," which weren't necessarily dangerous but for an old man could only add to his problems, notably high blood pressure. Genovese was a walking time bomb in that his blood pressure got dangerously high, so much so that he had to be put on tranquilizers at night to get the sleep he needed.

After his transfer to Leavenworth in July 1962, Genovese was assigned to the prison food services department for about a month before he was placed permanently in the hospital wing because of his health problems. The irony of this entire period of incarceration is that to all the wardens and prison staff, Genovese, the reputed boss of all crime in New York City and the country, was nothing but a deferential man who appreciated everything being done for him. He wasn't cranky, cantankerous, or abusive.

As the model prisoner he was, Genovese could receive visits and mail from his family. Surprisingly, despite the rancor that had torn apart their lives, his wife, Anna, made visits, as did his ever-loyal daughter Nancy and his adopted daughter Marie. But by 1966, as it became clear that Genovese wasn't going to get his conviction overturned, those visits were sometimes emotionally tough on everybody. Genovese preferred the women just stay away.

"He states that his wife and daughters do not come to see him because 'they would just break down and cry' and it is better that they don't come," prison officials said in Genovese's annual review in 1966. "He states the daughters have families of their own which makes it difficult for them to visit."

By 1967, Genovese was only getting visits from his brother Michael, his attorney, Wilfred Davis, and a number of Immigration and Naturalization Service officials, the latter showing up for reasons that are not clear from prison records. Letters of course still came from his daughters, his son, Philip, and Anna. One New York City woman wrote the prison chaplain to ask if she could send Genovese some religious material. The chaplain responded by thanking her and said Genovese was doing religious studies in his cell.

Genovese was a good inmate, but in terms of his health, that was another matter. Once a heavy smoker, Genoese finally quit smoking about a year after he was incarcerated, but by then the damage to his lungs had been done. His body was that of man old beyond his years. He had emphysema and clogged arteries, something his sedentary lifestyle in the prison hospital didn't help. As time went on, Genovese's medical problems began to hold him in a firmer grip. A prison mug shot of him around the time he was in the prison hospital showed an aging man, with wisps of gray hair and a lined face with skin that sagged in hangdog fashion. It was a far cry from the dark visage with penetrating eyes and upswept hair of the man who had once demanded respect in the American underworld.

By late January 1969, Genovese noticed that he was getting increasingly short of breath and sometimes he couldn't walk halfway across the exercise yard without getting winded. He also started to have increased swelling in his ankles, a sign of heart failure, and was overtaken by a feeling of malaise. A regimen of the drug digitalis did very little to help Genovese, and prison officials at Leavenworth saw enough deterioration in Genovese's condition that they sent him to the Medical Center for Federal Prisoners in Springfield, Missouri. It was a place familiar to Genovese since he had earlier been admitted for other heart episodes as well as surgery for a cancerous bladder tumor, which had been successfully removed.

As the days progressed, Genovese started to have more trouble breathing. He became cyanotic, which meant that he took on a bluish pallor because of a lack of blood oxygenation. While his heart rate seemed normal at seventy beats a minute, a cardiac "gallop" set in, meaning he had extra sounds that doctors detected when they listened with a stethoscope.

On February 12, Genovese's blood oxygenation dropped to 70 percent, a sign he was in some kind of respiratory failure. Genovese got a sudden case of diarrhea, complained of severe abdominal pain, and then collapsed. His skin was clammy and sweaty. On top of everything, Genovese was unresponsive. His condition was now critical, and hospital officials notified Genovese's daughter Nancy back in New Jersey by telegram of the sudden downturn in her father's condition.

The next day, February 13, a cardiac specialist was brought in who, after an examination, believed that Genovese had likely suffered from a pulmonary embolism, something that indicated he had an obstruction in a blood vessel blocking a coronary artery. Doctors intubated Genovese and gave him digitalis, but as the medical records stated, he would not pull through. At 1:25 A.M. on February 14, 1969, Genovese flatlined. He was dead.

The official death certificate for the biggest Mafia figure of the era said that 71-year-old Vito Genovese died of respiratory failure, preceded by a pulmonary embolism. Five years of arteriosclerotic heart disease also contributed to his demise, as did so many years of smoking inside and outside of the Alto Knights Club and other haunts in Manhattan's Little Italy. His old bladder cancer was also noted but didn't seem to have any impact on his dying. There was no mention of pancreatic cancer, as some news reports had stated. Anna Genovese was listed as his wife, although it had been years since she had visited him while he had been in custody. Prison officials asked Nancy if she would permit an autopsy: she declined. As she instructed, Genovese's body was prepared and shipped to the Anderson Funeral Home in Red Bank, New Jersey.

Mafia funerals had a reputation for being grandiose affairs, with enough flower cars to stock a botanical garden and processions that could best any a dead politician could have for the final ride to eternity. In 1928 when Frankie Yale, whom Genovese rubbed shoulders with in the days of Prohibition, was machine-gunned to death on orders from Al Capone, his funeral was unrivaled for the time. His casket was estimated to have cost $15,000, an extravagant sum and one subject to gross inflation by the newspapers. An estimated 150,000 onlookers lined the funeral route as his cortege—comprised of thirty-five flower cars and two hundred limousines—made its way to Brooklyn's Holy Cross Cemetery.

In the case of Genovese, things were much lower key. Mafia experts and cops expected the wake at the Anderson Funeral Home and the church funeral to be lavish, much like Willie Moretti had when he was slain in 1951 and thousands lined up outside the church in Cliffside Park. But if a grand event was expected for Don Vitone, what occurred was a disappointment. The one-day wake drew just over one hundred visitors, including some local politicians who paid respects to Genovese's son, Philip, who had been a local councilman. His sister, Nancy, Genovese's firstborn, also greeted those who visited.

At the church, only about 125 people, many of them women, were on hand for the service on February 17, 1969, inside St. Agnes Catholic Church in Genovese's old hometown of Atlantic Highlands. About one hundred of the curious lined up outside in the cold weather. None of the old New York and New Jersey Mafiosi showed up. The big boys might have been staying away to avoid FBI and press cameras. Some of them also probably had no love lost for Genovese. The biggest contingent was about thirty pupils from the fourth-grade class of the St. Agnes School, where Nancy taught, who sat dressed in maroon-and-white uniforms with white lace mantillas.

The Mass didn't have any eulogies. After an hour-long service, the procession of the hearse, four limousines, four private cars, and a station wagon filled with flowers left for St. John Cemetery in Middle Village, Queens. The small group arrived at the cemetery in time for a 1:00 P.M. graveside ceremony around the open outdoor Genovese family crypt, where the concrete slab had been moved back to allow access. Genovese's casket was placed in a copper outer container. A floral blanket of pink-and-white chrysanthemums, orchids, and lilies of the valley, with a ribbon bearing the words "Our Dad," adorned the casket.

The graveside service took about five minutes as a priest recited a prayer. The mourners and family left the snow-covered grounds. It was then that cemetery gravediggers lowered the casket into its niche. Genovese's long odyssey had come to an end as he rested with his parents, his first wife, Donata, and a few other relatives in the family plot. He also resided near some of his old mob confederates. Joseph Profaci's grand mausoleum was just about forty yards up the road, and the grave of Salvatore Maranzano, whom Genovese had played a role in killing, was also very nearby. In another mausoleum by a different cemetery road was Charles "Lucky" Luciano, who was buried with his mother and father and other relatives in a structure bearing the original family name, Lucania. Over the years, other Mafiosi would choose to be interred at St. John Cemetery: Carlo Gambino, John Gotti, Aniello Dellacroce, and Carmine Galante. There were enough of them, old-time and modern gangsters, that they could almost hold a spectral meeting of the Commission.

Journalists and FBI agents with telephoto lenses can always see what goes on at Mafia funerals. But the bigger challenge for them is to try and figure out when a Mafia boss dies who will take his place. The ground had not even thawed around Genovese's grave when FBI agents started getting intelligence reports from informants that there was some gossip that one Carl James Civella, a Mafioso from

Kansas City, might replace Genovese as head of his family. These reports were fanned by intelligence that a number of mobsters, including Civella, had met in Miami in early March 1969 to pick Genovese's successor. But the suggestion that Civella, a gangster outside of New York, would take over for Genovese seemed implausible. FBI files showed that one informant said it was not clear if Civella had his own crime family or had been part of Genovese's family.

One other aspect of the Miami meeting, according to the FBI report, was that Thomas Eboli, a longtime member of the Genovese clan, wasn't favored to take over the job or Genovese's old position on the ruling Commission. Closer to New York, one name that did surface as Genovese's successor was his old friend and underboss Gerardo "Jerry" Catena. According to one news report, Catena was tapped as the new boss during some kind of mob cruise from Florida to Haiti, possibly the meeting mentioned in early March. But Catena, who was 67 years old and ran his legitimate business from East Orange, New Jersey, was reported to have been reluctant to take the position, something that would have been understandable given the way the FBI kept hounding Mafia bosses.

Over the months and years, other names would emerge as Don Vitone's successor, and some gained more credence than others. One such name was Michael Miranda, an old mainstay of the crime family who had weathered good and bad times with Genovese, including an arrest in the old Boccia murder case. There was also Michael "Trigger Mike" Coppola, an old associate of the likes of Frank Costello and Joe Stracci, the old garment center schemer who was active in gambling activities in Miami.

If Eboli did make it to the top job in the Genovese crime family, as some in the FBI and NYPD suspected, his reign was short-lived. A dapper dresser who was known to sport a snap-brim gray straw hat, Eboli was involved in managing prizefighters and oversaw the Genovese family interests in the docks and nightclubs. When Genovese passed away, it was Eboli and some others who managed the crime family operations as a committee. But during testimony before an investigating committee, Eboli, who had suffered from heart problems, seemed irrational. It was shades of Willy Moretti all over again. The night of July 16, 1972, after he left the home of a girl-friend in Brooklyn, Eboli was shot dead. Five bullets punctured his skull on the left side as he sat with his chauffer in a Cadillac.

Police and some crime historians believe that two other crime family members profited from Eboli's killing: Vincent Gigante took over his gambling operations and Frank "Funzi" Tieri found himself as boss. The future leadership of Genovese's family was starting to emerge.

Epilogue

IN HIS LIFETIME, VITO GENOVESE USED his cunning, guile, and canny sense of Mafia politics to cement his rise to the top. In the days after World War Two and the Korean War, if there ever was a boss of all the bosses, Genovese was seen as the man to fit the bill. Until his conviction on the heroin case in 1959, he was lucky enough to escape the long arm of the law, particularly as the other bosses found themselves beleaguered by the federal government's efforts to tie them into the big Apalachin conspiracy, a classic case of overreach by prosecutors that ended in a stinging reversal of the convictions.

But as *The Deadly Don* detailed, Genovese made some costly strategic decisions about planning to hold the meeting in Apalachin that led to a disaster of bad publicity and seemingly never-ending investigations. Some have theorized and even outright stated that Genovese's mistakes angered others in the Mafia who then set him up to fail with Apalachin and in the drug cases. The case for the latter is advanced by Chuck Giancana, the half brother of legendary Chicago mob boss Sam Giancana, and Chuck's nephew Sam in their 1993 book *Double Cross: The Explosive Inside Story of the Mobster Who Controlled America.*

The Giancana book made numerous claims that the elder Giancana had ties to the CIA and had a hand in ordering the deaths of President John F. Kennedy and Marilyn Monroe, as well as a host of other crimes. But deep in the book, the authors related a conversa-

tion between two Chicago gangsters in which they discussed how
Nelson Cantellops was being used to set up Genovese in the big
heroin case. Cantellops, according to a man identified only as Willie,
was used by Giancana to set up Genovese. Cantellops was supposedly a soldier of Willie's and was used by Giancana as a "sap" to
screw Genovese with the help of some other Mob big shots. Giancana's motive was to get Genovese out of the picture because he
was seen as the only Mafia boss who would stand up to the grasping
power of the Chicago Mafia, or so it seemed.

"Since [Giancana] supplied the plan and the manpower, Lansky,
Gambino, Costello and Luciano supplied the dollars to finance the
narcotics caper that would ultimately frame Genovese. . . . The plan
worked perfectly; Genovese was arrested, thanks to Cantellops's
testimony, and sentenced to fifteen years in prison," the Giancanas
alleged in their book.

There is a kernel of known truth to that Giancana story, at least in
terms of Cantellops's travels. Cantellops did spend some time in
Chicago when he came to the States, but it was for a very short period, for a few days, he said, working in a restaurant before he left
for New York. If that is the case, it is improbable that he did enough
in his life as an itinerant petty criminal that he could be considered a
"soldier" in any Chicago crime group. More to the point, Costello
had an aversion to drug dealing, wanted respectability, and was already being watched closely by the federal government. Besides,
Costello had already "retired" from mob life after the assassination
attempt on him. All of which meant that Costello likely wouldn't
have been involved in financing heroin deals.

Lansky was too smart an operator, with too many dealings in
Cuba and Florida, to do risky drug financing, although the FBN
deemed him to be someone involved in the past with financing narcotics transactions. Gambino was also viewed by the FBN as a
Mafioso who had done drug financing, and Luciano was also seen
in the same light, operating from his base in Italy. But the authors of
Double Cross cite nothing but their own claims about conversations
with people who died long ago as proof for the Genovese set-up. In
addition, when it came time to prosecute the Genovese case, prose-

cutors charged garment businessman Benjamin Levine as the chief financier of the various heroin buys done by the conspirators.

Genovese went to his grave saying he was framed in the case, and given the thin, circumstantial nature of the evidence against him, one can understand why he believed that. The one piece of substantiation that Genovese knew Cantellops came from the fleeting conversation that FBN agents overheard in a restaurant. Genovese's remark that "he is all right" or words to that effect when referring to Cantellops could have meant anything. But it was from that slender proof that the rest of what Cantellops had to say seemed to be bolstered. Cantellops himself met a bloody end. He was killed in July 1965, reportedly knifed to death in a Bronx bar fight. He lies in a nondescript grave at Rosehill Cemetery in New Jersey

In his lifetime as the nation's big Mafia boss, Genovese was believed to have amassed a fortune estimated at about $33 million. He and Anna did live large for a time. They had enough to buy the big Red Hill estate in the 1930s and then a nicely furnished waterfront house in Atlantic Highlands. It was not that the Internal Revenue Service didn't look at Genovese: he did settle a case of back taxes for just over $160,000. But it seemed that Genovese hid whatever wealth he had very well.

In the end, Genovese's material life was encapsulated in a two-page last will and testament he signed on September 5, 1950. He was already in the throes of problems with Anna then. In the will, Genovese gave the bulk of his estate to his daughter Nancy, who was his executrix, and his son, Philip. There were no dollar amounts listed, but one attorney would later say Don Vitone left a fortune valued at about $2,000, to be split between his two natural children. Maria Genovese Esposito, who Genovese said under oath was his adopted child, got the grand sum of $5. For Anna, there was nothing.

During the lifetime of her adopted father, Maria is said to have disavowed him. But if the prison records are accurate, at some point Maria had a reconciliation with Genovese since she was listed as a visitor while he was in Springfield for the final years of his life. If his feelings towards her changed, Genovese never got the opportunity to change the will.

Yet the will and the paltry sum Genovese was reported to have at his death really don't tell the whole story. As it turned out, Genovese was frugal in prison. Records showed that over the years on a regular basis he purchased U.S. Savings Bonds with money taken from his commissary account, the account all prisoners have to make purchases from the prison stores. In Genovese's case, he was making purchases of bonds with face values of $250 to $500. Where he got the money to do that was unclear: it could have been from family or his Social Security benefits. In any case, Genovese had no use for the bonds while in custody, and he made daughter Nancy the beneficiary, so at his death an estimated $10,000 in bonds went to her.

As it turned out, Genovese also provided for Anna. Prison records show that Genovese was getting $106 a month in Social Security old age benefits in September 1961 after he began serving his sentence. His application for the benefit showed that he made $1,600 in 1960, although the source wasn't specified. In any case, Genovese was one of a number of inmates getting the benefit and presumably did so until his death in February 1969. As it turned out, despite all of the troubles they had in marriage, Genovese made Anna his Social Security beneficiary, so presumably for the rest of her life she received some part of his $106 monthly pension.

Such a strange, conflicted relationship Vito and Anna Genovese had. Under the code of the street, Genovese would have been justified to have her killed when she turned on him so publicly. But he never did, nor would he. They had a love-hate drama that locked them in a strange bond. Anna proved to be calculating, impetuous, and impulsive. Yet Genovese cared about and loved her for as long as both lived. Although the marital woes should have destroyed things, the man considered the ruthless head of the Mafia and his combative spouse in time came to their own secret truce and maintained a relationship to the end.

After her husband's death, Anna Genovese did work for a living and according to relatives was head of housekeeping services at the well-known Warwick Hotel in Manhattan. On January 4, 1982, Anna Petillo Genovese, said to be suffering from gall bladder problems, died in a Manhattan hospital. She was 78 years old. The funeral was handled by a funeral home on Staten Island. It was a low-key affair with nieces and nephews and some friends in attendance. No news items appeared in any of the local newspapers. The hearse took Anna to St. John Cemetery, where once again the Genovese family vault was opened and her casket was slipped into a niche near where her husband reposed. She would spend the rest of time with the crime boss she once told the world she feared but who in the end still cared deeply about her.

Notes

CHAPTER ONE

Information about the life and death of Donata Genovese can be found in a number of contemporary newspaper accounts at the time of her death in September 1931, which appeared in the *New York Times,* the *Standard Union,* the *Brooklyn Daily Eagle,* the *Ridge-wood Times,* the *Daily News,* and the *Brooklyn Times Union.* Information about the problems New York City had with tuberculosis was also reported in the *New York Times,* while medical information about miliary tuberculosis was found on Wikepedia.com. Dom Frasca's book *King of Crime* related some alleged details of Vito Genovese's relationship with Donata. Details of the estate Donata Genovese left when she died and the identification of the daughter she had from another relationship can be found in the records of Queens County Surrogate's Court.

CHAPTER TWO

Information about Vito Genovese's early years growing up in Italy and his migration to the United States in 1913 can be found in various sources, notably, the National Archives and Records Administration, where his application for U.S. citizenship is on file; Dom Frasca's *King of Crime*; Genovese's federal prisons records, which are also contained in the files of the National Archives; and his interview related to efforts to denaturalize him in the 1950s, which contains comments about his going into the U.S. Army in an effort to gain citizenship. Details of Genovese's various arrests in the 1920s are contained in newspaper accounts reported in the *New York Call*, the *Brooklyn Daily Eagle*, the *Daily News*, the *Daily Star*, the *Brooklyn Times Union*, the *Richmond Times Leader, and the Queens Leader-Observer*. Genovese's indictment on counterfeiting charges in 1930 made the news in the *Evening Star*, the *Bismarck Tribune*, and the *New York Times*. Genovese recounted his version of some of his arrests in a deposition he gave in September 1954 in connection with denaturalization proceedings contained in U.S. v. Vito Genovese (USDC DNJ) Civ. 1127-52. The indictment and related papers in the counterfeiting case are contained in the case file of U.S. v. Pericle Mannerini, et al. (USDC EDNY) case file 27071, on file with the National Archives. Formative events in the early years in the 1920s and 1930s in New York organized crime, including the assassinations of Joseph Masseria and Salvatore Maranzano, as well as the rise of Frank Costello and Charles "Lucky" Luciano through bootlegging, are found in Peter Maas's *The Valachi Papers* and Anthony M. DeStefano's *Top Hoodlum: Frank Costello, Prime Minister of The Mafia*.

CHAPTER THREE

A discussion of the early history of Greenwich Village can be found on Wikipedia. The Petillo family history is spelled out in cursory fashion in U.S. Census reports for 1920. Gerardo Vernotico's criminal history is described in a number of articles published in the *Evening Telegram* and the *Standard Union*. Vernotico's marriage to Anna Petillo is documented in copies of their marriage license on file in the New York City Municipal Archives. Anthony "Tony Bender" Strollo's criminal history is found in his rap sheet on file with the NYPD. Vernotico's murder in 1932 and the resulting police investigation were described in the *Daily News* and the *Standard Union* and the *Chicago Daily Tribune*. Anna Genovese's statements to congressional investigators can be found in the files of the Senate

Special Committee to Investigate Organized Crime in Interstate Commerce (1950–1951) in the National Archives. Vito Genovese's description of his marriages and the births of his children is contained in his naturalization papers on file with the National Archives in New York City. The purchase of Genovese's house in Red Hill and his renovation of it were described in articles in the *Daily Register*, the *Keyport Enterprise*, and the *Daily Record* and in an article at www.monmouthcountyparks.com. Genovese and Anna's travels to Europe in the late 1930s aboard the vessel SS *Conte de Savoia* are recounted in Dom Frasca's *King of Crime* and Genovese's immigration files. Information about the age of ocean liner travel and the SS *Conte de Savoia* was obtained from www.wikipedia.com.

CHAPTER FOUR

The life and times of Mayor Fiorello LaGuardia, as well as his run-ins with Tammany Hall politicians like Albert Marinelli, can be found in Alyn Brodsky's *The Great Mayor: Fiorello LaGuardia and the Making of the City of New York*. LaGuardia's campaign against gangsters like Frank Costello, Vito Genovese, and Charles Luciano is described in Anthony M. DeStefano's *Top Hoodlum: Frank Costello, Prime Minister of The Mafia*. Genovese's immigration records and citizenship application are found in the National Archives in New York City.

CHAPTER FIVE

Events leading up to the appointment of Thomas Dewey as special prosecutor and his prosecution of Charles Luciano on prostitution charges are described in Anthony M. DeStefano's *Top Hoodlum: Frank Costello, Prime Minister of The Mafia*

CHAPTER SIX

Thomas Dewey's efforts to disgrace Albert Marinelli and by implication Vito Genovese were described in various news articles of the period published in the *New York Times* and the *Daily News*. Efforts

by Dewey to investigate Frank Costello were described in Anthony
M. DeStefano's *Top Hoodlum: Frank Costello, Prime Minister of
The Mafia*. The destruction of Genovese's Red Hill mansion in New
Jersey by fire was described in the *Daily Register*, the *Keyport En-
terprise*, and the *Daily Record*. Dom Frasca's *King of Crime* re-
ported on Anna Genovese's travels to Europe.

CHAPTER SEVEN

The rise of Benito Mussolini and his campaign against the Mafia in
Italy, as well as Vito Genovese's close relationship with Italian Fas-
cists is detailed, in John Dickie's exhaustively researched book
Blood Brothers: The History of Italy's Three Mafias. Claims that
Anna Genovese traveled to Italy extensively to see her husband and
provided him with money and other assets are contained in interviews streamed in 2019 and 2020 for the podcast titled "Mob
Queens," produced by Jessica Bendinger and Michael Seligman.
Details of the Allied invasion of Italy are found in Carlo D'Este's
Patton: A Genius for War and historical surveys on Wikipedia, as
well as a communiqué from Patton found in the files of Charles Poletti and held at the Columbia University Rare Books and Manuscript Library. A discussion about the possible organized crime
connections to the assassination of publisher Carlo Tresca was
found in Nunzio Pernicone's *Carlo Tresca: Portrait of a Rebel*.

CHAPTER EIGHT

The history of the overthrow of Mussolini, his rescue by the German Army, and the subsequent advance by the Allied Forces during
the war is found in detail in reports compiled on Wikipedia and in
Carlo D'Este's *Patton: A Genius for War*. Conditions in cities like
Naples, particularly with the health of its residents during the Allied
advance, were detailed in a report by the U.S. Army Medical Department, Office of Medical History, prepared by Thomas B. Turner, M.D.,
and found at history.amedd.army.mil/booksdocs/wwii/civiliaffairs/
chapter9.htm, as well as the article " 'To Bury the Dead and to Feed
the Living': Allied Military Government in Sicily, 1943," by Cindy

Brown in *Canadian Military History*. The efforts of U.S. Army Sergeant Orange Dickey to investigate Genovese in Italy for black market activity and his cooperation in getting Genovese shipped back to the United States were described in Dickey's testimony in July 1958 during hearings of the Select Committee on Improper Activities in the Labor or Management Fields, Part 32. The legal troubles of Umberto Costello and his deportation to Italy were described in 1937 newspaper accounts in the *St. Louis Globe-Democrat* and the *St. Louis Globe-Dispatch*. Mussolini's capture and execution by partisans were described in Wikipedia.

CHAPTER NINE

Details of Ernest Rupolo's problems in connection with the Boccia homicide and other criminal matters were discussed in the *Daily News* and the *Brooklyn Daily Eagle*. A capsule summary of the career of Charles Poletti was found on Wikipedia.com. Poletti's anger and discussions about possible legal action over allegations he was close to Genovese are found in the collection of his papers held by the Columbia University Rare Books and Manuscript Library. The Poletti-Genovese allegations were described in Dom Frasca's *King of Crime*. A letter to all NYPD commands to be on the lookout for Genovese and five others was found in the files of the Kefauver Committee held in the National Archives pertaining to Genovese. Genovese's return to Brooklyn to stand trial on the Boccia murder case was reported by the *Brooklyn Daily Eagle,* the *Daily News*, and the *New York Times*.

CHAPTER TEN

Pretrial proceedings in the case against Vito Genovese for the murder of Ferdinand Boccia, including his arraignment, were described in the *New York Times*, the *Daily News,* and the *Brooklyn Daily Eagle*. Events leading up to the cooperation of Charles Luciano with authorities during World War Two have been described in a number of published accounts and were consolidated in Anthony M. DeStefano's *Top Hoodlum: Frank Costello, Prime Minister of The*

Mafia. A description of the last few days spent by Luciano on a ship in New York harbor was contained in a memorandum to Kefauver Committee counsel Rudolph Halley from Thomas Cahill dated March 15, 1951, found in the files of the committee held by the National Archives. Ernest Rupolo's claims that he was the object of a poison plot while in jail were reported in the *Daily News*. Events related to the 1945 dispute between Brooklyn District Attorney George J. Beldock and Mayor William O'Dwyer over the handling of the case against Genovese, including his return from Italy, were described in the *New York Times*, the *Brooklyn Daily Eagle*, and the *Daily News*, as well as in Dom Frasca's *King of Crime*.

CHAPTER ELEVEN

The trial of Vito Genovese in 1946 for the 1934 murder of Ferdinand Boccia was described in almost daily coverage in the *New York Times*, the *Daily News*, and the *Brooklyn Daily Eagle*. A portion of the trial transcript, mainly the testimony of Ernest Rupolo, was reproduced in Dom Frasca's *King of Crime*. The granting of freedom to Rupolo for his testimony by Judge Samuel Leibowitz was reported in the *Daily News*.

CHAPTER TWELVE

The situation after World War Two within the New York Mafia, particularly within the Luciano crime family, was described in George Wolf and Joseph Dimona's *Frank Costello: Prime Minister of the Underworld* and Peter Maas's *The Valachi Papers*. The famous Mafia summit in Havana with Charles Luciano, Vito Genovese, Frank Costello, and others has been described in many sources. In this book the main sources were Enrique Cirules's *The Mafia in Havana: A Caribbean Mob Story*, T. J. English's *Havana Nocturne: How the Mob Owned Cuba . . . and Then Lost It to the Revolution*, Martin Gosch and Richard Hammer's *The Last Testament of Lucky Luciano*, Selwyn Raab's *The Five Families: The Rise, Decline, and Resurgence of America's Most Powerful Mafia Empires*, and Anthony M. DeStefano's *Top Hoodlum: Frank Costello, Prime Minis-*

ter of The Mafia. Luciano's expulsion from Cuba was described in the *New York Times*.

CHAPTER THIRTEEN

Details of Genovese's business dealings in New Jersey and Manhattan were found in the files of the Kefauver Committee pertaining to Genovese in the National Archives, as well as articles in the *New York Times* and FBI files related to Genovese created in 1958. Details of the Italian lottery were found in a memorandum supplied to the Kefauver Committee and placed in its file on Genovese found in the National Archives. Sherman Willse's testimony to the 1958 McClellan Committee about Genovese and his associates is found in Part 32 of the record of the proceedings. Details of the 1949 New York City mayoral election were reported in the *New York Times* and the *Daily News*.

CHAPTER FOURTEEN

Personal information about Anna Genovese was obtained from interviews by the author with her relatives, notably Kate Harmon Gmehlin and two others who prefer not to be identified. Details of the matrimonial action are contained in papers filed in the case of *Anna Genovese v. Vito Genovese*, M 247-50, Superior Court of New Jersey Chancery Division, Monmouth County (1950). Details of the testimony of Frank Costello and others during the Kefauver Committee hearings were summarized in Anthony M. DeStefano's *Top Hoodlum: Frank Costello, Prime Minister of The Mafia*. Information about the efforts of investigators with the Kefauver Committee to subpoena Vito Genovese was found in the committee files related to Genovese. Articles in the *New York Times* and the *Daily News* detailed the testimony of a number of mobsters who appeared before the Kefauver Committee. Willie Moretti's testimony was the subject of an article in the *New York Times*. Details about events surrounding the murder of Moretti were found in Peter Maas's *The Valachi Papers*, the *New York Times*, and the *Daily News*.

CHAPTER FIFTEEN

The Genovese divorce and matrimonial action was heavily chronicled in the newspapers, namely the *Daily News*, the *Daily Record*, the *Courier-News*, the *Asbury Park Press*, the *Record,* the *Herald News*, and the *Central New Jersey Home News*. Anna Genovese's statements to congressional investigators in 1951 were found in the Kefauver Committee hearing materials, namely the file kept on Vito Genovese that is available at the National Archives.

CHAPTER SIXTEEN

Vito Genovese's denaturalization case is documented in the case file and transcripts of *U.S.A. v. Vito Genovese*, Civ. 1127-52 (USCD, DNJ, August 16, 1955) and the decision in *U.S.A. v. Vito Genovese* 133 F. Supp 820 (1955).

CHAPTER SEVENTEEN

Information about Vito Genovese's power and influence in the New York City garment industry was found in his FBI file. In a series of stories done by the author in 1977 for *Women's Wear Daily*, the history of the Mafia involvement in the garment industry, including the infamous gangsters involved, was detailed at length. Anna Genovese's testimony and the lack of information she provided to New Jersey authorities about her husband's alleged rackets on the waterfront were reported in the *Daily News*. Genovese's involvement in a steel fabricating company on Long Island was reported in *Newsday*.

CHAPTER EIGHTEEN

Information about Frank Costello's tax problems is found in Anthony M. DeStefano's *Top Hoodlum: Frank Costello, Prime Minister of The Mafia*. FBI files related to Vito Genovese reported a Mafia meeting in which Costello's loss of status was discussed. Genovese's maneuvering to usurp Costello's power and orchestrate his attempted assassination was discussed in Peter Maas's *The Valachi Papers*. Albert Anastasia's assassination was reported in many newspapers, notably the *New York Times*. Costello's reaction to Anastasia's murder was detailed in George Wolf and Joseph Dimona's *Frank Costello: Prime Minister of the Underworld*.

CHAPTER NINETEEN

Genovese's FBI file contains information about the pre-Apalachin meeting at the home of Ruggiero Boiardo. Biographic material on Boiardo was found in articles published in the *Record* at the time of his death in 1984. A detailed summary of the Apalachin meeting and its various participants was found in Arthur Reuter's report dated April 23, 1958: *The Activities and Associations of Persons Identified as Present at the Residence of Joseph Barbara Sr. at Apalachin, New York, on November 14, 1957, and the Reasons for Their Presence*. The overturning of the federal conspiracy convictions of certain attendees of the Apalachin meeting was reported in *U.S. v. Russell Bufalino, et al.* 285 F. 2d 408 (2nd Cir. 1960)

CHAPTER TWENTY

The buildup to the drug investigation of Vito Genovese was described in part in Renee Buse's *The Deadly Silence*. Information about possible drug dealing by Albert Anastasia was found in his subject file in the material of the Kefauver Committee held in the National Archives. A history of post–World War Two drug dealing by the Mafia in Italy is described in two reports published by the Italian Parliament (the Chamber of Deputies and the Senate of the Republic). Two chapters in particular were relevant: chapter one, "L'Impianto Mafioso," and chapter three, "L'Organizzazione."

CHAPTER TWENTY-ONE

Details about the drug dealing and personal history of Nelson Cantellops are found in the case file and transcript for *U.S. v. Alfredo Aviles et al.*, Cr. 156–157 (USDC SDNY 1958), and *United States v. Alfredo Aviles et al.*, 274 F. 2d 179 (2nd Circuit Court of Appeals, 1960). Agent Anthony Consoli's role in getting Cantellops to cooperate with the investigation of Genovese was described in Renee Buse's *The Deadly Silence*. James Hunt, the son of the late FBN investigator James Hunt, described details of his father's surveillance of Genovese in a bar that provided critical evidence for the prosecution.

CHAPTER TWENTY-TWO

The *New York Times* and the *Daily News* covered the indictment and arraignment of Vito Genovese on the narcotics case. The case file in *U.S. v. Aviles*, Cr 156-157 (USDC SDNY 1958) provided a description of the charges. *The Daily News* covered the murder of Cristoforo Rubino. The incident involving federal agent Benjamin Begendorf was described in material in the case file of *U.S. v. Aviles* and the decision in Benjamin R. *Begendorf v. the United States*, 340 F. 2d 362 (Ct. Cl. 1965).

CHAPTER TWENTY-THREE

Details of the trial of Vito Genovese and the testimony of Nelson Cantellops were found in the case file of *U.S. v. Aviles*. Sentencing proceedings in the case of Genovese were reported in the *New York Times* and the *Daily News*. Genovese's testimony before the State Commission of Investigation was reported in the *New York Times*. The capture of John Ormento and Carmine Galante was reported in the *New York Times* and the *Daily News*. Cantellops's attempted recantation was detailed in the case file of *U.S. v. Aviles* and reported in *U.S. v. Aviles*, 197 F. Supp 536 (1961).

CHAPTER TWENTY-FOUR

Vito Genovese's surrender was widely reported in the *New York Times* and the *Daily News*. Genovese's prison records were found in his file at the National Archives facility in College Park, Maryland, within Record Group 129, Entry No. A1 14-A, Boxes 33–35. The history of the Atlanta penitentiary was found in Wikipedia. Genovese's life in prison was described in his file at the National Archives.

CHAPTER TWENTY-FIVE

Vito Genovese's discussions with prison officials about Joseph Valachi were described in his prison file at the National Archives. Peter Maas's *The Valachi Papers* detailed Valachi's decision to co-operate, an event reported in the *New York Times* and the *Daily News*. Details of Genovese's prison life were found in his prison file held by the National Archives.

CHAPTER TWENTY-SIX

Information about Vito Genovese's physical decline in prison and his relationship with his various family members in his later years was found in his prison file held by the National Archives. Genovese's death was described in detail in his prison file, and his funeral was reported in the *Daily News* and the *New York Times*. FBI information about attempts to determine Genovese's successor were found in his file kept by the agency.

EPILOGUE

The Sam Giancana theory of Vito Genovese being set up by others in the mob was expounded in Sam and Chuck Giancana's *Double Cross: The Explosive Inside Story of the Mobster Who Controlled America*. Genovese's last will and testament detailed his various bequests. Genovese's communication with his various family members while in prison and his making Anna his beneficiary were described in his prison file kept by the National Archives. Kate Harmon Gmehlin, a relative of Anna, described her later life and death in an interview with the author.

Bibliography

BOOKS AND PUBLICATIONS

Allen, Oliver E. *The Tiger: The Rise and Fall of Tammany Hall.* New York: Addison-Wesley Publishing Company, 1993.

Brodsky, Alyn. *The Great Mayor: Fiorello LaGuardia and the Making of the City of New York.* New York: Truman Talley Books/St. Martin's Press, 2003.

Buse, Renee. *The Deadly Silence.* New York: Doubleday, 1965.

Cirules, Enrique. *The Mafia in Havana: A Caribbean Mob Story.* Translated by Douglas Edward LaPrade. New York: Ocean Press, 2004.

D'Este, Carlo. *Patton: A Genius for War.* New York: HarperCollins Publishers, 1995.

DeStefano, Anthony. *Top Hoodlum: Frank Costello, Prime Minister of the Mafia.* New York: Citadel Press, 2018.

Dickie, John. *Blood Brothers: The History of Italy's Three Mafias.* New York: PublicAffairs, 2014.

English, T. J. *Havana Nocturne: How the Mob Owned Cuba . . . and Then Lost It to the Revolution.* New York: William Morrow, 2007.

Frasca, Dom. *King of Crime.* New York: Crown, 1959.

Giancana, Sam, Chuck Giancana, and Bettina Giancana. *Double Cross: The Explosive Inside Story of the Mobster Who Controlled America.* New York: Warner Books, Inc., 1992.

Gosch, Martin A., and Richard Hammer. *The Last Testament of Lucky Luciano*. New York: Little Brown and Company, 1975.

Horan, James D. *The Mob's Man*. New York: Crown Publishers, Inc., 1959.

Hortis, Alexander C., and James B. Jacobs. *The Mob and the City: The Hidden History of How the Mafia Captured New York*. New York: Prometheus Books, 2014.

Jackson, Kenneth T. *The Encyclopedia of New York City*. New Haven, CT: Yale University Press, 1995.

Lacey, Robert. *Little Man: Meyer Lansky and the Gangster Life*. Boston: Little, Brown and Company, 1991.

Linnett, Richard. *In the Godfather Garden: The Long Life and Times of Ritchie "the Boot" Boiardo*. New Brunswick: Rutgers University Press, 2013.

Maas, Peter. *The Valachi Papers*. New York: Bantam Books, 1968.

McShane, Larry. *Chin: The Life and Crimes of Mafia Boss Vincent Gigante*. New York: Kensington Publishing Corp., 2016.

Mockridge, Norton, and Robert H. Prall. *The Big Fix: Graft And Corruption in the World's Largest City*. New York: Henry Holt and Company, 1954.

Newark, Tim. *Mafia Allies: The True Story of America's Secret Alliance with the Mafia*. New York: Zenith Press, 2007.

Pernicone, Nunzio. *Carlo Tresca: Portrait of a Rebel*. Oakland, CA, and Edinburgh: AK Press, 2010.

Peterson, Virgil W. *The Mob: 200 Years of Organized Crime in New York*. Ottawa, IL: Green Hill Publishers, Inc., 1983.

Raab, Selwyn. *The Five Families: The Rise, Decline, and Resurgence of America's Most Powerful Mafia Empires*. New York: Thomas Dunne Books, 2005.

Reavill, Gil. *Mafia Summit: J. Edgar Hoover, the Kennedy Brothers, and the Meeting that Unmasked the Mob*. New York: St. Martin's Press, 2013.

Rovner, Eduardo Sáenz. The Cuban Connection: *Drug Trafficking, Smuggling, and Gambling in Cuba from the 1920s to the Revolution*. Translated by Russ Davidson. Chapel Hill: The University of North Carolina Press, 2008.

Sciacca, Tony. *Luciano: The Man Who Modernized the American Mafia.* New York: Pinnacle Books, 1975.

Siragusa, Charles, as told to Robert Wiedrich. *The Trail of the Poppy: Behind the Mask of the Mafia.* Englewood Cliffs, NJ: Prentice-Hall, 1966.

Tripodi, Tom, with Joseph Desario. *Crusade: Undercover Against The Mafia and the KGB.* McLean, VA: Brassey's, 1993.

Valentine, George. *The Strength of the Wolf: The Secret History of America's War On Drugs.* London: Verso, 2006.

Wolf, George, and Joseph Dimona. *Frank Costello: Prime Minister of the Underworld.* New York: William Morrow and Company, 1974.

COURT CASES

In the Matter of the Application for Letters of Administration of the Goods, Chattels, and Credits which Were of Donata Genovese, Deceased: File No. 3303, Queens County Surrogate's Court (1934).

U.S. v. Alfredo Aviles et al., Cr. 156–157 (USDC SDNY, 1958).

Anna Genovese v. Vito Genovese, M 247-50, Superior Court of New Jersey Chancery Division, Monmouth County (1950).

United States v. Vito Genovese, Civ. 1127–52 (USDC, DNJ, 1952).

Vito Genovese v. United States of America, 65 Civ. 2764 (USDC SDNY, 1965).

COURT DECISIONS

Benjamin R. Begendorf v. the United States, 340 F. 2d 362 (Ct. Cl. 1965).

United States v. Alfredo Aviles et. al. 274 F. 2d 179 (2nd Circuit Court of Appeals, 1960).

United States v. Russell Bufalino et.al. 285 F. 2d 408 (2nd Circuit Court of Appeals, 1960).

United States v. Vito Genovese, Civ. 1127-52 (USDC, DNJ, August 16, 1955).

United States v. Vito Genovese,133 F. Supp 820 (1955).

GOVERNMENT REPORTS

Commissione d'inchiesta antimafia 1972–1976. This Italian parliamentary commission published a series of reports about the Mafia, and two chapters in particular where used in this book: chapter one, "L'Impianto Mafioso," and chapter three, "L'Organizzazione."

Hearings before the Special Committee to Investigate Organized Crime in Interstate Commerce, United States Senate, Eighty-First Congress (Second Session) and Eighty-Second Congress (First Session). Part 7, July 1950 to March 1951.

Hearings before the Select Committee on Improper Activities in the Labor or Management Field, United States Senate, Eighty-Fifth Congress (Second Session). Part 32, June 30 to July 3, 1958.

The Activities and Associations of Persons Identified as Present at the Residence of Joseph Barbara Sr. at Apalachin, New York, on November 14, 1957, and the Reasons for Their Presence. Report by Arthur Reuter, acting commissioner of investigation of the state of New York, to Averell Harriman, governor of the state of New York, April 23, 1958.

NEWSPAPERS AND PERIODICALS CONSULTED

Asbury Park Press (Asbury Park, New Jersey)
Brooklyn Times Union (Brooklyn, New York)
Chicago Tribune
Daily News (New York City)
Democrat and Chronicle (Rochester, New York)
Elmira Star-Gazette (Elmira, New York)
Evening Star (Washington, DC)
Evening Telegram (New York City)
Keyport Enterprise (Red Bank, New Jersey)
Long Island Daily Press
Matawan Journal (Matawan, New Jersey)
Newsday (Long Island)
Press and Sun-Bulletin (Binghamton, New York)
St. Louis Post-Dispatch (St. Louis, Missouri)

The Bismarck Tribune (Bismarck, North Dakota)

The Brooklyn Daily Eagle

The Buffalo Evening News (Buffalo, New York)

The Central New Jersey Home News (New Brunswick, New Jersey)

The Courier-News (Bridgewater, New Jersey)

The Daily Record (Long Branch, New Jersey)

The Daily Register (Red Bank, New Jersey)

The Daily Star (Queens, New York)

The Herald News (Passaic, New Jersey)

The Lancaster New Era (Lancaster, Pennsylvania)

The Morning Call (Paterson, New Jersey)

The New York Call (New York City)

The New York Post (New York City)

The New York Sun (New York City)

The New York Times (New York City)

The New York Tribune (New York City)

The Post-Star (Glens Falls, New York)

The Queens Leader-Observer (Queens, New York)

The Record (Hackensack, New Jersey)

The Richmond Times Leader (Queens, New York)

The Standard Union (Brooklyn, New York)

The Sun (New York City)

Times-Tribune (Scranton, Pennsylvania)

WEBSITES CONSULTED

www.americanmafia.com

www.bibliography.com

www.crimemagazine.com

www.fbi.gov

www.findagrave.com

www.fultonhistory.com

www.geni.com

history.amedd.army.mil

www.investopedia.com

www.loc.gov

www.monmouthcountyparks.com

www.nara.gov

www.newspapers.com

www.nyc.gov

www.nexis.com

podcast.mobqueens.com

www.theblackvault.com

www.thesmokinggun.com

www.wikipedia.org

www.youtube.com

Acknowledgments

These books about the old Mafia bosses tend to be modern archeological projects in that most of the people who were their contemporaries are long gone. That forces a writer to dig deep into the past, culling previously written materials, film clips, and official documents, as well as interviewing people who may have secondhand or thirdhand information about the subject. The job had the complication in the spring of 2020 of the coronavirus pandemic, which shut down a number of public research facilities. In the case of Vito Anthony Genovese, there were a number of people who helped me along the way and whom I want to acknowledge.

Fellow author Nick Pileggi, who has been a mentor by encouraging me on a number of book projects, provided me access to a rare copy of Dom Frasca's early biography on Genovese, titled *King of Crime*. Nick also was, as he has always been, a font of information about the formative years of the Mafia, particularly the 1940s and 1950s. We talked for hours, even while Nick was in the middle of working on the film *The Irishman*.

In Italy, author and Italian cuisine expert Rossano Del Zio worked tirelessly over many hours to translate parliamentary reports and other materials for me, which helped round out the story of narcotics dealing during the 1950s.

In law enforcement, NYPD Chief Thomas Conforti helped provide access to old records about some of the characters in the Genovese story.

Retired Drug Enforcement Administration official James Hunt, whose father was involved in the 1958 investigation of Genovese, provided recollections about his father's activities. Allison Guerriero also gets my thanks for recommending that I talk with Hunt.

Relatives of Genovese who provided information and merit my thanks are his grandson Philip Genovese Jr., as well as two people who are related distantly to Genovese: Kate Harmon Gmehlin and Frank Esposito.

Employees of the National Archives and Records Administration provided key reference help: Kevin Reilly (New York City), Carey Stuum (New York City), and Tom McAnear (College Park, Maryland).

Colleague John Doyle gets thanks for his enthusiasm and encouragement, while Ida Van Lindt provided some materials from the files of her late boss, Manhattan District Attorney Robert Morgenthau, who for a time served as Manhattan U.S. Attorney in the 1960s.

At *Newsday*, Laura Mann once again helped get me access to old photographs, while my editor, Monica Quintanilla, also provided assistance in my scheduling time off.

Thanks again to Gary Goldstein, my editor at Kensington, for guiding this book to fruition. My agent, Jill Marsal, gets my appreciation for handling the business side of this project.

Index